shobDolara
My Sylheti Dictionary

Sylheti-English English-Sylheti Dictionary
Subject-wise Sylheti-English Dictionary
With Verbs List and Tenses

Munayem Mayenin

3

shobDolara My Sylheti Dictionary

Copyrights Notice

No part of this book can be copied or reproduced in any manners, formats or means without prior written permission form its author Munayem Mayenin who asserts and holds the copyrights of this book under the UK, European and International Copyrights Laws.

shobDolara My Sylheti Dictionary

By Munayem Mayenin, London, United Kingdom

ISBN: 978-1-4709-4924-2

First Published: November 12, 2011

Price: £27

la ciela: singing the sacred words: la ciela

Book: Between your pages I carry hidden oceans, impossible islands, awesome landscapes, soul changing symphonies, miraculous openings and made up imsoniums. La ciela you are: voice of the sacred words, sublime words forever singing

Imsonium Books

4

eniara aral

aral bilor muk anonDor Qubi zeno eK; haraDin harabela
Kore khela ashmanor nilua nilua bilashi bahuloTa dhoria
shunDor. shobDohin bon, tilla ar uca uca PaYrh caia thaKe
bubar moTo zoban araia I shuBon arali sobir ganor mayaT.

eniara aral namor meye, ase eK aralir goBir bukur gohon
nilua zanor kuṯaT; cokur arhalo arhal arhal Tar lazuk lazuk
shob khela. canni raiTor rushnir moTon Tar Basha! Panir
cokuT aha eniara Porir moTon eK nari ze Tumar zanor maze

loia ay eK Pagol dhomKa boishag mashor dhomKa zhorhor
moTon! aha! Tar aT zeno kahinir Desh eK! aha! Tar alor angul
shob Quli Quli meli meli zaay ki BesTor DuniaBashani gan!

eniara siletor meye; zobano Tar Patharia fute zeno ashman
fulor lakhan zekhano Dunia-maTa khali ze mathia zain ki
anonDo ruPKotha. eniara mayar Porosh, eK mayadhari Paro!

silara shurma sOnet
November 12, 2011

sileti amar silara zoban

sileti amar silara zoban ar sobi Tar zeno
shurmar PaniT caYPaTa shobuz zhilmil
silara canni raiT ar sileti zoban zeno eKakar
zibonor gan ar noDi zeno eK mayar KobiTa

emon zibon aha manciTror cinnoBinnohin
mati mele Dankha tillaay ar PaYrhe PorboTe
sorhaay sorhaay cole ruPali Panir KobiTa
PaTTore PaTTore ciTrosobi Kocua PEYnar

kheTe kheTe shunar dhan bile bile ruPali masor
bilashi bisTar ar deUor dhoria ashmanor loge
zeno iTiKotha ruPKotha banaay niTTo niralaay

riTur chokre ay shomoyor biPul birat shob Dan
ganor shuror loge zanor Kemon bEla bazaay aha
silara maDobkundo ruPali Panir sruTor Tare Tare

silara shurma sOnet
November 7, 2011

Dedication

To the memories of Tassaduq Ahmed MBE (whom I used to address as Tassaduq Bhai) and Rosemary Ahmed from Germany (whom I never had the good fortune to meet but who touched and moved me, regardless, through Tassaduq Bhai as he told me their stories of falling, staying and continuing in and living love.

They had no children. I hope shobDolara My Sylheti Dictionary may become their child and carry their names as long as Sylheti lives on. Tassaduq Bhai came from gulaPgonj, the Rosemarket of Sylhet, the Beautiful Market, to find his Rosemary. I now plant both of them into this Aspern Grove of Sylheti Dictionary with my respect, regard, love and prayer for them. And, to those who will be using this dictionary, I urge that they say a prayer for both of them at the same time as their children would have done had they have any.

Tassaduq Bhai once said at an Annual General Conference of Desh Bikash (London) in the Autumn of 1993 at The Davenant Centre that he had never tried writing poetry other than once. And, lucky for us all attending, he read his only ever poem that I heard once and never read; yet, the words are stuck in my head, till now. I don't know whether it had ever been published anywhere but I do not think so. I publish it here and with the hope that anyone using this poem must always ensure that the Author of this piece is acknowledged with his full name (as Tassaduq Ahmed MBE). I would like to imagine that he met Rosemary somewhere in Munich at a Café when they were only letter-courting between London and Munich and could only see each other on shuttle visits; and with his characteristic wit, sarcasm, humour, mischievousness and humanity he spoke these lines to her who could not help choking with laughter; spilling her coffee all over the table getting all scarlet. So, here I title this piece as Rosemary's Lines.

rouzmerir lain

Tumaro birohe bondhu
ami Dine Dine muta hoi
Din o raTri sarha
ami sharabela zege roi

Rosemary's Lines

For the longing of you, darling,
I get fat every day.
I stay awake all the times
Except the days and the nights.
(Translation: Munayem Mayenin, London, England 2011)

In reality, however, Tassaduque Bhai lived in an infinite longing, love and bereavement of Rosemary after she had died; year after year, after year, after year till the day he died (all the time breathing in and out of her love that she had left for him).

Contents

sylheti aplhabet II sileti Akkor

Vowels

(11 Vowel Sounds)

A   a   aa

o   O   I   i

u   U   e   E

<u>Consonants</u>

(38 Consonant Sounds)

k kh KH K Q

g gh ng s

ch c j jh

T th D dh

t <u>t</u> d <u>d</u>

p P f b B

r l h sh

y m n rh

z zh Y w

sylheti sounds II dhOni/shobDo

There are 11 vowel sounds and 37 consonants and an additional sign that helps to write certain sound-blends making the total number of Sylheit sounds to 48 and total letters 49.

A is pronounced like the A in Aldgate or Auction

a is like English ark and not as in America, and, Andover, another etc.

aa like Ireland

o is like the in on or onion

O is like Bonn

I is like Finnish ii or Indigo

u is like put

U is like the woo in wool

e is like the e in Ben or Ken

E is like the e in Bear

A to W Sample of the Way Letters are Used to Write

Here is an example of how these letters are used in words.

1.Vowels

A: ATo lamba mathiona.

a: am, ami, amar

aa: aalla,(a village name in Sylhet) allaa (Allah, God), aami (a sweet and sour dried confection made from mango paste)

o: ono aow.

O: dhOni. bOni.

I: Ila Kam Kora Bala naay.

i: ina, mina, Dina

u: uzaneDi nouka baia zaowa koṭin.

U: Ula, Uli, Ulluk

e: eKzon, eKla

E: Ela Kora Bala naay. mEla manush,

2. Consonants

k: kiTa Koila? Kila zaow?

kh: PakhaniT zairani? khaniDani kila Oilo?

KH: KHichurhi randhrani?

K: kiTa Korra? Koi zaira? KoTo Dia kinla?

Q: Quabor kuno mani Ayni? Quab Dekhia Din zaibogini?

g: goruE dhan Khailailonu. gan gaowcain.

gh: ghune dhorilaise.

ng: rongcong Koria kiTa KorTaay.

s: soy tEKar mal becTaay KotEKaay?

ch: Pachjon manush.

c: caca nizor zan bacaow. caca Koi gela?

j: Panja lorha.

jh: jhorh ar.

T: Tin morar cin.

th:thana Daroga Koria ar kiTa Aibo!

D: DaDar bole mokkaT zaiona.

dh: DeKbaay nE KoTo dhano KoTo caul.

t: tilla Bangia Porhi gese.

t: Kamo khali t̠elat̠eli Korionacai.

d: Oba mia, khali dugdugi bazaile Kam Aiboni?

d̠: d̠uldoPki na bazaile abar kizaTor Anustan!

p: aPne amar borho prio manush.

P: aPa amare eK glash Pani Deow.

f: fufur barhiT zairam.

b: borho Bala Ailo, aPoD gelo!

B: Bala Ailo. Tain amar borho Bai.

r: rag Koria kiTa lab Aibo!

l: lal Payzoma Panjabi PinDia Koi sutlaay ba?

h: haay haay Kora!

sh: shabdhan Koria Diar, ar barhiona!

y: Kothaay Kothaay Ay Ay Koriona mia, zeTa maatho buzia maathio!

m: zomino moi Dilaisoni?

n: nana Koi zaira?

rh: beshi barhabarhi Koriona, morizibaay.

z: zeTa Qushi iTa Koriona, mon Dia Porho.

zh: mathaaT zhinzhin Korer. mathaar maze aKTa zhinnaTTi utlo.

Y: Tole Porhia heYe! PoYrha, caY, PoYrhram

w: low, neow, deow, khaow, waDa

Introduction

To work on a dictionary of a language for the first time, I realised as I came to do this first ever dictionary/shobDolara/shobDorugar of Sylheti, is not like the laying down of the foundation of a building; however, it is rather like laying down the foundation of a living architecture of an aspern grove. This architecture is living and growing. And, to start, must, therefore, mean, to literally, lay the first set of the asperns so that they carry on growing as the primary Author and Compiler and the successive generations of them carry on planting more and more aspern-word-trees with the people as they utilise the living aspern grove of the language developing it as they go and grow on living. I did not realise how hard this task would be when I had set out to do it. There was no reference book; there was no beginning but there must be a beginning. All I had was that what I had inside me of the entire living aspern grove of Sylheti that my Mother and Father had instilled in me and that grew with me as I worked in the maps and landscapes of the language.

No language in human history has ever been developed without human endeavours of creativity, ingenuity and imagination. Language is not simply a means to communicate which is only its hollowest of purposes; the language is a medium that captures what humanity not only is but what it aspires to be. Language is the means, medium and mechanics of human ingenuity, creativity, imagination and its vision of time-all that offers it the means to see its time within that framework. This is testified when Achiles says: They will be talking about this war for eternity to come; they will be talking about us and what we did here for all eternity.

A human, living in his/her simple present can only be capable of placing himself/herself in the flowing magnitude of all-time so to judge himself/herself against it, if he/she has the sense of that all-time. Being aware of not just what is or was or the immediate next but the all-past to the brief-present to the brief-future towards the flow of time to eternity is human's best feature which can only be expressed through and understood in language. It is not just the domain of the cities, the bankers, the financial bond and hedge junkies, though, it does all that; language is not just what I am but that what I aspire to be, where and why I aspire to be. Hows and what ifs of life is the businss of languge. Language offers the best means of asserting exististence since the fundamental proof of my agency is essentially asserted in language when the agency becomes self aware; when it asks questions and it does so using a language: Who am I? What am I? Why am I? Where am I? When am I? Where did I come from? Where am I going to? What for am I here? What is my being? What is my existence? The fact that something or someone inside my biological body is raising and, is capable of asking questions testifies the fact that that something or someone exists and that it is my being, my existence, my agency and, that testimony cannot be gained in any other way to begin with. That is why language is so fundamental and vital in our existence and life.

This dictionary is the beginning of that aspiration for Sylheti to become that medium to all the people who speak and use this language so that they begin to plant new asperns so that this grove grows and enriches as they enrich, as they live in the language and its bounty.

I realised this in 1978 when I was a young child: away from home in all senses of the word. I was near the sea, Bay of Bangla (I would rather call her Bangla Bay), South East of Bangladesh, in a place called, Noakhali which later in life, writing in English to a friend whom I came to know and love while in Noakhali, I affectionately called New Empty, near which the St Martin Island lives in the water-expanse of the sea and always gets lit up by awesome human endeavours and who always puts up an epic struggle of survival in the water and her wuthering weathering heights.

I could read and write Bangla but could not yet speak it fluently when I went to New Empty. Sylheti was my mother tongue. When I went to New Empty I found myself absolutely empty. It was like an Englishman who found himself in Munich except he did not speak a word of German and the Germans weren't going to speak English with him simply because he could not speak their language! So, like the Enlgish in Munich, I realised that people there did not speak Bangla at all, at least the Bangla I could read and write and I might be able to understand a little if I heard it spoken! But no one speaks English in Munich! Nor do they speak Spanish in Romania or Burma! And the New Emptians or the Noakhalis neither spoke Bangla nor Sylheti; unless they were engaged in official business when they would use Bangla with a very strong and unmistakable accent like the Sylhetis speaking Bangla or like the Scots speaking English.

In Noakhali they spoke in Noakhali dialect that I simply could not understand. I lost my home; I lost connections to my parents, family, friends and my language as well.

I learnt fast to speak and understand Noakhali and since I was a young child I had no accent and I began to speak like a Noakhali child. Having learnt Noakhali dialect as a necessity I still realised and lived the loss of my mother tongue in that early age and that experience stayed with me. Thus, briefly, like a lot of migrating children, I lost my mother tongue and had to adopt another tongue and made it my own. Noakhali, therefore, became my adopted mother tongue which gave way to English later on; which, however, was not a must but a free and wilful choice made under no duress or pressure long, long before I arrived in the UK in search of William Shakespeare's England to find her heart in the words of John Keats.

There, one day, sometime in the Autumn, probably in November 1978, I stood in a fish market where all the catfishes were glistening gold as they jumped up and down in a bustling arena of fishmongers, I rememberd what my mother used to say often: one country's tongue another country's swearing. *eK Deshor buli aroK Deshor gali.* This thought occurred to me when I looked at the countless number of a beautiful silver small fish and antoher dark golden brown fish equally alive like the catfishes on display. Since, by than, I came to know that the Sylheti names of these particular two fishes were absolutely a no-no-use in Noakhali dialect as they were absolute swear words and in reverse the Noakhali name of one of those fishes was an absolute swear word in Sylheti! I am not going to, I am afraid, enlighten you, readers, on this, here!

Ahyhow, when I came back to Sylhet, I carried Noakhali-Munich or my New Empty with me. Yet, my home began to refuse to accept and acknowledge me as one of its own. For people were asking people about me. Who is this boy? Asked the ones who could not recognise me (since I was away a while and grew a little) and they would be told who I was and they would not accept it. How could he be the Doctor's son! He speaks like a born Noakhali! Explanations helped.

Soon I fell back to my mother tongue and lost the Noakhali accent as well as the Noakhali dialect which I would later use at college and university when I came in touch with people from Noakhali to astound them with my 'native-speaking' skills! Therefore, I came to know well as to what it was like to lose one's mother tongue.

However, all the work that I have done for and in Sylheti is only to ensure that the Sylhetis do not lose their mother tongue for losing one's mother tongue is a grave loss that ensures a continual bereavement for a nation or people that will haunt them forever.

I have published Sylara My Sylheti Tutor and now, shobDolara My Sylheti Dictionary is being placed forward. The next one, hopefully, to be complete soon, is Larakoron My Sylheti Grammar. All this is my contributions to this Sylheti Aspern Grove and I shall continue to add to it as best as I could.

Yet, here, I leave it to all my students, both native and non-native Sylheti speakers and learners and the Sylheti people with the hope that they will continue to add to this Sylheti Aspern Grove.

It is time the creative Sylheti people take up writing, creating and translating in Sylheti so that this Grove carries on growing and extending life and living and all the splendours that they hold in the beautiful language of Sylheti of Sylhet: the Beautiful Market or the Stone's Market or the Rolling Stone or the Moving Stone or Move (you) Stone (whichever takes your fency, choose) or you would rather call her with affection, take up Silara. A language can never be a complete, whole and wholesome, younthful adult until it has learnt and done life's beautiful business of creating in it.

Sylheti was my Mother's tongue, my Father's tongue and my forefathers' tongue who spoke it and developed it and I do this for them to say and show Sylhet that it is time the Sylhetis wake up to call Sylheti their Mother Tongue and take her up in their all spheres of life.

And here, I would like to acknowledge my Sylheti students (most of whom are non native speakers of Sylheti) for they acted as my inspiration to carry on working in these pieces of works for they needed resources to continue learning Sylheti and I always felt an affectionate duty towards them.

This is the first publication of this dictionary, and as such, this will continue to be a work in progress, whereby, hopefully, it will get larger with time. And as I have worked with the language and developed writing in the script I needed to learn and remember everything like any other learners and therefore, there still may remain, despite my best efforts, descrepencies in spelling harmony across the pages of these books which I have continued to correct and hopefully, with time the harmony will be achieved.

33 years ago, today, when I was in New Empty where I found, experienced, seen, felt and lived a life that shaped me as to what I were to become and that life carried on living inside me as alive as anything else there is alive outside; so did live New Empty or Noakhali in my soul. Noakhali is forever going to be my New Empty near the St Martin Island.

St Martin Island that gets lit up by awesome human endeavours and puts up an epic struggle of survival in the water and her wuthering weathering heights. Beautiful! My New Empty is whether in Noakhali or in Sylhet or in the wider wonderful world.

I am publishing here as part of the dictionary a series of sonnets, titled 'silara shurma sOnet' (Silara Shurma Sonnets), for people to read and enjoy in the hope that more and more Sylheti poets will take up writing in Sylheti. It is about time Sylheti authors, poets, translators, researchers, academics, journalists and thinkers begin to belive that what they feel, think, imagine and write about is as much worthy of being written in Sylheti

(since they do all that in their heads in Sylheti) as of the people writing in any other lanaguages including Bangla.

When time shall ask us, "What have you Sylhetis got to show for, say, the time since the British Raj left Sylhet? what will we be able to show for this period of time? What poetry have we written? What epics have we written? What novels, what history, what other genres of writings have we to offer as proof of our being, of our life and living? Hason Raja and ShiTalong Shaha won't do since they did it in their time and we simply have nothing! Now, ask time back to show you what the Vitorian England has done and you shall need a few life times to venture and discover what it was that they were able to create. Same applies to Bangla Language. But Sylehti has nothing (other than what was created in the brief past written history of the language and sadly that still remain inaccessible to the populace).

This bare, baren and desolate emptiness against the expanse of eternity of Sylhet and Sylheti makes me feel terribly sad. I very much hope that Sylhet shall not continue to live to become emptiness in the human assembly of creativity and start writing in her tongue Sylheti; celebrating life, living and all that Sylhet is: a wonder, a Beautiful Market of Life.

Thank you for your time.

Munayem Mayenin

November 12, 2011
London, England, United Kingdom

Post Scrip:

shobDorugar: dictionary. shobDo=word, shobDor=word's ugar=a place. ugar is where in the country people store their paddy inside their homes in a specially built store room when the paddy is harvested and dried up. So, shobDorugar could translate as word-store-room or wordbank and hence, dictionary. ShobDolara My Sylheti ShodDorugar. In time to come, I hope, shobDolara might come to mean dictionary as well. MM

A

1

sharoDa holor shaDa saaTo nirala raiTor cannir dhola nouka lame
ar shoinkashimahin shaDa anonDor porioKol niribili mihin baTTir
norom norom moshlin Pushake eK Azana Duniar AmriTo khaia zaay.
canni raiTor Dilor ghorano Tara nace-Tara nace zeno Tara aiz Ai gese

canni raiTor modhubala-danKar Qushir maTal maTal eK daK. ar goTir
sutonTo deUo Tarar ruPali shorilor norom gorom shob ghran baTasho
mishe hasnahenar Abimol shughranor beakul zaDur lakhan niralaay.
KanDabaay baul Poth ate asTe dhire nimaTra behula shurma amar nirobe

bazaay Tair sruTor bElaa; Angor aynaT Tair dhoria rakhe canDor muk. ki
aDore Tare Tai boia ney shagoror Dike; mail mail DuroTTor Poth dhori
behula shurma gaay gan-shobDohin gaan ar canDor Kano dale modhu.

ami kinbrizor pinjirar BiTTor thaki ashman-shagoror Tiro ruPali maTal
canni Pagol baulor lakhan barhai amar Dui aT ze aTo Dunia Tulia
Dey mayar mohua eK; amar ruPali bElaa behula shurma zanor kutaT.

silara shurma sOnet

A Ailo Poyla siloti shorborno, the first vowel sound of the alphabet. It is pronounced as the A in Aldgage, Aldershot, Augment, Auction, Aldwych.

Ay: yes

Tumi BaT khaisoni? Have you eaten (rice)? Ay, khaisi. Yes, I have. Ay Ay Koriona. Don't (just) say, yes, yes. Haa haa, haa haa Kora; saying yes to everything.

Aowa: to become, to occur, to happen. ami Ailam jon. I am John (though literally it means I was John to mean I am John). korimor eK baichcha Aise (korim has had a baby to mean korim's wife has had a baby or it could, in English, be said as The Karims have had a baby.) ikta AiTo Parena. This can not happen or be happening. iktare Aowani lagbo. This has to be made possible to occur or happen. baichcha Aowaiso ebla Paalo.

Gave birth to a child, now look after it.

Aowani: to cause the occurrence. Baichcha Aowani. To bring a child (to this world). khali huruTa AoaileU AiTonaay iTare PaalaO lagbo. It's not good enough to give birth to children they have to be looked after and raised.

Amola: like this.
Amola Koro. Do it like this. Ola, Olakhan, ilakhan, Ila

Ahongkar: Pride. Arrogance. guman, mutamaatha. As in English Pride is used both in positive and negative sense.
Ahonkare amar buk fulia uter. Pride is swelling my breast.
Ahonkar PoTonor mul: Pride/arrogance is the cause of fall.
Read: Pride and Prejudice: Jane Austen

Ahongkar Kora: To pride or to be arongant

guman Kora: To show off pride, to be arrogant, to be arrogantly proud.

Ala: like this.
Ala Koro. Do it like this.

AToTa: so much/this much.
AToTa Diona. Don't give me this much.

ATo: too much, so much
ATo maath Bala naay. Too much talk is not good.

AKat: worthless, beKama.
I AKator Kotha maathio na. Do not speak about this worthless (person).

AKama: worthless
I AKamar Kotha maathio na. Do not speak about this worthless (person).
beKama, aKama, ApoDarTo

Azaga: place of no value.
I Azaga loia kiTa KorTa? What would you like to do buying this worthless place?
aazaga, bezaga, zEsakhan

Acina: unknown

I Acina zagaT ebla ami Koi zaiTam? In this unknown place where do I go now? ancina, anzana, Acin, Acina.

Azana: unknown.
ikta amar Azana. I do not know this/It is not known to me. zana naay, nazana, gIanor baira

AzaniT: in one's not knowing state of mind.
AzaniT asil. It was in my unknown (It wasn't known to me). Inadvertently.
Azanaay, AzaniTe, AzanTe
AzaniTe: unaware.
ikta amar AzaniTe Aise. It has happened without my knowledge.
AzanTe, AzaniTe, AzanTe

Azagor: python. Azagoror lakhan cole. (It) goes like a python. azagor, azagor shaP/haP

AzaT: class of no value.
AzaT manush. One without any value or class. bezaT (bad class), zaTnai, zaTsarha.

AzaciTe: without asking. AzaciTe paowa. Getting without asking.

AshubiDa/AshubiTa: difficulty.
ami borho AshubiDaT asi. I am in big difficulty. shomoishsha, aPoD, bipod, shoishsha, zhamela, benga, ghafla

ABab: hard time, poverty.
ebla ABabor shomoy. It is a hard time. AKal, aKal, baD shomoy, Dushshomoy, beDIn, Ashomoy, kuDin

AshomBob: impossible. ikta AshomBob. This is impossible. shomBob naay, beshomBob, namunkin

Alosh: lazy. igu eKta borho Alosh. He/she's a very lazy. ailsha, aalIa, alshia, alshe

Aloshbana: being lazy.
Aloshbana Koriona. Don't be lazy. alshiami, alIami.

Ashohaay/Ashoaay: helpless.
ami borho Ashoaay. I am very helpless. shohayhin, lokhBiksarha, lokhnai, befana

Ashomoy: bad time/hard time.
I Ashomoyo hE kiTa(kiTar) lagi aise? Why has he come in this bad time?
beshomoy, aKal, AKal

AKal: bad time, hard time, ominous time.
borho AKal Porhse. An ominous time has come/fallen/arrived. baD shomoy, beshomoy

AshanTo: unrestful.
I baichchata borho AshanTo. This child is very unrestful. shanTi nai, usrinkol, bisrinkol, besrinkol, Aicoi.

AshanTi: unrest, lack of piece, oppressive state. amar borho AshanTi lager. I am feeling very unrestful. shanTi nai. anchan, anchan Kora, zano kiTa Kora, zano kiTa kiTa Kora

Anacar: unfairness, tyranny.
ikta borho Anacar. This is very unfair. Anacar Kora, harassment. saTani, hoyrani, zalani, Kosto Deowa

AnaT: orphan.
AnaTor dhon maria khaowa borho PaP. Stealing off an orphan's assets is a big sin. eTim, befana.

AndhoKar: darkness.
AndhoKar namer. The darkness is descending. andhair, mishmisha, Kala. cIai

AKazor/Akamor: worthless.
AKamor zinish Koria kiTa laB? What's the point doing worthless things?
ApoDarTo.

AnaDi: beginning of time. AnaDi Kal dhoria Burbala PubeDi suruz uter ar
hanjabala canD uter. Since the beginning of time the sun has been rising in the east at dawn and the moon rising at dusk.

AnonTo: endless, eternity. ami AnonTKal dhoria Tumare Bala Paia zaimu. I will have been loving you for eternity/for endless time/forever.

Ashadharon: out of the ordinary, extraordinary. merilin monro eKzon Ashadharon mohila asla. Marilyn Monroe was an extraordinary woman.

ATol: bottomless, something that has no bottom, bottom can not be reached. atlantik mohashagor Ailo ATol. The Atlantic Ocean is bottomless.

Amaanisha: deep dark night/ ominous dark night. I Amaanishar raiT amar borho dor lager. In this ominous dark night I feel very scared.

AiDdhaPok: Professor. ADdhapok
Read: The Professor: Charolotte Bronté

Angsho: part of something. amar Anhsho Koi? Where is my share? Baag, tukra, hishsha, hissa

Ango: body. Ange Ange bish Korer. It is aching in every part of my body.

ABin: inseparable. Tara Dui Bai ABin. These two brothers are inseparable.

Arikkol: lantern. Arikkolta gelo Koi? Where is the lantern? (Where has the lantern disappeared?)

AYring: deer. Duita AYring. Two deer. maya AYring, mayahorin, horin

AKama:unusable/one that's useless. Ikta AKama. This is worthless.

Aghor: not one's place. Aghoro ghumani zayna. (One) can not sleep in other's place.
Ashomoy: untime, bad timing, wrong time.
borho Ashomoyo telifon Korso. You have called at a bad time.

Araz: tyranny of a ruler. I razaay Araz kaem Korse. This King has established tyranny.

ArozoKoTa: anarchy, tyranny.
Lal Dole Desho ArazoKoTa proTishta Korse. The Red Party has established anarchy in the country.

AnasTa: no confidence. Shobuz Dole Lal Dolor prodhan monTrir biruDdhe AnasTa anche. The Green Party has brought a No Confidenc Motion againt the Red Party Prime Minister. asTa Quai laowa, bishshash arai laowa

AgunTi: innumerable. ashmano AgunTi Teraa. There are countless stars in the sky. AgunTi mas dhorsi. I have caught countless fish.

AshoTTi: untrue.

Ikta AshoTTi. This is untrue.

AshoiTTo: untrue.
AshoiTTo Kotha Koiona. Don't tell untruth/lie.

Alosh: lazy.
Igu Aloshor baaDa. He/she is the laziest.

Agrim: advance.
Agrim beTon caowa shorom. To ask for salary in advance is embarrassing. agam,

Agrim Deowa: to give an advance. Agrim caowa
Amare Imashor beTonta Agrim Dibar bebosTa Korbani? Will you please arrange (my this month's) current month's salary in advance?

AlikiTo: unwritten
aDaloTo AlikiTo kothar kuno Dam nai. At court, there's no value in the unwritten words (to mean without evidence).

AniomiTo: irregular
aPnar sele goTo shara mash AniomiToBabe ishkulo aise. Your son has come to school irregularly all of last month.

Aniom: unruly, chaotic, outside the rule, mismanagement, misappropriation
Tumi shob shomoy Aniom Koro. You are always unruly.
Ishkulor tEKa loia birat Aniom Aise. There's a huge mismanagement with the school fund.

AnirDisto: uncertain, not scheduled, not cetain.
ishkul AnirDisto Kalor lagi bonDo Ai gese. The school has closed for an uncertain period of time.

ADrishsho: invisible
baTash Ailo ADrishsho zinish. Air in an invisible thing.

AKamor: useless
AKamor zinish Keu Poysha Dia Kineni? Does anyone buy worthless thing with money?

AKazor: useless, AKamor
AKazor math mathiona. Don't speak rubbish.

Aboshor: leisure
Abshor Paile Boita Porhlam One. If I had the time (leisure/not working) I would have read the book. nirai Aowa, shanTi Aowa, fursoT, fusroT, fursoT Paowa, fusroT Paowa

Abshore/Aboshore/niralaay/sobresiTre: in leisure/ in the free time
Tumi nizor Abshore Tumar nizor Kam Korio. You do your own work at your own time.

AbosTa: state, situation, circumstance
rugir AbosTa baD Ai gese. The patient's situation has deteriorated.
Tarar ArToniTik AbosTa besh Bala naay. There financial situation is not very good.

AshomBob: impossible, not possible
am gaso ayfol dhora Ashombob.
It is impossible for a mango tree to produce apple.

Aboishsho: of course, certainly, sure, must
aPne ikta Aboissho Korba. You must do it. nishchiT, nishchoy, nishchoI.

AboishshoI: absolutely sure/certain
aPne ikta AboishshoI Korba. You must do it.

ABinash: that what does not die
manshor Bala Kam Ailo ABinash thaKe. People's good deeds are deathless, immortal.

ABinashi: eternal, immortal
eKta Bala shilpoKormo Ailo ABinashi. A good piece of art is eternal.

AgrogoTi: progress, advancement, forward
aPnar Kamor kuno AgrogoTi Ailoni?
Have you had any progress in your work? aguani, agroshor Aowa, Bala Aowa, unnoTi Aowa, aguaia zaowa,

Agoinno: innumerable
ashmano Agoinno Teraa. There are countless stars in the sky.

AgunTi: innumerable
kheTo AgunTi moric dhorse. In the field/garden/nursery there are countless chillies.
shimashoingka nai, shimahin, gonra baire

Agula: these ones

Agula shoraow. Move these away.

Agulain: these ones
Agulain hObayDi horaow. Move these there.

Anurag: love, affection
zamai bour maze Aunurag na thaKle shongsharo mair lageU. If there's no love between husband and wife there is bound to be troubles/fights/arguments in the family.

Anuzug: complain
amlaTonTroy Anuzug buzena. Burearcracy does not undstand complaints.

AzukTi: lacking logic/ration
AzukTir math mathiona. Don't speak irrationally.

Azuiggo: unsuitable, unskilled
I Azuiggore Ke Kam Dibo? Who is going to give this unsuitable/unskilled a job?

Azaaga: unsuitable place/unworthy place
I AzaagaT boiona. Don't sit in this unsuitable place.

AzaagaT: in a bad place

Anami: unknown

ABoy: unafraid, brave, fearless.
hE ABoy cola fira Kore. He moves about fearlessly.

Anunoy: making earnest request/ beseeching/begging
ami aPnare Anunoy Koria Koi I Kamta aPne Koroina zeno. I beseech you please don't do this. binoy, Anurudh, Anurudh Koria Kowa, Qub Koria Kowa

a
2

lukoKotha manushor muke muke bacia thakia zaay azar azar bosor. manshor muko Tara khani Paay-Pani Paay bacia thaKar-zagia thaKar; zela ase bacia aizO shazolalor masor kahini kichcha KoToshoTo bosor dhoria hOu masor lakhan zera aizO shazolaror Pukrir Panir nagorik.

DanobOKol Pailo noya aDesh; shazolale nisheD Disoin Tara zaTe ar manush na khaay. manushur khoTi zeno Tara ar na lekhe Tarar Kame Kaze; kinTu amra Taile Kemne bacmu baba kripar Poran! uTTore shazolal Dilen TaDer ek proTigga shunDor. bishshash rakho shobe

allaar uPre. Tain Tumrar khani Diba Pataia porTek Din; azar azar bosor dhori zoTo Din Tumra thaKbaay bacia khani aibo Tumrar muko utia. er Pore iTiaash Aia gelo eK; DanobOKol boDlia gelo borho borho maso.

Kala Kala gozar masor Dol Bashia utlo shazolalor Pukrir PaniT; aizO hI mas bacia ase ar azar manush PorTek Din loia ay Tarar khani Dur Desh thaki. I mas ar I zaDur kahini aizO bacia ase siletor bukur matiT.

silara shurma sOnet

a Ailo Dui nombor siloti Akkor.
uchcharon: as in understand, upper, utmost, **absolutely not like** Anna, Hannah, Sarah, man, van.

am: mango.
am mita fol. Mango is a sweet fruit.

ami: the agency of I.
ami eKzon manush. I am a human being

amar: mine, my. mor
ikta amar Boi. This is my book.

amra: we, us.
amra shombare hekniT zaimu. We will go to Hackney on Monday.

amrar: our, ours.
aPne amrar barhiT aila na. You did not come to our house.

amrarU: ours (asserting). amrarU I Kam Kora lagbo. We will have to do this job
(ourselves).

abhaowa: Weather. BabgoTik, PorisTiTi.
Read: Wuthering Heights: Emily Brontë

azana: unknown. azana zaga. Unknown place.
azana zagaT Kare gia zikai. In this unknown place who do I go to ask?

azab: pain, suffering (suffering at death bed) or in hell. ami borho azabo asi. I am in
serious pain.

alaa: the rice that has not been boiled, normal rice, not boiled rice. ami alaa caulor BaT
khai. I eat normal rice (as opposed to brown or boiled rice)

aulia: pious man
shazolal eKzon aulia asla. Shah Jalal was a pius man/godly person.

azan: prayer call. At the time of the five prayers of the day a prayer call is made on loud
speaker calling people to pray.

ata: walk. ata shaisTor lagi Bala. Walking is good for health.

atani: to get walking done as is walking a dog. ami amar kukurre ataniT/ataT loia
geslam. I went to walk my dog.

ataa: wholegrain flour. ataa Dia caaPaTi banani Ay. Chapati is made from atta flour.

alamoT: sign. rugir Bala Aowar kuno alamoT nai. There's no sign for the patient to get
better.

anaa: 1/16th of a taka. shullo anaa bicar Korio. Jugde (something) fairly. shullo anaay eK
tEKa Ay. Sixteen anaas make a taka.

ana: to bring. Tebulor uPoror Boita ano. Bring the book that's on the table.
ani, anoin, ano, anos, ane (I, you-formal, you-close, you-informal, he/she-informal)
anani: to get something brought. ghoro khani rakia Otol Tone ananir DorKar kiTa?
What's the point getting food from a restaurant when there's food at home?
ana: without. ana Tele kila ranDoin? How can one cook without oil?

anaanash: pineapple. anaanashor bagan. Pineapple garden/plantation. anaanash
khaowar baDeU Dudh khaile shoril kharaP Korbo. If one drinks milk immediately aftetr
eating pineapple one wil be sick.

anaTele: without oil. anaTele mas biran Kora zaay na. One can not fry fish without oil.

anTanzi: guess/without a clue/without a basis. anTazi maathiona. Don't speak without a
basis.

anaiPanai: creating a fuss/giving lame excuses. anaiPanai Korio na. Don't give miserable
excuses!

anarhi: naïve/inexperienced. anarhir lakhan Kam Koriona. Don't work like a novice.

aowa: to come. aPne obayDi aukka. Could you please come this way?

aOr: lake. sileto shoTo shoTo aor ase. There are hundreds of lakes in Sylhet

aOla: haOla. in the care of. allaar aOla Korlam. I leave (you) to Allah's care.

ag: front/ahead/too early. lainor ag. front of the queue. hE age gese. He went ahead. age
age maatha Bala naay. Speaking too early is not good.

agaa: top of a tree/tip. gasor agaa. Tree top. culor agaa. Tip of the hair.

agam: ahead. agam khobor. News learnt ahead of time.

aghaa: to open one's bowel (col), informal. Formal: Paykhana Kora.

agami: shamneDi, BobishshoTe. future/advance/day ahead.
asha Kori aPnar agami Din Bala zaibo. I hope you future goes well/I wish you a happy
future.
ami agami Kail fulam zaimu. I will go to Fulham tomorrow.

agamiT: shamneDi. BobishshoTe. in the future. agamiTe abar Dekha Aibo. See you in the future.

asha: hope. asha sarha manush bacTo Parena. People can not live without hope. naTashar asha Ailo Tan QuabOKol. Natasha's hopes are her dreams.

asha Kora: to hope.
ami asha Kori. I hope.
ami asha Kori inDiraay PorikkaT Balo Korbo.
I hope Indira would do well in (her) exams.

araani: to lose. Tan shoron shoKTi araai gese. His ability to remember has been lost.

aram: rest/comfortable. ki aramor zibon! What a comfortable life.

aram Kora: to rest/to live comfortably. Tain Kam Tone aia aram Korra. Having got back from work he is resting.

aram Deowa: to make comfortable. I zuTataay amare borho aram Der. These shoes are very comfortable.

aram Paowa: to feel relief. beDnar ushoD khaowar loge logeU Qub aram Paisi. Immediately after taking the pain killer I felt the relief.

ari: saw. ari Dia gas ciroin. You saw a tree with a saw.

ashik: lover. ashik sarha premor muillo Ke buzbo? Who else could understand the value of love (without being) a lover?

arif:good person. Tain eKzon arif manush. He is a good person.

aiz: today. aiz shunDor Din. It is a beautiful day.

aizku: on today. aizku aiTam ParTam naay. I can not come today.

andhair: darkness. andhairo kunTa Dekha zayna. Nothing is seen in the dark.

acanoK: amazing/out of the ordinary/strange. I To borho acanoK Kotha! This is strange!

azgubi: unbelievable. Ila azgubi Kotha zibone hunchina. I have never heard such a strange thing!

azar	thousand.
amrha	a sour fruit/useless/pointless
amon	a type of paddy
amonUra	the field where amon paddy is grown
amUdfurTi	enjoying
aguani	to ahead/progress
ashami	a defendant
ashaami	Assamese
ashman	sky, aKash, akash, biman
ashmani	of the sky/of heaven/heavenly
aK	line/scribble
aKa	to draw
aKani	to teach drawing/getting something drawn/to scribble
agla	separate
aglani	to separate
agonmash	name of a month
alaP	chatting
alaP Kora	to chat/to discuss

amma: Mother. Mum. ammu, ammi, ammazan, ammizan, ammuzan, maizi, maa, maTa

33

Read: Mother: Maxim Gorky

abba: Daddy, father. PiTa, pita. baba, abbu, abbi, abbazan, babazan, bazan, baPzan.
Read: Sylvia Plath

aa

3

shunar dhanor kheTo shimahin agonmashor roiD zhori Porhe
zeno eK maTal uTshob niralaay alor noDi Aia megh Aia zhore;
baTashor Torongila Dushto deU ay Dourhi Dourhi shagoror
dhola dhola deUor lakhan. eKtar uPre aroKta deU Bangia Porhe

zeno Tara nirai ashir zhorna eK. cairobaay Qushir miTali tania lamaay
ani Quabor Dunia eK siletor zominor kocua norom gaar Taza Taijjub
mayaT. gramo gramo ashar baTTi gan Aia ute Dinor moholla zurhi
ashamnor rong sobishob aKe agamir mayaBora eK anonDor Dinor.

ki gan lekhmu ami? ki Dia anmu ami amar I gorib golaT I gan? kila
silet Tumi dhoinno mati! Tumar namor banan dhoinno, Tumi zeno
mar zobanor shuaagor soa. ami cesta Kori borho Dia mon zaTe amar

zoban Paay hasakur Basha-hasakur cerag baTTir rushnaI zar shoKTi
bole zoban amar Aibo Tumar golar shurma-Konti azob shunDor ze
shunDuror shuTa Dia ami gathmu Qushir kinarahin I siloti boyaan.

silara shurma sOnet

aa Ailo siloti Tin nombor Akkor.
uchcharon: as in under, aha

aalla: name of village in Sylhet. On the other hand, **allaa:** allaar nam neow. Pray to
Allah. allaah, allaaTala, allaaPaK

aaToki: taking one's only hope or source of dependence. Ila amare aaToki Korio na.
don't make me hopeless/helpless like this.

aami: dried mango. Kaca am katia hukaia aami banani Ay. aami is made by drying
chopped up green/unrippen mango

aaga: to open one's bowel (colloquial use). baichchatar agaTe borho Kosto Ar. The child
is hurting very much when opening his/her bowel (referring to constipation).

Constipation: Paykhana Koshan, Paykhana Koshan Aowa.

aaṭaa: glue. Katlor aataa. jackfruit's glue.

aaṭaani: to tighten something. aataaia bandho. Tie it tighly.

Aagaani: to go ahead. aaggaaia zaow. Go foreard, go ahead.

Aacani/aacaia Delkha: to test (the market), aazani, aazaia Dekha.

aazani: bring closer. noukata aro aazaowcain. Bring the boat closer. KanDaani, Birhani, KanDaabaay ana, KanDaa lagani.

aazam: the person who does the circumscision (which is Sylhet is a family run business whereby an aazam's son might end up becoming an aazam himself).

aahazari/aahazari Kora: Crying inconsolably (as in when someone's loved one has just died.

aanja: To chop a fish on its sides without sepating it.

aanja-aanji: Hugging, particularly after the Eid prayers. kulakuli, gola milani.

aaowa: the eggs hen lays without mating with a cockrell.

aalamotT: sign. Dinor aalamoT Bala nay. The day does not look be good

O

4

amar zanor kut̲aT Dukko eK zagia thakia Kore gan harabela.
Katol Pakir moTo gan gaay I Dukko amar DinraiT-khali gaay
gan: amar koTTo Duk! amar KoTTo Duk! ar ami ati Acina
Potho buko loia Dur Duniar Dur shob acanoK Quabor Desh

zara shagoror Panir Tolor barhia ut̲a coror lakhan barhia ut̲Te
thaKe niralaay. nicuP Duniar eK anguror loTar moTo zibon amar
baia ut̲e rushnir macango. shurma noDi TobuO moioTorO Kotha
Koia zaay zaTe ami mono raki zibon o moioTor zugol nibash-Bitar

Kotha. ma amar, mono Ay, KoiTa amare: eK Deshor buli, babu,
mono rakio, AiTo Pare aroK Deshor kuno gali. zuDio manshor
zobanshob shunDoror Kori zaay ki azob bonDona-sonDona aha!

shurma noDir Pani burhigonga Taki kuno Binno kisu naay; naay
kinTu AinnomoTo Bolga kimba Ioki noDir PaniO. shob noDi, Pani
ar gan manshor eK zinDegirI ekI anonDo o Dukkor gathar bagan!

silara shurma sOnet

oba: Hello/hello, listen. oba! obayDi hunocain. Hello dear, listen. (informal)

otaa: This one. otaa obayDi Deowcain. Pass this one this way.

oKta: This one

otaaU: Definitely this one

oKtaaU: Definitely this one

oU: Here. Ono, Ino, ikano, Okhano

oUnU: Definitely here

ogu: This one (boy or girl or it)

oguin: These (boys or girls or these)

ogula: These ones (things)

ogulain: These ones (things)

oguTa: This one (thing)

oguinTain: These ones(things)

oaayDi: This way.

obarhi: This household

orfias: Orpheus, the greek god of Music.
Read: Rene Maria Rilke

O

5

maghur masor cikcik zhilimili camrhar shunaT haraDin
shuruz zoli-Purhi ki baTTir acanoK shuna zoma Kori zaay
zanTaay caowni Tumi aiz? zanTaay caowni Tumi urhal bilor
aU aU deUor maze ki azob acanoK biraz coli zaay? aOrOKlor

Panir aynaT ki lazuk nizomuk Dekhe modhumoTi ou bisTor
ashamn zar shuinoTar mokhmoli culo ciroinor mayar moTon
boia zaay aha ki Im shumonTo baTashor Amol angul shob aha!
Qushir mukTa Kore zholmol zanor monikutar manikor aarhi

zeno uclia uclia Porthe Bora gangor uTalPaTal zuboTi Angor
buzi shanTi nai ATo Tar zan Bora gan ATo Tar Bora gan zan!
hithano balish ase nice eri nirail loTar eK aKalia baKalia Desh!

zanor monDira baze coukor noDir Qula Desho zeno aha fulor
condon ar bashor zharhor sonDo milimishi haon mashor megho
daUkor gan anonDor gang Aia boia zaay zibonor ei kichchakahini

silara shurma sOnet

Ono: Here

Okhan: Here

Okhano: In here

Omaa: Exclamation/surprise/pleasantly shocked

Ommaa: Exclamation/surprise/pleasantly shocked

OKol: all, everything, shoKol, shoKolTa, hoKolTa, shobTa

I

6

Parul Pagla Purhi siletor kun zeno gauT eK zonmia bacia
gesil eKDin. Quabor Dorhi Dia Paowo Tai KoTo Din KoTo
KoTo bar uṯse namse amluki gasor ruPali mathaar shanTo
ceragor AYringor coukor moTo Desho; zuan shoril mono

Tair thoi thoi zoubonor khoihin Torol moDor moTo shagor
eK gan gaisil eK Din: khali eK Quabor dhUashar moTo kuno
eK Duroir ashmanor soa Paia. ze Poroshor zaDu Tar couko
heDin ruisil KoTo modhu-Quabor KoTo shiulir koTo cera!

heDin gasor uPre Tai boisil eK Porir lakhan shuna roiDor
PaniT Bizaia Tair shumoTTo shunDor shunar zaDur moTo
Dui Paow Dia meli; Dekhsilni Tai nizor Dui couke ki Duniar

Amisal baTTi Aia Tair meghomala Kala culo shunar aguin eK
khulia Disil eK AshomBob moha alorhon! kinTu ze asil ubaia
amluki TolaT Tar aTTa shikar Koria nisil AzonTapuror Parule.

silara shurma sOnet

Ila	Like this. Ila Kam Kora Bala nay.
Ilaa	To move. hobayDi Iloincain. Could you please move that way?
Im cold!	Cold. ze Ime dhorse! (I am) feeling terribly cold. ze Im Porhse! What a
Imani	Cold spell of winter. Imani Porhse. Terribly cold!
Ish	Expression of sympathy (if someone gets hurt in front of one, one says: Ish!)
Ilm/Ilim	Knowledge/knowledge of the unknown world

I   This (I, note, is not pronounced as English I! 'I' signifies near: ino-here hIno- there)

i

7

aral bilor muk anonDor Qubi zeno eK; haraDin harabela
Kore khela ashmanor nilua nilua bilashi bahuloTa dhoria
shunDor. shobDohin bon, tilla ar uca uca PaYrh caia thaKe
bubar moTo zoban araia I shuBon arali sobir ganor mayaT.

eniara aral namor meye, ase eK aralir goBir bukur gohon
nilua zanor kuṯaT; cokur arhalo arhal arhal Tar lazuk lazuk
shob khela. canni raiTor rushnir moTon Tar Basha! Panir
cokuT aha eniara Porir moTon eK nari ze Tumar zanor maze

loia ay eK Pagol dhomKa boishag mashor dhomKa zhorhor
moTon! aha! Tar aT zeno kahinir Desh eK! aha! Tar alor angul
shob Quli Quli meli meli zaay ki BesTor DuniaBashani gan!

eniara siletor meye; zobano Tar Patharia fute zeno ashman
fulor lakhan zekhano Dunia-maTa khali ze mathia zain ki
anonDo ruPKotha. eniara mayar Porosh, eK mayadhari Paro!

silara shurma sOnet

iD	Eid
ikan	Here, this.
ikano	In here
inDara	Water well. IDaara.
iTa	This. iTa kiTa? What's this?
iTain	These.
ishkul (primary),	school, skul, iskul, shkul, biDDaloy, Patshala (primary), Pashshala

iman   Faith

imam   Imam(priest).

imamoTi Kora: When the imam leads a prayer (nomaz/namaz, one of five a day) standing in front of the congregation he is said to be doing imamoTi or imamoTi Kora or nomaz/namaz PoYrhani: to lead a prayer (as in a namaz) where as to lead a prayer (not nomaz but a general prayer to God) is Dua Kora but Dua Korani is if one organises an imam to come round to one's house and joins and leads other people to a special recitation of the Quran and holy scriptures and then all the congregation prays. That could be done at a Mosque as well.

ibar   This time, this year.

ikanTa   This thing, this one.

ikhanTa   This thing, this one

iaarana   Friendship. ebla Kamor shomoy; iaarana baaDe Korbaay. Now it's working time; you may do your friendships later.

iaar   Friend

iaarbondhu   Friends/companions/mates, pals

india   India, BaroT, BaroTborsho

igula: These. Igulaay Ino kiTa Korer? What are these doing here?

iTTaDi: Etc. am, Katol, zam iTTaDi. Mangos, jack fruits, berries etc

imon: shunDor, a male name, this mind.

iaan: North East, the north east corner of a house. iaan Deowa: to lay the foundation of a new house by putting up a pole in the North East corner.

iarki: Joke, dOng, dOng Kora, iarki Kora: to joke around, iarki mara: to joke around

isaa: prawn, isaa mas, isrhe, ichrhi, ichrhi mas

ichcha: wish, ichcha Kora: to wish, ichcha Aowa: to feel like (doing something). amar am khaibar borho ichcha Korer. I am feeling like having mango very much.

ichcha shoKTi: Will power, willingness, wilfulness.

ingsha: hatred, feeling resentment, jealousey. ingshani: to hate/resent/feel jealous

u

uzan	High land or the higher up the river's path
uPor	Up
uPre	(On) the up, uPreDi: upward
uTTor	north/answer

Read: Northanger Abbey: Jane Austen

uTTre	On the north. uTreDi: northbound
uTTreDi	Towards the north/northward/northbound
ubani	To stand up, to wait
utan	Yard outside one's house
ulta	Opposite, biPoriT
ukkaa	Hookah
ukil	Solicitor. edBuket, ainzibi, ainbiD.
ukaloTi	The profession of being a solicitor
ukaloTnama	Affidavit
uaa	Breath
uaa falani	To breathe. uaa lowa, shash neowa, Dom neowa/lowa
uaa lowa	To breathe.. shash falani. shash lowa.
ukauki	Loiter about
ukauki Kora	To loiter about. ukauki Deowa/mara.

ujjol	Bright/burning bright. zholmola, zholmol Kora. zhikmiki Kora.
uzala	Illuminated

unnish   19. ami unnish nombor Dibosh shoroniT thaki. I live at 19 Dibosh Shoroni (Dibosh Street).

uciT	Ought to be/righteous (AnuciT not wise/immoral)
ukoin	Head lice
urI	when a lot of people at night call out together to attract attention so to get help (when they are attacked by robbers).
unDal	Kitchen. unDakhal, randha ghor, ranna ghor, roshOi. roshOi ghor,
ranna ghor	

uDla: naked, bare. lemta, nengta, KaPorhchuPorh sarha, ana KaPrhe.

unDur: mouse

unDakhal: Kitchen.

um: warmth, umla/umli ghorom: luke warm

um Deowa: when a hen sits on her eggs what she does is said to be um Deowa.

ulta: opposite. ultaPalta: all mixed up, does not make sense.

ugar: a special room built inside the house to store dried up paddy.

ucnic: up and down

uTal PaTal: stormy, waving, unrestful, incessant

uDan: Untime, bad time

urhukkol: Plane, air plane, air bus

uTla: boiling

ushol: to pay off
ushol Kora: to pay off a debt, to get the most out of something (like a piece of garment)

ummoT: The followers of prophet Mohammed (SM) are referred as ummoT (a community of followers). ummoT together makes up the umma or ummah

uPash: hungry, hunger

uPashi: Hungry

uPobash: Hunger

uPobash Kora: Staying hungry.

utka: Vomiting

ulaauta: Cholera. Pendemic of Cholera

U

Ula: Tom cat/male cat

Uli: Female cat

Ulluk: Dear/idiot

Uri: a Sylheti green beans

Ura: leaking from the roof

Ut: Camel

Usta: Kick on something,

Usta khaowa: To bump onto something.

UstabIstaa: Something that has no wroth. UstabIstaar zinish: things that have no worth or value (and thus suffer disrespect or careless treatment).

Uthan: Being difficult.

Uthan Kora: being contrary, being difficult, being silly

Ucaton: Sense of unrestfulness, sense of longing.

Uar: Pillow cover. Ushar.

UPol: Name of a fresh water fish (that does not have much following! (as in it is held in very contemptful esteem!)

Ush: Sense. hUsh, hUsh buDdhi.

e

eKzon: One person.

eKta: One thing

eKla: alone. eKlaguli, nishshongo.

eggaro: 11. eggaro ambagan shoroK. 11 Ambagan Road.

ebla: Now. ekhon, One, Okhon.

ekhon: now.

ekhano: Together. All together. Mixed up. Mixed.

ei: Calling out (informal). This.

ei ma: One would call his daughter: ei ma, obaayDi hunocai. Darling, listen. O ma, obaayDi hunocai. Darling, listen.

ema: Another expression ofr ei ma, O ma. Darling, love, dear. Beautiful.
Read: Emma: Jane Austen.

ei ze Bai: Calling out to someone formally (man) to stop someone to ask for help

ei ze Boin: Calling out to someone formally (woman) to stop someone to ask for help

eKakar: Mixed up, blended, entwine

ebong: And. o, ar.

eshaa: The fifth prayer of the day (and the second and last of the evening).

eshaar AKT. The time of praying the prayer of eshaa.

eshaar nomaz: The prayer of eshaa.

eTeqab: In the month of Ramadan some people (who can) might go and live in the mosque full time in order to pray continuously as they fast and while most would do that from the 27th of Ramadan til Eid Day. This practice is called eTeqab.

enTar: countless. Lot of.

eta: This one.

eru: Too little, little.

eruTa: A little. Very little.

eKzora/eKzera: A little

eloPaTarhi: Running without direction.

enda: Egg, dim, boiDa.

eboTorhi: Up until now.

E

Ela: Neglect, abandonment, ignoring. Abohela, Abohela Kora. Showing contempt.

Ela Kora: To neglect, to ignore, to show contempt.

EnglaPengla: Very thin (lack of nourishment).

Elani: To move something, to bend something, to shift something.

Erhani: To laugh in a silly way, to laugh without knowing why.

EbrhaTebrha: Uneven, jagged.

EOT: Winter, winter time, dry season.

k

kebla	The way to Makkah
keblamuka	Towards Makkah
kuno shomoy	Sometime
kuno shomoyU naay	Never

Read: Never Let Me Go: Kazuo Ishiguro

kono shomoy naay	Hardly
kiTa	What
kila	How
kil	blow/punch
kilani	To hit/blow/punch
kina	To buy
kinra	Buyer, lowra, qreTa
kiba	If/whether. kimba, kingba
kun	Which/angle
kuna	Angle/corner
kunakuni	Diagonal
kunTa	Something
kunDin	What/which day
kun shomoy	What time

kun baala	What time
kunozor	Bad intention/ dirty look
kuTTa	Dog (is a highly derogatory swear word)
kuTTi	Bitch (is a highly derogatory swear word)
kula	A Sylheti kitchen item used in food preparation
kinara	Near/bank (of a river, pond)
kisu	Some
kisukunTa	Something
kichcha	Story
kIran	Low cast/farmer (derogatory)
kicoK	Noisy
kiar	A Sylheti land measuring unit
kia	A plant used to make sitting mats
kiTab	Religious books, books
kiTab kuran	Religious matter, religious scripture
kinTu	But. kinTuk
kinTu kinTu Kora	To hasitate. amTa amTa Kora.
kiano/kunkhano/kunano kubai/kuai	Where
kur	Lap (when one is holding a baby)
kurkuri Kora	To make crispy sounds

kira	To swear (to make an absolute oath), pledge, oath
kira Kora:	To swear
kickici Kora	When a lot of birds gather and make a lot of noise
kiron	Sunrays. rushni, rushnai,

kh

khaowa	To eat/drink
khaowani	To feed
khaowra	One that eats
khaowaowra	One that feeds
khela	Play/game/sport
khelani	To play
kheirh	Game
kherhual/kherhual	Sportman
khana	Food
khani	Food
khola	Place where harvest is gathered, dried and sorted out
khobis	Evil/dirty/with bad habbits
khan	A family title
khonDokar/khonKar	A family title
kharaP	Bad
khal	Animal skin
khaaYlaa	To take the skin off a slaughtered animal
khala	Maternal aunty. moi, mashi (Hindus use this word)
khazna	Tax

khoi	Fluffy rice
khobor	News. shongbaD, shombaD, PaTTa, barTa, khobor barTa, khUz.
kholoi	Basket
khoborDaar	Warning or prohibitive word used to warn or prohibit someone trying to do something that is aginst the law/norm of the land or the community
khUz	News
khUz lowa	To try to find out news about someone
khaash zomi	Government owned land
khaacari dail	A type of lentil
khasha	The best
khamoKa	For no reason/ to no avail
khanoKa khazanchi	chef/butler
khaishloT	Habbit/bad habbit
khablakhabli	To try and eat thoughtlessly, pinching food, grabbing food
khashia	A tribe in Sylhet

khaab: Dream

khaab Dekha: To dream

khoTi: Loss, harm, damage.
Read: Damages: Josephine Hart.

KH

KHiTTa	Field/ patch
KHicurhi	A dish made of lentils, rice and often meat
KHicurhi banani	To make a mess
KHicani	To beat up someone (a threat)
KHicrha	One that is too persistent (in a negative way)
KHica	Wallet (not a European wallet)
KHiTKHiT/KHiTKHiTi	A sense of disgust/discomfort because of wetness.
KHiTKHiT/KHiTKHiTi Kora	To feel a sense of nosea/ discomfort because of being wet

K

Kal: shomoy.

Kaalbela: Bad time. Time of misery. Time of death and destruction. Aweful time. Ominous time. The last time (in the sense of last day or judgement day).
Read: Kalevala: Finnish Epic: Compiler and Editor: Dr Elias Lönnrot

Kaalor bOlaa: The angel of death. The messenger of death.

Kaal: Death. Angel of death.

KaalE dhora: Death catching up with one.

KaaYl: Deaf.

Kam	Work
Kam Kora	To work
Kaz	Work
KamKaz	Work
Kamor	Something of use/value
Kamla	Worker
Kamani	To shave/ earn
Kaman	Cannon
Kamrhani	To bite, muscle pain, pain, bitting pain.
Kala	Black, cIai, kala, Kalo
Kana	Blind.
Kaca	Unripe/young/naïve

KanDa	To cry
KanDaa	Near
Kora	To do
Korani	To get something done
Kowa	To say/speak
Kowani	To get someone speak or tell
Kowra	One that is speaking
Kotha	Speech/the fact/the thing/the matter
Kocua	Green. shobuz
Kolom	Pen
Kolla	Head
Kaua	Crow, kak, KaK
Ka Ka Kora	To crow
Kangla	A fish
Kangal	One that wants to eat everything as if they had never seen these food items
Ke	Who (singular)
Ke Ke	Who (plural)
Kene	Why, kiTar Daay, kiTar lagi, kiTallagi
Kar	Whose (singular)
Karar	Whose (plural)

Kelaa	Who (Tui)
Keta	Who (Tui)
Kegu	Who (Tui)

KerKeri Kora: If there is sand in a sandwich it is described as such.

Kolera: Cholera. Ulauta. kolera. **Read: Love in the Time of Cholera: Gabriel Garcia Marquez.**

Q

Qub: Very, very much, much

Qubi: Beauty

Quab: Dream. shoPno, khab, shopon, shoPon.
Tain Koila: adhunik Kalor monobiggan Quab ki zinish ikta buze Kori ami mone Korina.
He/she said: I do not think modern psychology understands what dream is.

Quab Dekha: To dream. manshe ze Quab DekhTo Pare oKtaU Ailo monushoTTor
borho Proman. The big proof of humanity is in that fact that humans can dream.

Qun: Blood. Murder

Qun Kora: To murder/to kill

Quni: Murderer/killer

QunaaQuni: Murderous

Qiaal: Awareness, alertness

Qulna: Name of a district

Qula: Open/to open

Qulani: To get opened

Qula Dile: With open heart, without reservation

Qulasha: Open, detailed, descriptive

Qulasha Koria Kowa: To tell everything honestly/ in details

Qua: Dew. shara raiT Qua Porhia ghashre ruPali Korilise. All night dew fell making the
grass silver.

Qua Porha: Dew falling

Qur: Hoop

QIra: Cucumber. shosha.

QIra kheT: Cucumber field

Qirani: To milk (a cow/goat)

Qica: Money bag (Not a wallet, however)

Qicuni: Convulsion

Qila: Toothpick. Qilail

Qilail: Tooth pick

QianoT: Losing money, particularly, if the money was given to in trust. If A asks B to keep some money for him in trust and A then spends it. That is a QianoT. The money in question is amanoT. Losing trust.

Qunta: Pinching

Qunta Deowa: To pinch

Qunta mara: To pinch

Quta: Pole.

QUta Deowa: To remind someone that they owe one something. If one tells their friend that they had lent them money the friend concerned would be offended because his friend reminded him of his favour: QUta Deowa.

Quashar: In Sylheti, apparently, there's no word for snow or snow fall. For ice we have borof/boraf and borof/boraf is used for snow as well. Qua is dew that appears in silver white colour. megh is for rain and clounds. So, shobDolara proposes Quashar (Qua and shar from Tushar, the Bangla word for snow) for snow. Substitue words for snow as Quamegh, Quadhla (dhola-white), forshamegh (bright white rain), shaDamegh (white rain). Therefore, Quashar Deowa, Quashar Porha and Quashar Aowa for snow fall. (Quamegh Porha, Quadhla Porha, forshamegh Porha, shaDamegh Porha etc for snow fall). And another word for snow could be: ImuTTorashar: Im is cold, north is related to cold north wing and shar from Quashar and thus ImuTTorashar. Snow. May be, for poetic purposes!

Quashar Deowa: Snow fall

Quashar Porha: Snow fall

Quashar Aowa: Snow fall

Quasha: Fog. dhuasha: smog

g

gan	Song
gan gaowa	To sing
gaayoK	Singer (male), gaayika (female
gaT	Hole
gamla	Big bowl
gaTaa	to pierce
gIT	Song
gITi	Songs
gIla	To swallow
gona	To count. gonona Kora
gonani	To get someone counting
goru	Cattle
gorumi Kora	Behaving/speaking like a cow/ fool
gadha	Donkey. Stupid
gonda	A unit of four
gunda	A ruffian/thug
ganda	Big
gala	To break
galaT	Near by, adjacent

gOla	To melt
golaa	Neck
goTo	Gone/past
goTo Kail	Yesterday
goTo bosor	Last year
gondar	Rhinocerous
gondaror camrha	Hard skin/ nothing gets to someone
ganabazna Kora	Having fun/ singing and merry making
gas	Tree
gesh	Gas
garhaa	To push something in the ground
gaarha	A muddy hole
guTa	To push/poke
guTani	To poke
guTaguTa Kora	to poke about
gulli	Tablet, bullet. borhi.
gulli Kora	To shoot
gul	Field
gUl	Round
gumrha	Sad. gumra

gumra	sad. bezar
gUaani	To waste
gulab/gulaP/gulap	Rose
genjam	Trouble. Difficulty.
genjam lagani	To create trouble
golTi	Mistake
goloTi	Mistake .
golTi Kora	To make a mistake
golDa	Big
golDa chingrhi	King Prawn
goyro	Absent
gorazir	Absent
goP	Chat, talk, story
goP Kora	To chat, to talk
goP mara	To tell lies, to tell porkies, to big up
guPal	A name, sod, simpleton
gusha	Anger
gusha Kora	To get angry, to mind
gusT	Meat, flesh
gulmal	Problem, difficulty

gulmal laga	A difficulty arising
gulmal Kora	To create trouble
gese	went, towards.
genji	Vest
gaa	Body
gaaT	In the body
gau	Village
gram	Village
gang	River
gangkul	Riverbank
ganja	Cannabis
ganjurhi	Canabis addict
guna	Sin. PaP
gunagar	Sinner. PaPi
guP	Moushtach. mus
guPon	Secret
guPoniO	Confidential
guPTo	Hidden, secret
gun	Quality, merit
guta	Round size fruit or seed

gutti	A round size ball for games
gutta	Game (as in one game), scoring a point
gutani	To put away
guTam	Button. buTam
guTa	Hit with the head
guTani	Hitting with the head
guit	A herd of cattle
gullasut	A Sylheti game
guz	Hump
guza	Humpback
gua	beetle nut. shupari
gU	faeces
gondho	odour. baD gondho
gondhail	Something that has started to smell, gone off
gitta	Tie. shoKTo Kori gitta bandho. Tie it hard.
giTa	The Hindu Bhagovat Geeta
gom	Wheat
gangcil	Sea gull

gh

ghor	House, household.
ghoro	In the house
ghorhi	Clock/watch
ghonta	Hour/bell
ghI	Butter/butter ghee
ghoshani	Wiping, scrubbing
ghash	Grass
ghush	Bribe
ghush Deowa	To bribe
ghush khaowa	To take bride. ghursh neowa. ghush caowa. To demand a bribe
ghUsh	One from the family that works as dairy family unit
ghUla	Muddy
ghin	hatred, loathing, deetesting
ghinPiT	Sense of abomination
ghinghin Kora	To feel a sense of deep abhorance/ hatred/ disgust
ghinna	Deep sense of abhorance
gham	Sweat
ghama	To sweat
ghamani	To make someone sweat

ghaa	Infection caused open wound
ghengheni Kora	Whinging/ speaking when no one wants to hear
ghun dhora	Wood getting eaten by worms
ghura	To spin/to go round

ghurha: Horse, stallion. Ashsho
Read: Ted Hughes

ghurhsoar: Horse ryder

ghurhi	meyer
ghurghur Kora	To go about as though having a bad intention to do something untoward
ghuraghuri Kora	Going about wasting time
ghum	Sleep
ghumani	To sleep
ghushi	Punch
ghushi mara	To punch

ng

No Sylheti word begins with this sound.

rong	Colour
rongcong	Shining
<u>d</u>ong	Joke
<u>d</u>ong Kora	To joke/ to muck about
Banga	To break
BangTi	Change/coin
baingoin	Aubergine/tomato/bilaTi baingoin.
bangla	Bangla (Bengali)

S

sorha	Rhyme
sOrha	Brook
sOrTa	Beetlenut cutter
saana	To make a mess
sagol	Goat
sagi	She goat
saaT	Roof
saTani	To annoy/harass/to give a hard time
saaTTi	Umbrella
salom	Dish/curry
sarha	To let go/ to divorce
sIna	Breast/chest
sIngol	Cane
sola	Bag/sack
sOla	Getting angry/angry outburst
sOnDo	Metre (poetry), rhythm
sOnDomil	Rhyming
sOnDomilani	To rhyme

sUBieT iUnion: Soviet Union

**Read: Imperium: Ryszard Kapuscinski. Translation: Klara Glowczewska
The Ten Days That Shock The World: Jack Reed**

samana: Things, material

sabal: Child

saai: ash, dust

sUta: Run

sUtonTo: That what is running

sUbasUbi: In a hurry, mayhem

shuzon: Good person, good people

shumon: good person, one with a good mind (male), shumona (female)

shuruchi: Good taste

shuruchishil: One with good taste

shuDorshon: handsome

shumoTTo: Full of youth and vitality (female), used to describe a young girl who has become a woman.

shuDin: Good days.

shuTa: Thread

shura: Alcohol

shur: melody, tune

shuza: Easy

shobiTa: Feminine name for the sun (Literary)

ch

In Sylheti the ch sound is used rarely since c is used most frequently instead of ch

chana   Chickpeas

chanachur   Bombay mix

C

cear   Chair

caoawaa   To look

caowYa   To want/need

caY   Tea

caP   Pressure

caPa   Introvert

cePa   Bent/dented

cera   Young plant

cEra   Appearance/look

cIna   Known

ciK   Scream

cin   Mark/spot

cillani   Shouting

cErag   Light/lamp

can/canD: Moon
Read: Ted Hughes

canDni/caDni/conni/canni   Moon light

cOK/khOrhi mati   Chalk

cOla   To move

coloia	Social/topical/up to date
conna	Forehead
can KoPali	The cow with a white patch on her head
conDon	Jewels
cUna	The paste made of lime stone
cUna PaTTor	Limestone
conDoni	Moon light
caanDa	Part/share/any money given to charity
caKa	Wheel
couk	Eye. noyon.
couka	Something that has a joint
couKat	Door step
col	Fashionable/topical/ up to date/tradition
coicoi	Screaming/making lot of noise by children
coicoi Kora	Children making lot of noise
cokkor	Turning round/rounds
cokkor Deowa	Doing rounds
cokro	Wheel, cycle.
corKa	Wheel
cuYka	Sharp
cuk	Anger

cukami	Being angry
cukTi	Contract/agreement
cur	Thief
curi	Theft
curi Kora	To steal
cubani	Putting someone under water
cUsha	To lick
cUshani	To get a child lick something (a lolly)
cUkaa	Sour
cuP	Quiet. nirai. nishchup
cuP Kora	To stay quiet
cuP thaKa	To stay quiet
cuP mara	To not speak (to stay silent)
cukumbuDai	One that does not use his brain but only shows anger
cEra	Feature/countenance/appearance
cair	Four
cairta	Four items
cain	A household item used to rid the rice or wheat off any unwanted item in it
caDDor	Shawl

coDri/couDri/choudhuri	A family title
cOYa	To plough the land
coPcoP	Quickly
coPcoPa	Moist/watery grass bed
caYP	Pressure
caYP Deowa	To apply pressure. zaTa, zaTa Deowa, zaTa mara.
caYPa	Introvert
caraa	Ability
caraahin	Helpless
caowa	To look
cal	Roof
caul	Rice (uncooked rice)
cOrha	Canary
corhani	Slapping
cotKona	Slap
cOti	A paste dried to make a savory item off mangoes
caati	A mat made of bamboo
caPaTi	Chapaty
canaa	Chick peas
cara	Plant
caakha	To taste out

caakia Dekha	To taste out something
carhal	One that makes pottery, a professional potter.
camar	Shoesmith
cabaani	To chew
cabani	Ache/pain in the body/muscle
caang	A hanging kitchen construstions that hangs from the roof
cUnga	A bambo used to blow air through it
cUnga Purha	To use bambo to cook a special kind of rice to make a savory item of food for a party/feast/special occasion
cIk	Screaming
cIk Deowa	Scream out
cIkani	To scream
cin	Mark
cinno	Sign/mark
cina	Known
cIna baDam	Chinese nut/ground nut
cIna	China/Chinese
cinTa	Worry
cinTa Kora	To worry
ciz/cis	Splinter of wood when got into one's skin.
cIz	Thing/a thing/ something

cirol	Cut out as in a leave that is cut out from its sides like decoration paper
coilTa	A sour fruit
ceTona/coiTonno	Consciouness. Ush, hUsh
coshma	spectacles/glasses
coshom	Sense of honour and humanity
coroTa	A type of wild tree
cora	To graze (cattle)
coiT mash	The penultimate month of Bangladeshi year
couDDo	fourteen
courasTa/ coumuki/coumuna/ coumuhoni/comuna	a junction with two roads crossing creating four roads (cou=four)
cuDa	to fuck (swear word)
cuTra	nettles

j

In Sylheti, like the sound ch, j is not often used since j is replaced by z and zh sounds.

joy: Win. zoy

joy porajoy: Winning and losing. zoy Porazoy

jannaT: Heaven

jonom: Being born

jonom mati: Birth place

juni: Vagina. zuni, zuniPoth.

jounoTa: Sex, sexual, of or about sex. zounoTa.
Read: Second Sex: Simone de Beauvoir

jh

jhorna: Waterfall. kund, kundo, jolproBaT

jhorh: Storm
Read: Leaf Storm: Gabriel Garcia Marquez.

jhora: Wilting

T

Tin: Three. Tin Din. Three days/

Tan: His/her. Tan name kiTa? What's his/her name? (aPne)

Tar: His. Tar garhi. His car. (Tumi/Tui)

Tara: They (aPne)

Tarar: Theirs.

Tain: He/she (aPne)

Tanor: His/hers (aPne).

Tal: Beat

Taal gas: Sweet palm tree

Tala: Lock/to lock.

Tarla mara/Deowa: To lock.

Teraa: Star. Taraa.

Tol: Bottom/beneath. nic (below) .

Tola: bottom. Paor Tola (foot), zuTar Tola (sole)

Tokhon: Than

Taza: Fresh

TorTaza: Fresh

Terha: Bent

Tez: Zeal/strength/vitality/heat

Til: Sesame, beauty spot

TiTTa: Bitter, sour

Tingun: Three times

Tash: Card (game)

Tash khela: To play cards, card game

TaTrangi: The sensation one has when (his/ her urine is infected) urinating.

Talash/Tallash: To search, to look for, to look up

ToKTa: Wood planks used to make furniture.

Ton: Health

Tone: From

Tarha: Hurry

Tarha Kora: To hurry up

Tarha Deowa: To hurry someone up

TarhaTarhi Kora: To hurry up

Tamsha: Fun

Tamsha/ Tamasha Kora: To joke. Tamosha/Tamaish Kora.

Tama: Copper

Taraa: Star

ToPon: A clothing item that men wear in everyday life. Another word is lungi or longi.

TeKTani: To harass

TeKTo Kora: To harass or wear someone out

Tufan: Storm

Tula: To put something away

Tulaa: Cotton used in pillows

Taijjub: Amazed, speechless

TelismaTi: Out of the world activity, astonishing, unheard of, magic

Tela: With oil

Tel: Oil

TemoTo: Like that

Taana: Tired, worn out

TaaK laga: To get dazzled, to get amazed

TaaK lagani: To make (someone) dazzled or astonished

Tar baDe/TabaDe: After that

Tar Pore: After that

Tik: Determination. Swear to do or not do something with such volition and resolve that one will deem to be absolute about it and one will never break that oath.

Tik bandha: To get determined

Tik Kora: To swear (to do or not do something)

Toba: To pray for forgiveness (from God), promise to do or not do something

Toba Kora: To pray for forgiveness or promise to do or not do something

Tosla: Cooking saucepan

Tuba: Mess

Tuba lagani: To make a mess (of clothes etc)

Tumba: Sulking face, swollen face (as a result of one being sulky)

Tumba fulani: To make a sulking face

Tulshi: A plant used in Hindu temples and prayers

TiTTa: Bitter

Tishna: Thirst. Tishna, Testa

Tishna laga: To feel thirsty

Tish: Thirty. Trish, Tirish

th

thal/thala/thali: Plate

thaana: Police station. Pulish steshon.

thaKa: To stay

thoa: To keep

thamaa: To stop

thamaani: To cause something to stop/come to a halt

thUrha: A little

thubani: To pick (fruit)

thuk Deowa/thuk falani: To spit, to spit (in the sense of expressing hatred or disgust or contempt).

thorthOri Kora: shaking violently.

thabani: To slap

thomki zaowa: To come to a sudden holt

thOwa: To put away.

thankila: Longstanding resident of a place, honourable, known, well regarded.

D

Daa: A Sylhei kitchen knife with two legs made of galvanised iron on which it stands up.

Dan: To give/gift/present

Daan: Turn (in a game)

Deowa: To give

DaTa: One that gives (to charity)

DaT: Tooth/teeth

Dol: Group/political party

Din: Day

Dena: Debt

Dabi: Right (one has a right)

Dourha: To run

Dourhani: To run

Dur: Far

Duroi: Far

DurDin: Bad times, famine

Dukko: Sorrow/pain/suffering

DukkiTo: Sorry. Dukki: unhappy

Dushshomoy: Bad times

Dushmon: Enemy

Dushmoni: Enmosity, adversity

Dushmoni Kora: To commit acts of enmosity

Durbeboar: Mistreatment

DushcinTa: Worry/anxiety/concern

DuschcinTa Kora: To worry

Durgondho: Odour/bad smell

Dukan: Shop

DukanDar: Shopkeeper. Dukani, Dukanor malik. bebshaI.

Duibar: Twice

Dubai: Dubai

DiTiobar: Second time. Duinombor bar.

DonDo: Punishment. Suffering. Paying for one's deed.

Dosh: Ten. Dosh: society, community

Doshom/Dosh nombor: Tenth

Dom: Breath

Dom neowa: To breathe.

Dom lowa: To take a break.

Doma: sto stop

Domani: To get someone to stop

Dojjal: The Angel of death. Anti Christ.

Dolil: Document, papers, evidence.

Dolil PoTro: Evidence.

Dolal: Agent (mostly used as in a negative sense, often as a swear word). Collaborator.

Dolali/Dalali Kora: to act as an agent. To act dishourably

Dola: A rounded dry piece of earth.

Dolbol: Gang, group

Der: Late.

Deri: Late

Deri Kora: To be late

DemaK: To show off. To be full of oneself.

DimaK: Brain/head/Intelligence: DimaK khatai Kam Koro. Act using your head.

DimaK khatani: to use one's head.

Dina: A female name. Dina is the faminine of Din (Day)

Din: Day

Digra: Tying (a goat) with a long rope to hold it in a limited area so that it can not go away. Dorhi, roshi.

DIk: Direction.

DigonTo: Horizon.

Dil: heart, mind

Dilara: Two hearts.

Dila: Full of heart

Dilaara: With heart

DiP: Island. Panirzomi, PanirBumi, Panirmati, PanirBita, zoldanga, joldanga

**Read: The Island: Victoria Hislop
Ellis Island: Kate Kerrigan**

Disha: Direction. Sense of Direction.

Dibanisha: Day and night. Dibanishi.

DinBor: All day.

DiPanTor: Sending away to a remote island (as a punishment).

Dikka: Teaching.

Dikka Deowa: To teach (by a spiritual teacher). From Socrates to Plato.

Dikka laB Kora: To receive an education (from a spiritual teacher).

DinKal: The Times, bad times

Deowa: To give.

Deowani: To get things given

Deowaani: Public (law)

Deowaani ain: Public law

Dekhani: To show

DErha: One and half time.

Digun: Double. Duigun.

Dristi: Vision

DristiBongi: View point

Daag: Dent, mark, cut

Daga: Swindle

Daga Deowa: To defraud, to swindle

dh

dhakka: Push. tela

dhakka Deowa: To push. dhakka mara.

dhakka mara: To push.

dhakka khaowa: To get hit. To get a shock

dhakkadhakki: Pushing and shoving

dhakkadhakki Kora: To push and shove

dhoKol zaowa: Going over difficult phase.

dhir: Slow. Gengle.

dhirsTir: Calm, quiet, reliable, in command

dhaU dhaU: The sound of the flame burning furiously

dhaU dhaU Koria zola: Fire burning furiously

dhoraa:The earth

dhoroTi: The earth

dhoraa maTa: Mother earth

dhoroTi maTa: mother earth

dhorshon: Rape

dhorshon Kora: To rape

dhorshiTo/DorshiTa: Rape, rape victim

dhOTa: Gasping for air. Terribly exhausted so that one can hardly breathe

dhongshon: To bite (a snake biting).

dhongshon Kora: (a snake) to bite

dhamali: A communal event of dance and song

dhangorh: big, fat (people)

dhongsho: destruction

dhongsho Aowa: To get something destroyed, ruined

dhongsho Kora: To get something destroyed.

dhumdham: Big celebration

dhuma: Smoke

dhora: To catch/to hold

dhormo: Religion

dhormoKormo: Religious deeds.

dhormik: Pious. dharmik

dhormiO: About religion

dhoirjo: Patience

dhoirjo dhora: To be patient

dhunD: Trance

dhar: Sharp

dharani: Sharpening

dharaa: Flow. bonghodhara: flow of bloodline, flow of a river

dharaPaT: The book of number tables.

dhorTobibbo: That what is to be supposed, a priori, presupposed

dhOla: White. shaDa, Amol, Porishkar, forsha

dhoni: Rich

dhOni: Sound, word

dhomoK: To shout, to disapprove, to warn

dhomKa: sudden, gust. dhomKa baTash. Sudden wind. Gust of wind

dhakka: To push

dhaara: Section of a law

dhamacaPa: Hiding, covering up.

dhamacaPa Deowa: To hide, to cover up.

dhamacaPa Dibar cesta Kora: Try to cover up

dhaaga: Piercing

dhaaga Deowa: To pierce (ear or nose piercing)

dhaTu: Root, metal, mineral, semen

dharani: To sharpen

dharail: Sharp

dhanDa: business, motto, daze

dhormoshala: religious place

dhoPdhoP Koria ata: To walk with making thumping sounds

dhoPdhoP Kora: To make big noice

dhosh: Fall

dhosh nama: falling down, crumpling down, mud slide

dhorna Deowa: To pay a visit (to get something from the rich relation)

dhubi: Washerman. dhuPa.

dhuni: wood fire

dhuna: To beat up

dhuna Deowa: To beat someone up badly

dhomKa: gust

dhomKa baTash: Gust of wind

dhuTi: The piece of white cloth a Hindu man would wear.

t

tEKa: Money/Bangladeshi currency Taka

tan: Pull

tana: To pull

tenga: Sour

tEngra: A small fish.

tengraa: One that is rude, antisocial, lacking social tact

tePa: Shadowy place (under a big tree where no other plant will grow)

tiPa: Press. Massage (Done by family member in time of pain)

tika: Immunisation.

tIka: To survive. To bear

tilla: Hillock. tila.

tal: One lacking commonsense

tin: Tin

tana Deowa   To speak with an accent. tana Dia mathaa.

tulli: Roof.

tola: Wild cat

tontona: Ripe, hard and ripe.

tomtom: horse carriage. ghurhar garhi

toK: Sour

tukra: Piece, Part, nugget

tukra tukra: Fragment.
Read: Fragments: Poems, Intimate Notes, Letters: Marilyn Monroe.
The Fight at Finnsburg (Finnsburg Fragments): Old English Epic Poem.

tukra tukra Kora: To break something in piece, chopping something in many pieces.

tuPi: Cap

tuPatuPi: Children's picnic

tukri: A bamboo made basket

tuma: piece. A piece of apple, a piece of land

tuma tuma Kora: To cut something into pieces

tungtang: The sound one makes when stirring tea or coffee with the spoon

tuktuka: soft, fresh

tia: Parrot

tiP: Thumb print (for those who can not sign their name)

TiP Deowa: To put a thumb print

ṭ

ṭelaa: Push

ṭelaa Deowa: To push

ṭelaaṭeli Kora: Pushing and shoving

ṭOga: To cheat, to defraud, to swindle

ṭOg: Cheat

ṭikana: Address, nibash, mukam

ṭanda: Cold

ṭanda laga: To feel cold

ṭanda Porha: Cold to begin or fall

ṭasha: To put too much in a bag or basket.

ṭengaa: Pole. lati, Quti

ṭuli: Skull

ṭusha: Blow, punch

ṭushi: Blow, punch

ṭul: Empty

ṭukrani: To peck

ṭaat: Pretence, pretentious pride

ṭaat Dekhani: Keeping up appearance

ṭaat bozaay rakha: To try and keep up appearance

ṭUt: Lip

ṭahor: Guess. ṭaor

ṭahor Kora: To guess. ṭaor Kora

ṭuka: Knock

ṭukaṭuki: Knocking on

ṭuka mara: To knock

ṭuka Deowa: To knock

ṭukaṭuki Kora: To knock (a series of knocks that children might do as part of a game)

ṭunga: Paper bags used in shops

ṭaanga: Big wheel barrow. ṭelagarhi

ṭEsh: Lean

ṭEsh Deowa: To lean

ṭelagarhi: A big wheel barrow or cart

tEng: Leg (generally animals but colloquially for human legs as well)

d

dail: dail Dia bred khaow. Eat bread with lentils. NoakhaliT dail fole. Lentins grow in Noakhali.

dain: Right (Side)

daine: On the right

dan: Right (Side)

dane: Right (side)

dam: A bamboo made mat used to dry paddy and other food items

daK: Call, post, mail

daKa: To call.

daKaa: An animal (goat, cow etc) in heat

daki laowa: An animal to be in heat

daK Deowa: To call out

daala: A bamboo made item used in household chores.

dal: Branch, twig

dim: Egg, boiDa, enda

dima: Hen that is with eggs (laying eggs)

dunga: Paper bags

danKa: Wing. Dana, Pakha, PaKna

dula: To get dislocated. To move

dor: Fear. doraileU dor; na doraile nai. Fear exists when one is afraid; when one is not fear does not exist.

dorBoy: Fear. dorothir dorBoy nai. Dorothy is fearless.

dor Kora: o feel fear, to be afraid, to be scared.

dorani: To be afraid/fearful/scared

digi Deowa: To try to reach out for something

danda: Cane, pole

degar: knife, dagger.

dugdugi: drum

denga: A plant eaten as vegitable. data

deta: shoot (of a plant)

deki: A young cow

dEm: Side way shoot from a plant or tree

defol: A sour fruit eaten with food

dibi: Bottle. shishi, buTol

dabba: Tin, bottle, container

dibba: Tin, bottle, container

duba: To sing

dubani: To cause something to sink

dub: To go in the water

dub Deowa: To swim in, jump in, get wet

deKa: Ox

deki: Young cow

d̲

d̲aK: mail/post/call

d̲ekka: Push

d̲ekka Deowa: To push

d̲eki: A Sylheti wooden appliance to process the paddy into rice or grind rice into flour

d̲Ia: Push, hit

d̲Ia khaowa: To get hit on the head (as in walking onto a wall or door and get hit)

d̲eua: Wooden spoon to stir

d̲eU: Wave

d̲Engura: Fall over

d̲Engura khaowa: To fall and roll over

d̲ul: Drum. d̲uldoPi
Read: The Tin Drum: Günter Grass

p

prokriTi: Nature

prokriTo: Real

prokash: T appear/to be published/to be known

pran: Life/life energy

promiTias: the greek mythological character who brought light for humans.
Read: Prometheus Unbound: Percy Byshe Shelley

proTiruP: Likewise image, representation, doppelganger. **Read: The World As Will and Representation: Arthur Schopenhauer, Translation: E. F. J. Payne.**

In Sylheit this sound is very rare since it is replaced by P sound and generally where p is joined with another consonant followed by a vowel the sound is p but at the beginning of words and at the end it is mostly P.

P

Pan   A green leaf that is eaten with beetle nut

Pani   Water

Paow   Lleg/foot

PaTa   Leaf/page

PaTaa   To set up

PaTal: Underworld, underground
Read: Notes from Underground: Fyodor Dostoevsky. Translation: Larissa Volkhonsky and Richard Pevear

PaTalrel: Underground railway, tube train, tube lines.

Pala   To raise/to care/turn (taking turn)

Pal   Herd

Palong   Bed

Palki   A special carriage that is carried by men at wedding carrying the bride

Por   Not one's own

PinDa   To wear

Palaani   To throw

Poysha   Money/change

PoYrha   To read

Porha   To fall

Pas   Five

Pagol   Mad, crazy, insane, eccentric

Panna   Jewel

PIt   Back

Pic   Behind

Pai   One penny (Bangladeshi Poysha)

Paowa   To receive/to get get

Purha   To burn

Purhani   To get something burn

Pua   Boy, son, child, sele, baloK

Purhi   girl, daughter, meye, balika

Puli   Poom, kokko, Kamra, rUm

PuTa   Place where one's house stands

PaTTa   News, whereabouts. khobor, barTa, shombaD

PaTla   Light (weight)

PiPrha   Ant

Picla   Slimy/bad natured/naughty

Pobon: Air, wind

Pub: East

PubeDi: Eastward

Purbo: East

Putki: Bottom (of human body).

Puran: Old

Pishach: Cruel. Pichash, Pashondo, Pashan
Pir: Saint, saintly, godly

Pinjira: Cage

Pinjor: Ribcage, cage
Pukoir: A larg pond where people bathe. Pushkundi, Pushkunni

PeK: Mud

Paki: Bird. pakhi.
Read: Birdsong: Sebastian Faulks

Pakna: Ripe

Panjegana: Society, the Village Concil

PanchaiT: The Village Council, society, community

Pur: Village

Purno: Complete, whole. Pura, PuraPuri, purnango

Porisrom: Labour, Labourious

Porisrom Kora: To work hard

Pona: Newly bred fish, young fish

Palta: contra

PoTro: Leaf, letter (writing a letter to a friend)

Pokko: Side

Poircoy: Identity. PoriciTi, aTTo PoriciTi, nizor Poricoy. Known.

Read: Identity: Milan Kundera.

PoloK: Blink

Puzi: Capital. puji.
Read: Das Kapital: Karl Marx

PuzibaD: Capitalism.

PuzibaDi: Capitalist

Puzi biniUg Kora: To invest (capital)

f

fol	Fruit
fola	Grown (paddy in the field)
ful	Flower. kushum, Pushpo
folmul	Fruts
faal	Jump
fall Deowa	To jump
fon	Telephone
fIsh	Fees
fITa	Ribbon
fulaa	Swelling/to swell/to mind
fulfula	Fashionably dressed
fulconDon	Make up for a bride
fara	Torn
fari zaowa	To get torn
foysala	Resolution.
foysala Aowa	To get something resolved
foysala Kora	To resolve something
foshaD	Trouble
foshaDi	Troublesome

foshaD Parha	To creat troube
foshaD Kora	To make trouble
foshaD lagani	To cause trouble

faaYK: Gap. (Beware, it is not pronounced anything near like the English word you are thinking of!). mazkhanor khali zaaga. mazkhanor shuinnoTa
Read: Mind the Gap: Jeremy Miles.

fuYlaa	To take off the feathers of a chicken when cleaning it
fuY	Blowing of air from the mouth (and the same done by a priest for someone to get better as a way of prayer)
fufu	Paternal aunt. Pishi, Pishima (usually Hindus use these words)
fufa	husband of fufu. Pishemoshai, Pishu (Hindus use these words)
fika	Without. fika caY. Tea without milk
fika caY	Tea without milk
fikir	Being slimy/fishy
fikor	Being slimy/fishy
fikir Kora	To find a way
fikirbazi Kora	The act of being fishy
fiTa	Ribbon
fiTa Kata	To cut a ribbon to open something/ opening of something, a shop etc
fira	To turn
firia	Having turned round

firia aowa	To come back
firani	To cause coming back or stopping something happening
faana	Tiredness/exhaustion
fanaa	Release/let go
fanaa Deowa	To forgive/ release/let go
finki	Gushing out of blood
fen	The thick sauce that people drink made when rice is being cooked
fena	Foam
fena fena Kora	To break something to dust
falani	To jump up and down
faaYash	Fertile/fertilizer
fash	Pass
fash Kora	To pass
faYsh	Tight
faYshi	Death sentence
faYshi Aowa	To die by hanging
faYshi Deowa	To hang someone (by a court)
faYsh laga	Someone getting tangled up in their neck
fal Deowa	To jump
falafali	Jump about

falafali Kora	To jump up and about
fail Kora	To finish up a work on a piece of wood
fInish Kora	To kill off something
fInish Deowa	To take a break/finishing something
fInIsh Kora	To give something the final subtle and delicate touch when working on a piece of art or wood work
faTTi	Bad luck.
faTTi Aowa	To get misfortune
faTTi	A special occasion to celebrate one's life after he/she has been dead for a week on which a special feast is organised.
fata	To tear/fracture
fatani	To cause a breaking/fracture/tear
fatafati Kando	A huge affair
fatafati mair	A big fight
faraK/faroK	Gap/difference/distance between two things. faaYK
fEra	Measle
fara	To tear
farani	To cause something to be torn
fari laowa	To get something (a saree) getting torn
forsa	Documents of lands/any document

formaish	To ask someone to do something (bring me a glass of water, do this, do that etc)
formaish Deowa	To ask one to do something
formaish huna	To listen and do what is asked of one (normally younger ones)
forashi	French
forash Uri	French beans

b

buz: Sense. Understanding
Read: Sense and Sensibility: Jane Austen

buza: To understand.

bUza: Load, burden.

buz Deowa: To make something understood. To console.

bUza lowa: To lift a load, to lift a burden.

buzani: To explain, to make something understood, to persuade.
Read: Persuasion: Jane Austen

bol	Strength/power/energy/football
bola	To roll something
bowa	To sit
bala	Turn (one's turn)
balaa	Beautiful girl, beautiful young woman, princess, maiden
bala	Time
bela/beil	Time
balaa	Powder. ghurha, saai
bEla	Violine
bagan	Garden
barhi	House/home
bisna	bed (as in made bed not the bed)

bangla	Bangla Language. Bangla land. The Land of Bangla (Now Bangladesh and Poshchim Bong in India).
bangali	Bangaali Nation. Bangaali means anyone born of Bangaali parents that means people of Bangladesh and Poshchim Bong (India). All Bangaalis in Bangladesh are Bangladeshi but all Bangladeshis are not Bangaalis since there are other smaller nations, groups and entities of people who were born in Bangladesh yet they are not of Bangaali origin. The English term Bengali to mean both Bangla Land and Bangaali people should not be used as the name of the land has been Bangla all along and the people have always been Bangaali.
bengoli	bengoli has derived a new meaning in Sylheti. It means people from other parts of Bangladesh and are therefore not Sylhetis but bengoli. There is no negative connotation implied in the usage since it is used generally all over Sylhet.

bogoposhagor: The Bay of Bengal. The way we do not support the names of Bengal and Bengali for Bangla and Bangaali we oppose the the term Bay of Bengal for bongoposhagor. So, these are some alternatives: bongoshagor, banglaposhagor, banglashagor, banglajol, Bangla Bay. Bay Bangla. These words can be used as they are in English as name for the Bay. **Same goes to Royal Bengal Tiger: Royal Bangla Tiger is the best term.**

bikal	Evening
birhal	Cat. bilai, billi, mekur
biman	Plane. urhukkol
bia	Marriage/wedding
bia Kora	To get married (man)
bia bowa	To get married (woman)
bazar	Market
bazar Kora	To shop
bezar	Sad

bemar   Illness/ill

bemari   Ill person/patient

beshomar   A lot

beshi   A lot

bebat   Stupid

beiman   Lier/betrayer

bish   twenty/pain/poison

baTash   Air

baTash Deowa   Wind to blow

baki   The rest/buying thing on credit

baazani   To play (an instrutment)

bash: bamboo.

basha: House in the city

bashabarhi: Accommodation in the city. House, flat

barha: To grow, to incrase

barhabarhi: Go beyond one's limit, transgrassion.

barthTi: Additional

bakka: A lot

besh: A lot

baD: Bad

BaaDe: afterward

beng: frog

bel: A hard shelled fruit

banan: Spelling

banan Kora: To spell

banani: To make

banaroshi: eK zaTor KaPorh/sharhi. benaroshi sharhi.

beta: man. beta manush

beti: Woman. beti manush, nari, mohila, zuboTi

balish: Pillow

bali: Sand

balika: Girl. Purhi, zuboTi, meye

betha: Pain. beDna, Kosto, Dukko, Duk

beTToy: Without fail

beTon: Salary

bag: Tiger. shEr, shEre khan, shEr khan.
Read: The Tiger's Wife: Téa Obreht

begar: Without pay.

beshomar: A great many

beDokhol: Losing occupation of a land or property

benami: Without a name. benami citi: nameless lettter

bicarbuDdhi: Judgement. bicarbibechona, bichar shoKTi, bicar khomoTa. **Read: Critique of Pure Reason:: Immanuel Kant, Translation: Marcus Weigelt. Critique of Jugdement: Immanuel Kant, Translation: Werner S Pluhar**

B

Bala	Good, well, okay
Boy	Fear. Remember not to pronounc Boy (as the word English word, boy!)
Baaga	To flee/to run away
Boydor	Fear.
Boydor nai	Fearless.
Bai	Brother
Baia/Baisab	Addressing one's older brother
Boin	Sister
Bian	Morning
BaT	Cooked rice
Baanga	To break
Baangla	Change (money). BaangTi, Poysha
BUr	Dawn.
Bur	Raft. Bura, Buri
BuT	Ghost. preT, PeroT, Ashoriri aTTa, BuT PeroT, zinBuT, zinnaT
BUt	Vote.
BUt Deowa	To cast one's vote
BUto Darhani	To stand for election. BUto ubani, BUto kharhani, BUt khela

Bugol	Geography
Bugaa	To suffer
Bugani	To cause suffering
BuganTi	Suffering, ordeal, nightmare
Bula	To forget
Buli zaowa	To forget
BulaBala	Simple. saimon Ailo eK BulaBala manush. Simon is a simple man.
Bul Porha	To forget
Bul Kora	To make a mistake
Bul zana	To know something that was wrong as in when one says: dorset inglendor razdhani (Dorset is the capital city of England) one has known something to be wrong or incorrect.
Bua	Fake. Bua PasPut, fake passport
Basha	Language. buli, zoban, Kotha
Baasha	To float (one is floating)
Baashani	To float (something)
Boi	Book. kiTab, PusTok, gronTo
BoiPoTro	Books
Boish	Buffallo
Boisaal	Earth quack. Buisaal.
Bui	When paddy is grinded the skin comes off. Bui is that paddy skin together

as a lump of soft, almost weightless material that is used in household business such as lighting a fire etc

BOnda   Fraud, fraudster, imposter.

BOndami   Pretence, prentending, impersonating to gain something.

BOndami Kora: To defraud by pretending to be something, somebody else. BOndor KamU Ailo BOndami Kora. The job of a fraudster is to defraud.

BElKa: A sylheti fishing device to catch fish. BElcha

BEt: Water Lily's fruit. haluk, shaluk

Ban: Making up something or pretending, acting.

Ban Kora: acting up, pretending

Banji: Infirtile woman. baanji.

Baiggo: Fate, luck. KoPal, ToKDir

Baiggoban: Lucky (man)

BaiggoboTi: Lucky (woman)

BUg: Food. Feast

Bul: Wrong, mistake, incorrect

Bushi: Bui. When paddy is grinded the skin comes off. Bui is that paddy skin together as a lump of soft, almost weightless material that is used in household business such as lighting a fire etc

BIta: Foundation of one's house, the place where one's house stands

Bingul: Bumble bee

Binno: Separate. Different. Bin

BIkka: Begging

BIkari: Beggar

BIkkuk: Beggar

BIkka Kora: To beg

Baata: Lower, low land

BorTa: Chutney.

Bora: To fill up. Full, complete. Pura, Purno

Bosla: loose clothes, clothers that do not fit

Bongi: To act up, pretendign

Bongi Kora: Act up, to pretend

Bari: Heavy

Biki: muki. muki alu. Biki is a children's expression of the word muki which is potato like vegetable that is sticky when cooked.

Biki alu: muki, muki alu, Biki. Literally, Vicky Potatoe. Children's expression of the word muki.

Barhatia: Tenant.
Read: The Tenant of Wildfell Hall: Anne Brontë

r

raza: King.

rani: Queen.

razokio: Royal. Majestic. rajokio

rijjo: Kingdom, country, land

razoiTTi: Kingship/rule/reign. razoTTo

razkumari: Princess. razarkumari. razPuTri

razkumar: Prince. razarkumar, razPuTro

rag: Anger. ghusa

rag Kora: To get angry

ragani: To cause anger (to someone)

rog: Vein, shiraa, uPoshiraa

rug: Illness. bemar, AsuhsToTa

rugi: Ill, patient. rugini: female patient

ruga: Appear ill or thin

ruk: Wood

rua: To plant

rakha: To keep

rasTa: Road, street, path, way
Read: On the Road: Jack Kerouac

raiT: Night. raT, raTri, andhair.

randha: To cook. ranna, ranna Kora, PaaYK Kora, PaaYk Kora

radha: Radha, the lover of Krishna. radhika, radhe, radhi, rai, krishnomoTi, krishnoshuagi, krishna.

rosh: Juice. Sense of humour

roshoi: store room, kitchen

roshoi ghor: store room, kitchen

roKTo: Blood. lOu

roKTaroKTi: Bloody, murderous

rong: Colour

rongila: colourful, handsome, beautiful

rongin: Colourful

rongconga: Colourful.

rong Deowa: To paint (a wall or house or anything else). rong Kora

rangTa: Wrapper.

rasTa: Road, street

rIsh: Vendetta

rIshbanDa: To be fixed with a vendetta

ruPa: Silver

ruPali: Silver (colour)

ruP: Beauty. rup

ruPoboTi: Isabel. Beautiful woman. rupoboTi

ruPoshi: Isabel. Beautiful woman. ruposhi

rul Kora: To draw lines (When one is writing)

1

la: No. na. la generally denotes a negative sense of whatever word it is added to as a suffix. However, la could be found at the beginning of words as part of them and not as suffix: lamani: to lower. lama: You lower, lamaa: lowland

laraz: Not willing, not supportive of, not agreed

larazi: Not agreeing to what's proposed, not willing, unwilling

lara: To stir (children's version of larha to mean stir and to shake: zhaara)
Read: Lara: Lord George Gordon Byron.

larha: To stir. TorKarita larhocain. Please, stir the curry.

laarha: One that has no companion/loner.

la la Kora: Don't waffle (Expression used with young children), don't talk too much. Shoosh!

labrhra: Chutney, when a lot of different vegetables are used in one dish.

lakhrhi: Wood (to cook). Kat, cEli.

lamaa: Lowland

lama: To get down, to lower

laU: Green Sylheti pumpkin

laz: Shyness. lojja, loijja, shorom

lazuk: Shy. shorminDa, loijjaboTi

latom: spinning top.

latia: Lose character (male) as in terms of women, womanizer. boDmash. Womaniser. Rogue.

lagal: Reach.

lagal Paowa: To meet someone (who one was seeking)

larhai: War, fight, battle

larhai laga: War to break out

larhai baza: War to break out

larhai Aowa: War to begin

lamba: Long. Tall

lamba Kora: To lengthen something. To delay.

lamba Aowa: Someone deliberately trying to be unhelpful or showing off

lamba mathaa: To show off, to tell porkies, to tell lies

lambalambi: Across, diagonally. Lombalombi.

lagani: To enjoin something. To speak behind one's back.

laganibazani: To talk behind people's back.

lagaowra: One that talks behind people's back. (Male). Can not be trusted.

lagauri: One that talks behind people's back. (Female). Can not be trusted.

lakh: One hundred thousand. eK lakh

lagh: Animosity, row, dispute

lagh thaKa: Animosity being present

lagh badha: Animosity being created

laso mas: Name of a fish

lash: Corpse, dead body. murDa.

lash sarhi Deowa: Body to loosen up, feeling weak due to exhaustion, tiredness

langol: Plough.

langol Deowa: To plough

laasi: A drink made of milk.

lachchi: A sweet dish made of vermicelli. shemai, shaOi

laB: Profit

lai PaTa: A speicial kind of mustard leaf

laPaTTa: Gone missing/gone without news. niquz, nikhuj
lazuab: Lost for word. lazobab.

laacani: To shake

lannoT: Shame. Curse

laat: Governor (In the British Raj). Acting like one is a 'lat'.

laat shab: Governor (In the British Raj). Acting like one is a 'lat shab'.

lagail: Joined, connected.

lagaTar: Continuous. AbbahoTo, AbbahoToBabe, colia zaowa

laPanga: Bastard. Identitiless.

lati: Pole. golla, sIngla, sIngol

latikhela: A Sylheti game played by two players with bamboo or wooden poles.
latikheirh

lath: Kick

lath mara: To kick

latial: One that fights with a pole and works for a landlord

laga: To need, to harass. laga is used as a verbal suffix as well. groom laga, ṭanda laga etc

lagalagi: Causing trouble, harassing

lagalagi Kora: To harass

logno: Moment, expected moment. logon.

lobon: salt, nun, nimoK, nunTa.

long: One kind of dry chilly

longla: Name of a place.

lobong: A Spice

loslosa: Soft (food)

loshKosha: loose

loT: Vine. loTi

loTa: A vegetable

lokhai: The only son of a mother.

lowa: To hold/to buy

lOu: Blood. roKTo

luYa: Iron. luha

log: Companion

loge: Along with, with

logi: Oar

lila: Melodrama, illusion, play acting

lorha: To move

logno: Moment, expected moment. logon.

lobon: salt, nun, nimoK, nunTa.

lilaboTi: Beautiful, full of mystique, full of charm

lilua: Blue. nilua, nil

lika: To write. lekha.

likaa: To suck (a lolly)

lingo: Gender. Penis.

lim: Not letting anyone know of something

lim Deowa: To let anyone know of something

lipsha: Greed

lipshakur: Greedy. lipshakhur

lekha: To write. But lekia: having written

lekhok: Writer. Author.

lekika: Female Author

letleta: Runny (as in a food item)

letleti: Friendship being too friendly. letfeti

lEta: To lower onself (physically lowering oneself to pick something up.

lesh: Touch of something. Sign of something

leshmaTro: Sing of something being present

lenjurh: Tail. lezurh

lezurh: Tail.

lengurh: Tail

lengrha: Lame

lengta: Naked (a child)

lengti: A piece of clothing worn by boys covering their bottom.

lembu: Lemon. Lebu

lecu: lychees

lePa: To whitewash floors and walls with white mud

lePaPa: Dress

lePaPa DurusT: Well dressed

lenaDena: Transaction. Denalena

leD: Cowdung

leDa: Cowdung

lem: Lamp. baTTi, cerag.

lukani: To hide.

lukai laowa: To hide

luBaani: To use something as a bite to someone

luB Dekhani: To make someone greedy

lUfa: To catch something

luta: A saucer for water. boDna

lula: Lame

luf: Loaf of bread

h

haowa	Air. baTash
haTKora	A special Sylheti lemon type fruit that's eaten as a vegetable. shaTKora
haT	Variation of shaT (seven)
hoTTa	Murder. Qun. zane mari laowa.

Read: No Honnote (That What Does Not Die): Matreyi Devi

hamani	To enter. dUka, BiTre zaowa, probesh Kora
heman	Animal, innocent animal, wild animals
heman zanoar	Innocent animal/helpless creature
haola	In the care of. loge, shathe
haloT	State. AbosTa
hala	One's wife's younger brother. shala
hali	One's wife's younger sister. shali
hoKOl	All/everyone
hoKlOr	Of everyone
hoKOlTa	Everything. shobTa, shob
haraDin	All day. sharaDin, shomusToDin, shomuDoy Din.
habaa	Dumb
hUra	To wipe (the floor)

huruTa	Children. baichchain, huruTain, huruTamuruTa, selemeye, seleshonTan, baichchaKaichcha, baichchaKaichchain
huru	Small/young. shuru, kuti, kutimuti, suto, sutomuto, TiTkini, oTukuni, oToguni
huruTain	Children
haya	Sense of honour
hayaT	One's total life-span/life time/life
hIka	To learn
hIkani	To teach
hImani	Cold. Im, ţanda
hIlaani	To cause something move

hUga: A silver coloured small fish

hOgra: A sylheti fishing device that is lowered in the water and left there for fish to be caught in it.

hoz: Haj, pilgrimage to Makkah.
Read: Childe Harold's Pilgrimage: Lord George Gordon Bryon

hoz Kora: To do the haj pilgrimage

hozo zaowa: To go to Makkah for haj

aazi: One who has been to the pilgrimage to Makkah is called an 'aazi'. aazi shab. hazi, hazishab

hasaa: Truth, true.

hara: To finish. shara.

hari laowa: To finish, complte. shari laowa.

hanDani: To push something in. d̲Ukani

haari: One kind of robin. Shari

halka: Light (weight). PaTla, uzon Kom
Read: The Unbearable Weight of Beign: Milan Kundera

sh

shaT   Seven. haT

shan   Pride. shan showkoT, gobBo, Ahongkar

shanDar   One with pride and honour/honourable

shamna   Front

shikha   Flame. moshal, aguin, aguinor lofki
Read: The Mysterious Flame of Queen Loana: Umberto Eco

shomman   Honour

shoril   Health, body, wellness, well being

shoKOl   All/everyone

shob   All

shobTa   All/everything

shoKOlTa   Everything

shuag   Effection. maya, mayamomoTa, sneho

shuru   Beginning

shuru Kora: To begin

shara   All/everything. sharaTa, sharati

shaar: Fertiliser. faash.

shaar ala: With fertiliser (the soil where fertiliser is used). shaarala.

shaarli: nam.
Read: Shirley: Charlotte Brontë

shEra	The best. baasa, khasha
sIna	Chest
shiana	Clever
shian	Clever/grown up
shimana	Border/perimeter. shimanTo
shaDa	White/tobacco
shil	Stone/rock. hIl
shila	Stone, rock. PaTTor
shik	Iron bar
shinDur	The sepia colour paste/powder used at Hindu wedding
shanTi	Peace
shanTona	Condolence
shikar	Hunting

shikari: Hunter
shikarir Kam Ailo shikar Kora. The hunter's job is to hunt.
hE Ailo shikari shoBabor. He is of a hunter's nature (meaning someone very shrewed).

shorgo: Heaven. BEsT, behesT, Aloka. shaT BEsT. Seven Heaven.
Read: Paradise Lost: John Milton. Paradise Regained: John Milton

shoT: Honest.
korim shab Aila eKzon shoT manush. Mr Karim is an honest man.

shoiTTo: true/truth.
shob shomoy shoiTTo Koibaay. Always tell the truth.
shoiTTo Koria Kow. Tell me the truth, promise me.

shoTTi: True.
hE zeKta Kor ikta shoTTini? Is it true what he is saying?

shoTTiKar: True. Real
shoTTiKar kotha Ailo hE hoKlore dhuka Dise. The truth is he deceived everyone.

shoTTiKaror: True. Real.
alim Ailo eKzon shoTTiKaror manush. Alim is a true man.

shoiTTo Koria: Truly. shoiTTo Koria Kow. Tell it truthfully. Say it the way it is.

shoKTo: Hard/strong. I zinishta To borho shoKTo. This is (this thing) very hard.
shoKTo Koria: Strongly

shoKTi: Strength/power.
shoriro kuno shoKTi nai. There's no strength in (my) body.

shoKTir zur: With the strength of power. shoKTir zure hoKolTa Kora zaay na.
Everything cannot be done by force.

shola: Stick. eKshota shola. One hundred stick(s).

sholaforamish: Counsel, conspire.
holaforamish Koria Kam Kora uciT. It is advisable to act after taking counsel.
Tara guPone guPone kita sholaforamish Kore? What are they conspiring about secretly.

sholaforamish Kora: To discuss.
zinishta loia sholaforamish Kora DorKar. It is necessary to discuss this matter.

shagor: Sea. shomuDro, Doria. mohashagor (ocean), gOr shagor (ocean),
mohashomuDro (ocean)
Read: Isabel and the Sea: George Millar.

shomoy: time. beil, bela, bala

shomaz: Society. shomproDaay, Dosh.

shomazTonTro: Socialism. shaimmobaD: communism.

shomoy Bromon: Time Travel.

Read: The Time Traveller's Wife: Audrey Niffenegger.

shal: Year. bosor, bochchor, shon (as in year 1984)
Read: 1984: George Orwell

y

No word begins with y but always it is used at the middle or end of words

ay: Come. obaay ay. (You) come here.

aay: Income. Tumar bosoro aay KoTo? What is your annual income?

zoy: Victory. Libiar biDrohi zuDdhaOKle zuDdho zoy Kori laise. The Libyan rebels have won the war.

roy: Staying, living. (He) stays, lives.

shoy: Bearing. (hE) Kosto shoy. He bears pain or he suffers.

shOy: Habbit

paay: Getting, receiving. (hE) paay. (He) gets/receives.

m

ma	Mother. maa, amma, ammu, maaTa, mai, maizi
maa	Mum
man	Honour
mai	Mum
mui	I (some parts of Sylhet uses it more than others)
mor	Mine (some parts of Sylhet uses it more than others)
mon	Mind
moha	Great.

moharani: Empress, the great queen, the great empress. moharani Biktoria, moharani kethrin (Russia).
Read: Becoming Queen: Kate Williams.
Queen Vitoria: A Personal History: Christopher Hibbert

manush	People/humans
maPa	To measure
moza	Tasty
maflar	Scarf
meP	Map. manciTro
monDa	Down turn/business not doing well
magna	Free
maanga	Expensive, rare, scarce

mEla	A lot/much
melaa	A fair/fete
mOi	Aunt (mother's sister)
moi	Ladder
mOua	Aunt's husband (mOi's husband)
moua	A pest that destroys paddy fields
mala	Floral garland, necklace

maya: Love/affection/illusion/magic/mystical/full of mystery
Read: One Hundred Love Sonnets: Pablo Neruda

mou	Honey. modhu, misti, mita
modhu	Honey
mathaa	To speak
maatha	Head
mathaani	To say hello to someone, to talk to someone
maDan	Midday
maz/mazkhan	Middle
morhoK	Epidemic (in animals)
morki	Epidemic (in humans), cholera
mOrhki	Container where people keep rice
mUrI	Toilet
murI	Ppuffed rice/rice crisp

minar	The high tower of a mosque where the Imam stands up to make the prayer calls
misha	To mix (with people
mishani	To mix
mishal	Mixed. milail.
moshla	Spice
murug	Chicken
murga	Cockerel
murgi	Hen. demi: young hen
mullaa	Student of any Islamic schools (madrasha)
miasaab	Imam of a mosque
mia	added with one's name to show respect
mara	To beat up
marani	To get (someone) beaten up
maraowra	One that gets (someone) beaten up
manja	To scrape something to clean (clean a utensil)
maizla	Middle (child). mezo
maizom	Middle (child)
mazhari	Medium size
mayabi	One that is adoreable (female)
mayadhari	One that is very affectionate (female)

makhani	To mix (rice/food)
magaa	To beg
magi	Prostitute
miTa	Friend. bondhu, miTro, shathi
miTali	Friendship
mikaIl	Angel Michael

mukTi: Liberty
Read: On Liberty and Other Essays: John Stuart Mill

mukTo: At Liberty, free. shadhin, nizshadhin.

mukTa: Pearl.
Read: The Pearl: John Steinbeck
Girl with a Pearl Earring: Tracy Chevalier

mirki: Epilepsy. mirki bemar. mirkiE dhora: getting a seizure.

mirkI mas: A type of fish

mita: Sweet

mIta: Wiping out

mItani: To wipe out

mirabazar: Name of a market in Sylhet

mirash: One's lands/wealth/asset

mirashdhari: To show off one's power of lands etc

mikuani: To show one's tongue (children's act)

mukam: Home/house/grave or shrine of a saintly person which is regularly attended

mazar: Shrine of a saintly person which is regularly attended

masum: Innocent (children are described as masum and often it means children/child)

man shomman: Honour

manDa: low demand. monDa.

monDa: Sluggish
muT: Urine

muTa: To urinate

muTani: To take a child to toilet or to urinate

murTa: A green bamboo like plant that is used to make prayer and other mats. muTra

mura: Twist

mura mara: To give a twist/turn

mOKa: To rot (wood)

mOki zaowa: To rot away (wood)

misa: Lie, untrue

misa maatha: To lie

misarir: Of lies as opposed to the truth (hasarir)

misak: Tooth brush

misak Kora: To brush one's teeth

mozak: Joke

mozak Kora: To say or do something as a joke

mozaki: Comedy

mozaki Kora: To say or do something as a joke

moza: Delicious

mozaDar: Tasty

mOzani: To place something in water and keep it there to rot as in jute plants are cut and placed under water to get the fibre
moualu: Sweet potato

mouPuk: Vees/honey bees

mora	To die
mriTTu	Death. moioT
moron	Death
moiOT	Death
moiOTmati	Funeral
mouT	Death
mohashoy	Mr
mohagIani	Great knowledgeable person
mohan	Great
mohabir	Great warrior/hero
mohobboT	Love
mohoboTor	Love's
moholla	Part of a village
mohila	Woman

moyla	Dirty
moshaa	Mosquito
musaa	Wo wipe
monDo	Bad
monDo Kora	To do bad
monDo caowa	To wish bad
mon Dia Kora	To do something with full mind
macan	The support built for vinal plants. Trellis
mangaa	To seek/to want/to beg
maKorh	Spider. maKorhsha
maKorhsha	Spider
maKal	A type of bamboo. Worthless
maKal	Dumb/stupid/simpleton
maKal fol	Worthless
magur	Cat fish
mugoir	Wooden hammer, hammer
mugol	The Mughals
mongla	Originating from the Mughals
mongol	Good. Kollan, Bala, shuBo
mongol Kora	To good
mongol caowa	To wish/pray for good

monozug	Attention
monobaD	Row
monobibaD	Row/dispute, falling out
monorug	Mental illness
monu	A name
moshur	Known (a secret is out as in moshur)
moshur Aowa	A secret is out
moshari/moshori	Mosquito net
moshnoD	Royal throne
mosiD/moshjiD	Mosque. allaar ghor
monDir	Temple
monDira	Cymble
moshkora	Joke
mogra	Lazy
mogrami Kora	Being lazy
malik	Owner
malikana	Ownership
maliki	Ownership
malikana Dabi Kora	To claim ownership
malikana Dekhani	To show/claim ownership

mina	Female name
minara	Female name
miabibi	Man and woman
muki	A potato like sticky (once cooked) vegetable. Biki, Biki alu
mula	Raddish
mEla	Too much/enough
mela Deowa	To get going
mela Kora	To start/to set out
moyDa	Self raising flour
mola	To make a paste/dough
moKa	A type of small fish
mishti	Sweet

manushoTTo: Humanity. manobikoTa, manubikoTa, monushoTTo, insaniaT
Read: Existentialism and Humanism: Jean Paul Sartre.

moyna: Mynah bird. moyna Paki

manoshi: Muse. manushi, monika, monor manush, monomanobi, monoproTima. kolPoloTa, kolpoloTa, kolpoTara, kolpolara, KolPolara

monik: Beautiful, beautiful light, beautiful rays of the sun, jewel-like, shunDor, shunDor alo, shurzor shunDor alo, monir moTo. shurzor monik shuna Tumar DuicokuT Dui shorgor zhOrna Aia bOy: To your two eyes like two heaven-waterfalls flow in the beautiful gold sun-rays.

monika: Beautiful like a jewel, muse, maiden in one's mind, muse, source of inspiration. monomanobi, manushi, manoshi, monoloTa, monolara, monokolpoloTa, monokolpolara, monomayalara, mayalara.

Biktoria okampo robinDronathor lekhalekiT monika hIshabe Anupreronar uTsho Aia asla. Victoria Okampo had been the muse acting as insparation-source in Rabindranath Tagore's writings. **Read: Rabindranath Tagore, Victoria Okampo, Jeebonanada Dash.**

n

na	No. naa, naa naa.
naay	Not
nam	Name/ fame

Read: The Name of the Rose: Umberto Eco

namoTa	Number table
nam Kora	to praise someone
nam lowa	To think about someone
nami	Famous
namani	To take something down
naca	To dance
naTi	Grandson
naTni	Granddaughter
naTinaTni	Grandchildren
nirai	silent, solitude. niraicirai.

Nirala: Solitude. nishshonggo, ekakiTTo, eKla
Read: One Hundred Years of Solitude: Gabriel Garcia Marquez

nishcuP	Quiet/silent (a person)
nimrazi	Agreeing with silence/ unwillingly agreeing
nimaTra	One that does not speak much

nicinTa	One that has no worry (hakuna ma tata!!). A happy go lucky person may be described as one being 'nicinTa'. Not worked up.
nic	Down/below
nica	Something that is at the bottom or at a low position
nicu zaga/zomi	Low land, laama, Baati, Baata
nizor	One's own
niz	oneself.
nize	By one self
nize nize	By one self
nisTar	Escape. mukTi
nisTar nai	No escape
niTTo	Always. shobshomoy, shorboDa
niTTo Din	All the time
nibani	To put the light off (of a lantern or candle), put the fire off
nishan	Flag. PoTaka, boTaka
niruTTor	Silent/no answer
niroPekko	Neutral
nirbacon	Election. BUt
nirBor	Reliance
nikot	Near

nun	Salt. lobon, nuna, nunTa, nimoK
nunTa	Salty
nimoK	Salt
nil/nilua	Blue
nac	Dance
naca	To dance
nacani	To cause (someone) dance
naga	A type of chilli, presumed to be the hottest in the world.
naaga	An Indian nation some members of which live in Sylhet
nairhkol/narikel	Coconut
narhua	Non Sylheti from other parts of Bangladesh (derogatory)
narhi	Pulse
narha	Stir
nari	Woman
naaiOr	When married women go to stay with their own family/relatives
nao	Boat
nouka	Boat
nononD	Sister in law (of a married woman) who is younger than her husband
nosha	Bridegroom, DamanD

nisha	Addiction
nishakur	Addicted/drunk
niba	To go off (the candle goes off)
nimaTri	One that does not speak (female)
nika	Marriage/wedding
nikanama	The wedding registration document (terms of that document)
nazanTe	Without knowing
naDan	Sod/poor thing
nishana	Marks
nisharaiT	Deep night/dead of night
nirghum	No sleep, sleepless
nikhorhi	Name of a river
nishPoTTi	Resolution, resolving
ninDa	Bad name, to criticise
naowa	To bathe, ghushol Kora, snan Kora, shinan Kora, hinan Kora
naowani	To give someone a bath
nama	To get off
nacar	Helpless
nasTa/nashTa	Breakfast
nasTa Kora	To have breakfast

naasTi	No/negation/negative, impossible
naPara	Being unable to do
naKanicubani	Highly harassed, highly embarassed
naK	Nose
nIurha	Being grateful
nali	Leaves from a type of jute plant eaten as a vegetable
nala	Spring/canal
naali	Vessel/blood vessel
nila	Female name deriving from nil (blue)
nil/nilua	Blue
nima	Female name
nIm	Name of tree leaves of which is bitter and used as pain relief medicine. Its branch is used as tootbrush.
naki	Nasal
nakua	One that speaks with a strong nasal sound
naurhi	Connective wooden structure connecting two roofs
neTa	Leader. murobbi
neTri	Female leader
neTagiri	Leadership
neTagiri Kora	To show off
neTagiri Dekhani	To show off

nilla	A curry with a very thin sauce
nirgun	No quality
niazari	A state of nothing to do, lack of activity
nimki	A salty sundry
niramish	Aegeterian food/dishes
niramisha	Without meat or protein
noya	New. noTun
nobodong	New and exotic behaviours
natoK	Play/drama.
naittoKar	Playwright. natoKlekhra, natoK lekhok
nobin	New/young
noTun	New
noani	To lower something
nouzuan	Youth
norTon KorTon	Trying to be fashionable
nabaDaba/naowaDaowa	To have a bath
nouk	Nail
neul	A type of badger
niTniT	Often
nirBezal	Pure

nishPaP	Innocent. masum, PobiTro
nishcoy	Certain
nishciT	Certain
nishchiT Kora	To make sure
nishchiT Aowa	To be certain
nagal	In reach. lagal
nungra	Dirty. moyla, Kachrha
nurgrami	To be dirty/ dirty habbit/ to do a dirty thing
nongor	Anchor
nagor/laang	The man with whom a woman is having an illicit affair maug: the woman with whom a man is having an affair
nagunTi	Innumerable
nariTTo	Womanhood
nobi	Prophet
nobuOTi	Prophethood
nobab	King/fashionable
nobabi	Being fashionable
nobabi Kora	To show off one's fashionableness
noTo	Lowering
noTo Aowa	To lower oneself (from position of pride as in being humbled) or kneeling down to pray

noTI	Punishment
noTiPoTro	Documents
noKTi	Tiny dot of a distance
noKTa	The rope with which an animal is tied to
nol	Yardstick used to measure land's measurements
nola	A bamboo
noDi	River. noD (male), noDi (female). noDnoDi: rivers. gaang
noDnoDi	Rivers
nailon	nylon
nomro	Polite/amicable/soft
nomaz	Prayer (one of the five prayers of the day). Not prayer in the ordinary English sense of the word. namaz
nomazi	One that prays five times without miss. namazi
namzaDa	Well known/honourable/reputable
nalish	Complain
nalish Kora	To complain
naKari	Nose
naDan	Worthless, poor sod
naDai	Worthless
naDia	na Dia. Without giving
na Kora	To say no.

nanga	Without the sheath of a sword. Naked (as naked sword) not a human though.
	nanga Torowal Dia Dunia zoy Kora zaay na. The world can not be conqured by naked swords. aleksandare nanga Torowalor zure Dunia zoy Korar cEsta Korsla kinTu Tar zoy aiz Koi? AinnoDike, sokretisor aTo ziboneO hoyToba Torbarir soaU lagsil na kinTu Tar cinTaBabna kila Duniare ciroKalor lagi zoy Korlo! Alexander had tried to conqure the world with naked sword but where is his victory today? On the other hand, a sword might never have touched Socretes' hand, yet how his thoughts won the world forever! **Read: The Trial and Death of Socretes: Plato. Translation: Benjamin Jowett. Ed: Emma Woolerton**
naTasha	A name. Krishna's hope. naT is another name for Krishna. asha is hope. naTasha=naTor asha, naT's hope. Krishna's hope. Since Krishna is lord, naT means god as well. It means husband as well. Therefore, naTasha could mean husband's hope. Read: After You: Letters of Love and Loss to a Husband and Father: Natasha McElhone.

rh

rh is not used at the beginning of any Sylheti word. It is always used at the middle of before the last vowel of the word.

barhi	House/home/household
Barha	Rent
garhi	Car
sharhi	Saree
sarha	To let go
Parha	To pick (fruit from the tree)
Karha	To snatch
KaKrha	Crab
Kamorh	Bite/a bite /a mouthful
KaKorh	Small broken pebble in rice
PoYrha	To read
PoYrhani	To teach
Porha	To fall
zharha	To shake

Z

zaTa	Pressure
zaTa mara	To press/to put pressure
zaTa Deowa	To press/to give a press
zeTa	That/these/those

zeTaU: That/these/those (added a stress)

zEla: The way/ like this/like the way

zEno: Where/wherever

zesaTa: Anything/whatever

ze: That (this means that)

zeU: Whoever/whosoever

zein: That/Who. Whoever.
zein mathra hEin I Kam Korba. He/she who is talking about it will work on it.
Read: Jane Eyre: Charlotte Brontë

zaan: Whose. Zaan Kam Tain Korba. He/she will do it whose job it is.

zana	To know
zomin	Land. mati, Bumi
zamanoT	Deposit
zaT	Type/category/class
zaTi	Nation
zaTiala	One with a sense of good identity

zaowa	To go
zagani	To wake someone up
zamai	Husband. PoTi, shami
zaga	Place/place/seat
zugazug	Communication
zugazug bebosTa	Communication system/network
zugani	To provide
zual	Yoke
zagir	Lodging
zIna	Non marital sexual intercourse (consensual)
ziaPoT	Invite to a special meal/feast
ziaPoT khaowa	To attend a feast
ziaPoT khaowani	To organise and offer a feast
zindegi	Life

zbion: Life
Read: Doctor Zhivago: Boris Pasternak

zindegani	Life
zibanu	Germ
zila	District. zela, zilla
zilaPi/zulaPi	A sweet
zuar	High tide

zuan	Youth/young
zuboTi	Young woman
zukTi	Logic
zukTiTorko	Debate, discourse
zukTimoTo	Following reason/logic, according to
zonom/zonmo	Birth
zonom mati	Birth place/land of one's birth
zunaK	Moon light, ray of light
zunaki	Fire fly
zinipuk/zinipuka	Fire fly
zinnaT	Ghost
zannaT	Heaven
zinaa	Getting out of control (children making a lot of noise)
zini zaowa	To get mad in mayhem (chidren creating havoc)
zIn	Creatures made of fire referred in the Kuran
zinPori	Other worldly creatures (fairies etc)
zibra/ziPra	Tongue (not language)
zibra/ziPra lamba Aowa	One's desire to eat growing to an unusual level
zama	Shirt
zamaKaPorh	Clothing

zaamaT/zomaT	A congregation at a mosque praying
zua	Gambling
zua khela	To gamble
zua dhora	To place a bet. bazi dhora: to bet
zuarhi	Gambler
zuani	Youth
zuani Kora	To show off youth
zuani Dekhani/zuanki Dekhani to	To show off youth
zuanni	Ahighly youthful and chubby young woman (negative use)
zuboK	Young man
zuboTi	Young woman
zekhan	Where/there
zekhano	In/at where
zekuno	Something/anything/nothing
ziTa/zibonTo	Living thing, alive
zaU	Rice cooked very soft for ill people
zesa	Any
zesaTa	Anything
zesagu	Anyone (Tui)
zebla	When

zUk	Leech
zukTi	Logic
zuTa	Shoes
zuTazhUrha	Pair of shoes
zuTa mara/zuTa Deowa	To beat someone with one's shoes (both literally and metaphorically) which is the highest form of dishonour/disrespect/ ridicule that can be done to a person.
zuTa khaowa	To be humiliated
zUrha	Pair
zurhaa	To put together (items of a household)
zurha	Joint of a table or wall or other things
zhurhani	To get/put together household items
zurha lagani	To get something connected
zonTrona	Harassment/hassle/trouble/pain
zonTrona Kora	To harass/hassle
zonTrona Deowa	To harass/hassle
zala	To burn/pain/suffering
zaala	Seed
zalani	To burn
zalai	Marshland
zIani	To keep live fish in water at home

zIol	The fish that can be kept alive in water at home for later eating (not all the fish can be kept alive like this)
zIol mas	The fish that can be ketp alive at home in water
zibon	Life
zigor	Heart/sole energy of a person/centre of one's being
zikani	To ask. ziggasha/ziggasha Kora, Pusa
zirani	To take a rest
zir	Earth worm
zira	Cardmium
zUka	Measure/make an estimate
zUkani	To ask someone to do the estimation
zugani	To supply
zugan	Supply
zuganDar	Supplier
zola	To burn
zaga	Land/place/space
zEra	Argument (for the sake of it)
zEra Kora	To argue
zagazomi	Land/one's land holding
zomana	Epoc/period of time/epoch/era
zomin	Land

zominDar	Landlord/olden days Lords of the Manors
zomizoma	One's landholding
zoma	To deposit
zomani	To save
zoma Kora	To save/to gather
zumla	Everything together without any classification
zaaynomaz	Prayer mat
zaTra	To get going
zaaTraa	Village theatre
zaTra Kora	To set out
zanu	Leg
zanuParha	To sit on one's legs folded
zug	Addition
zUg	Era/epoc
zukTo	Connected
zuDDo	War/battle
zUla	One's own
zuanki	Youth
zuanki Dekhani	To show off one's youth
zugali	Apprentice (of a carpenter)

zugali Kora	To work as an apprentice
zobo	Slaughtering primarily of an animal
zobo Kora	To slaughter an animal
zobai Kora	To slaughter an animal
zoPa	To get something off by heart
zonoza	Funeral, the prayer done at a funeral
zonoza PoYrha	To attend and do the funeral prayer and burry the dead
zonozaT zaowa	To attend a funeral. moioT mati
zoban	Tongue/one's word/language. Tongue (in the mouth)
zobanDar	One that keeps his/her word
zonun	Mad, particularly of love
zolDi	Hurry
zolDi zolDi	In a hurry
zolDi Kora	To hurry up
zolashoy	Marshland
zor	Fever/temperature
zor zor Kora	To feel feverish/fever coming on
zor uṭa	Fever starting.
zora	Illness. Death. zoramriTTu
zoramriTTu	Desease and death

zoraay dhora	Too many illness catching up with someone
zanDa	Gone off
zanDar	With life/living
zanoar	Animal/beast
zaowa	To go
zaowani	To cause one to go
zilloTi	Poverty/suffering in destitution
zilloTi Kora	To suffer from destitution
zikir	Pray/to meditate/to call the names of God
zikir Kora	To pray/to meditate
zilkani	Sharp tingling pain (caused by inflamed vains/blood vessels)
zaata	Spear
zusna	Moon light. jusna, juTsna
zusna raiT	Moonlit night
zuar	tide/high tide
zuarBata/Bati	High/low tide/tide
zur	Power/strength/force
zurazuri Kora	To try and force something on something or someone

zh

zhinzhin Kora zhinzhini Kora	The pins and needles sensation
zhinnaTTi uta	A sharp painful sensation (if one's elbow is hit by something hard)
zhonzhon Kora	The sounds of ornaments
zhIari	One would call one's daughter's sister in law a zhIari
zhim dhora	To reach a state of freeze (thinking)
zhimani	To sit (closed eyed) and probably think
zhara	To shake
zharani	To get someone to shake
zhora	To wilt/to wither away
zhOr	Poison
zhonzhoni	Toy that makes rattling noise
zhorna	Waterfall. kund, kundo, zolproBaT, zolpropaT
zharha	To take the poison off the body of a snake bite (by a person whose profession it is to do so who is called an Uza)
zharhani	To get an Uza take the snake poison out of one's body
zhaYTa	Anything/whatever
zhaYTa Kora	To do whatever one likes/being unreasonable
zhaI	Slimy place/cold, wet and slimy place

zhaIuna	Slimy/dirty place
zhaarua	Bastard. Punga (male), Pungi (female)
zhaPta	Co claw up something/snatching
zhaPta mara	To snatch up
zhaPtazhaPti Kora	To snatch up (without manners)
zhUna	Ripe (fruit like coconuts)
zhuPrha/zhuPrhi	Poor man's hut
zhuor	The prayer in the early afternoon
zhuoror AKT	The time of the zhuor prayer
zhirzhir	Soft sound of the wind blowing gently over the trees
zhirzhir baTash Deowa	Soft and gentle wind
zhaPa	Bamboo made basket/container where people keep paddy
zhogrha	Quarrel. Kazia, Dorbar, foshaD, feshaD, zhogrhazhati.
zhogrhazhati	Quarrel
zhanda	Flag
zhunda	Set of things
zhoKmoki Kora	To sparkle
zhoKmoK	Sparkle/sparkling/shining
zhotPot	Quick
zhotPot Kora	To do something quickly

zhotaPot	Quick
zhOra	To wilt
zhOri zaowa	To wilt, fallen down (flower falling down from tree)
zhurzhuri	Sound of rice falling
zhuri Kora	To break something into small particles
zhoPzhoPi Kora	To splash out in water
zhut	False/fake/lie
zhuta	False/lie

Y

This is not a letter representing any sound. This is a sign to instruct the reader where they see this sign sitting between two letters that these two letters should be pronounced almost separately and in a way that these two separate sounds are bridged together forming the words. This is very uniquely a Sylheti device.

PoYrha: to read. The two separte syllables would almost be pronouncd as though they were separate monosyllabic words. Po rha. Yet, they are not two separate syllable but connected in a slow-motion delayed manner which is what I call 'bridging'.

Po rha these Po and rha sounds are pronounced as though they are separate sounds but they are pronounced in such a way that they are almost bridged.

But look, Porha   To fall.

But this Y could sit at the end of a one syllable word:

caY where ca is pronounced in a way that no air is pressed out of the mouth even though the mouth is open when the sound is pronounced. It can only be expressed in the manner of gently breaking on your car. You break but stop the pressing on the break ever so gently. caY in which the 'a' sound almost float-froze so that the syllable is closed to the 'a'.

caYPaTa   Tea leaf

Another point in Sylheti script there are no upper or lower case letters. The letters that look like English upper case letters are not meant to be upper case and, thus, you must not call them as such. The best way to name them would be to call their phonetic sound out. Therefore, A is Aow, a is (ah), aa (aah), T is Tah, B is Vah etc.

W

w sounds as wa as in was, war ward etc but in Sylheti no word begins with w sound rather wa is made with oa or owa if it is at the beginning of a word.

w is always used at the middle and end of words.

khaowa	To eat, to drink.
khaowani	To feed
zaowa	To go
Deowa	To give
neowa	To take
bowa	To sit
bowani	To help sit
bOwani	To get something carried
rowa	To stay

dhowa: To wash

showa: To bear

thowa: To put away, to tidy away

Verbs

Verbs

Group A i
Group A ii
Group A iii
Group B i
Group B ii
Group B iii
Group C i
Group C ii
Group C iii
Group D
Group E
Group F
Group G
Group I
Group J
Group K
Group L
Group M
Group N
Group O
Group P
Group Q
Group R

Verbs

In Sylheti there are verbs that are, like any other languages, very important, in terms of forming meaningful sentences, that are used in communicating and, thus without proper understanding of how these verbs are used and how they work, it is not going to be possible for anyone to speak Sylheti. There are different types of verbs which can be placed in different groups. Each group follows a regular pattern. In order to grasp how they work we need to look at each group.

Group A. i

These verbs ends with a and aa as their verbal suffix. You take the root of the verbs and add the suffix to suit your need. zana: to know: zan+a. Now, add the necessary suffix depending on your tense form and subject of the sentence. Remember, the suffixes must be in line with the status of the subject. So ami zani and aPne zanoin but he zane. I know, you know (you being aPne) and he knows (he being referred as Tui).

To know	zana
To read	PoYrha
To write	lekha
To hold/to catch/to arrest	dhora
To speak	maatha
To stay/to be	thaKa
To hear/listen	huna
To learn	hIka
To walk	ata
To understand	buza
To do	Kora
To hit	mara
To measure	maPa
To move	hOra
Dekha	to see
To touch	soaa
To put away	thoaa
To keep	rakha
To call	daKa
To put on a dress	PinDa
To cry	KanDa
To cook	randha
To beat someone up	rUndhaa
To raise something up/pick up	Tula
To cover	daaKa
To rot	Poca
To ripe	PaKa
To buy	kina
To shout like roaring	gunjYra
To move	shora
To urinate	mutha

To open one's bowel	agaa
To move	lorha
To pick unwanted items off	bacaa
To touch	soa
To plant	rua

Present: Kora-to do

In the following table sentences are as follows
Positive sentence
Negagtive sentence
Positive question
Negative question
shoKal noyta Tone: since 9 in the morning
(shombar Tone: since Monday
Pac ghonta dhoria: for five hours
Pac Din dhoria: for five days
Pac mash dhoria: for five months
Pac bosor dhoria: for five years)

Subject	Simple Present	Present Continuous	Present Perfect	Present Perfect Continuous
ami/amra	Kori. Korna. Korini? Korinani?	Koriar/Korram. Koriarna/Korramna. Koriarni?/Korramni? Koriarnani?/Korramni?	Korsi. Korsina. Korsini? Korsinani?	shoKal noyta Tone Koriar/Korram, shoKal nota Tone Koriarna/Korramna shoKal noyta Tone Koriarni/Korramni? shoKal noyta Tone Koriarnani/Korramnani?
aPne/aPnara Tain/Tara	Koroin. Koroinna. Koroinni? Koroinnani?	Korra Korrana Korrani? Korranani?	Korsoin Korsoinna Korsoinni? Korsoinnani?	shoKal noyta Tone Korra shoKal nota Tone Korrana shoKal noyta Tone Korrani shoKal noyta Tone Korranani?
Tumi/TumiTain	Koro Korona. Koroni? Koronani?	Korraay Korraayna Korrayni? Korraaynani?	Korso . Korsona Korsoni? Korsonani?	shoKal noyta Tone Korraay shoKal nota Tone Korraayna shoKal noyta Tone Korraayni? shoKal noyta Tone Korraaynani?
Tui/Tumra/Tura	Koros Korosna. Korosni? Korosnani?	Korre Korrena Korreni? Korrenani?	KorsoT KorsoTna KorsoTni? KorsoTnani?	shoKal noyta Tone Korre shoKal nota Tone Korrena shoKal noyta Tone Korreni? shoKal noyta Tone Korrenani?

Past: Kora-to do

In the following table sentences are as follows
Positive sentence
Negagtive sentence
Positive question
Negative question
shoKal noyta Tone: since 9 in the morning
(shombar Tone: since Monday
Pac ghonta dhoria: for five hours
Pac Din dhoria: for five days
Pac mash dhoria: for five months
Pac bosor dhoria: for five years)

Subject	Simple Past	Past Continuous	Past Perfect	Past Perfect Continuous
ami/amra	Korlam Korlamna. Korlamni? Korlamnani?	KoraT aslam KoraT aslamna KoraT aslamni? KoraT aslamnani?	Korslam Korslamna. Korslamni? Korslamnani?	shoKal noyta Tone KoraT aslam shoKal nota Tone KoraT aslamna shoKal noyta Tone KoraT aslamni? shoKal noyta Tone KoraT aslamnani?
aPne/aPnara Tain/Tara	Korla Korlana. Korlani? Korlanani?	KoraT asla KoraT aslana KoraT aslani? KoraT aslanani?	Korsla Korslana Korslani? Korslanani?	shoKal noyta Tone KoraT asla shoKal nota Tone KoraT aslana shoKal noyta Tone KoraT aslani? shoKal noyta Tone KoraT aslanani?
Tumi/TumiTain	Korlaay Korlaayna. Korlaayni? Korlaaynani?	KoraT aslaay KoraT aslaayna KoraT aslaayni? KoraT aslaaynani?	Korslaay Korslaayna Korslaayni? Korslaaynani?	shoKal noyta Tone KoraT aslaay shoKal nota Tone KoraT aslaayna shoKal noyta Tone KoraT aslaayni? shoKal noyta Tone KoraT aslaaynani?
Tui/Tumra/Tura	Korle Korlena. Korleni? Korlenanani?	KoraT asle KoraT aslena KoraT asleni? KoraT aslenani?	Korsle Korslena Korsleni? Korslenani?	shoKal noyta Tone KoraT asle shoKal nota Tone KoraT aslena shoKal noyta Tone KoraT asleni? shoKal noyta Tone KoraT aslenani?

Future: Kora-to do

In the following table sentences are as follows
Positive sentence
Negagtive sentence
Positive question
Negative question
shoKal noyta Tone: since 9 in the morning
(shombar Tone: since Monday
Pac ghonta dhoria: for five hours
Pac Din dhoria: for five days
Pac mash dhoria: for five months
Pac bosor dhoria: for five years)

Subject	Simple Future	Future Continuous	Future Perfect	Future Perfect Continuous
ami/amra	Kormu KorTamnaay. Kormuni? KorTamnaayni?	KoraT thaKmu KoraT thaKTamnaay KoraT thaKmuni? KoraT thaKTamnaayni?	Korlam One Koria harlam Onena. Korlam Oneni? Korlam Onenani?	shoKal noyta Tone KoraT thaKlam One shoKal nota Tone KoraT thaKlam Onena shoKal noyta Tone KoraT thaKlam Oneni? shoKal noyta Tcne KoraT thaKlam Onenani?
aPne/aPnara Tain/Tara	Korba KorTanaay. Korbani? KorTanaayni?	KoraT thaKba KoraT thaKTanaay KoraT thaKbani? KoraT thaKTanaayni?	Korla One Korla Onena. Korla Oneni? Korla Onenani?	shoKal noyta Tone KoraT thaKla One shoKal nota Tone KoraT thaKla Onena shoKal noyta Tone KoraT thaKla Oneni? shoKal noyta Tone KoraT thaKla Onenani?
Tumi/TumiTain	Korbaay KorTaynaay. Korbaayni? KorTanaaynaayni?	KoraT thaKbaay KoraT thaKTaynaay KoraT thaKbaayni? KoraT thaKTaaynaayni?	Korlaay One Korlaay Onena. Korlaay Oneni? Korlaay Onenani?	shoKal noyta Tone KoraT thaKlaay One shoKal nota Tone KoraT thaKlaay Onena shoKal noyta Tone KoraT thaKlaay Oneni? shoKal noyta Tone KoraT thaKlaay Onenani?
Tui/Tumra/Tura	Korbe KorTenaay KorTenaayni? KorTenaayni?	KoraT thaKbe KoraT thaKTenaay KoraT thaKbeni? KoraT thaKTenaayni?	Korle One Korle Onena Korle Oneni? Korle Onenanni?	shoKal noyta Tone KoraT thaKle One shoKal nota Tone KoraT thaKle Onena shoKal noyta Tone KoraT thaKle Onenni? shoKal noyta Tone KoraT thaKle Onenani?

Conditional Present: Kora-to do

In the following table sentences are as follows
Positive sentence
Negagtive sentence
Positive question
Negative question
shoKal noyta Tone: since 9 in the morning
(shombar Tone: since Monday
Pac ghonta dhoria: for five hours
Pac Din dhoria: for five days
Pac mash dhoria: for five months
Pac bosor dhoria: for five years)

Subject	Simple Future	Future Continuous	Future Perfect	Future Perfect Continuous
ami/amra	KorTe Pari KorTe naO Pari. KorTe Parini? KorTe Parinani?	KoraT thaKTe Pari KoraT thaKTe naO Pari KoraT thaKe Parini? KoraT thaKe Parinani?	Koria thaKe Pari Koria thaKTe naO Pari. Koria thaKTe Parini? Koria thaKTe Parinani?	shoKal noyta Tone Koria thaKTe Pari shoKal nota Tone Koria thaKTe naO Pari shoKal noyta Tone Koria thaKTe Parini? shoKal noyta Tone Koria thaKTe Parinani?
aPne/aPnara Tain/Tara	KorTa Paroin KorTa naO Paroin. KorTa Paroinni? KorTa Paroinnani?	KoraT thaKTa Paroin KoraT thaKTa naO Paroin KoraT thaKa Paroinni? KoraT thaKa Paroinnani?	Koria thaKa Paroin Koria thaKTa naO Paroin. Koria thaKTa Paroini? Koria thaKTa Paroinnani?	shoKal noyta Tone Koria thaKTa Paroin shoKal nota Tone Koria thaKTa naO Paroin shoKal noyta Tone Koria thaKTa Paroinni? shoKal noyta Tone Koria thaKTa Paroinnani?
Tumi/TumiTain	KorTaay Paro KorTaay naO Paro. KorTaay Paroni? KorTaay Paronani?	KoraT thaKTaay Paro KoraT thaKTaay naO Paro KoraT thaKaay Paroini? KoraT thaKaay Paronani?	Koria thaKTaay Paro Koria thaKTaay naO Paro. Koria thaKTaay Paroni? Koria thaKTaay Paronani?	shoKal noyta Tone Koria thaKTaay Paro shoKal nota Tone Koria thaKTaay naO Paro shoKal noyta Tone Koria thaKTaay Paroni? shoKal noyta Tone Koria thaKTaay Paronani?
Tui/Tumra/Tura	KorTe Paros KorTe naO Paros. KorTe Parosni? KorTe Parosnani?	KoraT thaKTe Paros KoraT thaKTe naO Paros KoraT thaKe Parosni? KoraT thaKe Parosnani?	Koria thaKTe Paros Koria thaKTe naO Paros. Koria thaKTe Parosni? Koria thaKTe Parosnani?	shoKal noyta Tone Koria thaKTe Paros shoKal nota Tone Koria thaKTe naO Paro shoKal noyta Tone Koria thaKTe Parosni? shoKal noyta Tone Koria thaKTe Parosnani?

Conditional Past: Kora-to do

In the following table sentences are as follows
Positive sentence
Negagtive sentence
Positive question
Negative question
shoKal noyta Tone: since 9 in the morning
(shombar Tone: since Monday
Pac ghonta dhoria: for five hours
Pac Din dhoria: for five days
Pac mash dhoria: for five months
Pac bosor dhoria: for five years)

Subject	Simple	continuous	Perfect	Perfect Continuous
ami/amra	KorTam ParTam KorTam naO ParTam. KorTam ParTamni? KorTam ParTamnaayni?	KoraT thaKTe ParTam KoraT thaKTe naO ParTam KoraT thaKTe ParTamni? KoraT thaKTe ParTam nani?	Koria harlam One Koria harlam na One. Koria harlam na Oneni? Koria harlam Onenani?	shoKal noyta Tone KoraT thaKTe ParTam shoKal nota Tone KoraT thaKTe naO ParTam shoKal noyta Tone KoraT thaKTe ParTamni? shoKal noyta Tone KoraT thaKTe ParTamnani?
aPne/aPnara Tain/Tara	KorTa Paroin KorTa naO Paroin. KorTa Paroinni? KorTa Paroinnani?	KoraT thaKTa Paroin KoraT thaKTa naO Paroin KoraT thaKa Paroinni? KoraT thaKa Paroinnani?	Koria harla One Koria harla One na. Koria harla Oneni? Koria harla One nani?	shoKal noyta Tone Koria thaKTa Paroin shoKal nota Tone Koria thaKTa naO Paroin shoKal noyta Tone Koria thaKTa Paroinni? shoKal noyta Tone Koria thaKTa Paroinnani?
Tumi/TumiTain	KorTaay Paro KorTaay naO Paro. KorTaay Paroni? KorTaay Paronani?	KoraT thaKTaay Paro KoraT thaKTaay naO Paro KoraT thaKaay Paroini? KoraT thaKaay Paronani?	Koria harlaay One Koria harlaay One na. Koria harlaay Oneni? Koria harlaay Onenani?	shoKal noyta Tone Koria thaKTaay Paro shoKal nota Tone Koria thaKTaay naO Paro shoKal noyta Tone Koria thaKTaay Paroni? shoKal noyta Tone Koria thaKTaay Paronani?
Tui/Tumra/Tura	KorTe Paros KorTe naO Paros. KorTe Parosni? KorTe Parosnani?	KoraT thaKTe Paros KoraT thaKTe naO Paros KoraT thaKe Parosni? KoraT thaKe Parosnani?	Koria harle One Koria harle One na. Koria harle Oneni?thaKTe Parosni? Koria harle Onenanii?	shoKal noyta Tone Koria thaKTe Paros shoKal nota Tone Koria thaKTe naO Paro shoKal noyta Tone Koria thaKTe Parosni? shoKal noyta Tone Koria thaKTe Parosnani?

Conditional Future: Kora-to do

In the following table sentences are as follows
Positive sentence
Negagtive sentence
Positive question
Negative question
shoKal noyta Tone: since 9 in the morning
(shombar Tone: since Monday
Pac ghonta dhoria: for five hours
Pac Din dhoria: for five days
Pac mash dhoria: for five months
Pac bosor dhoria: for five years)

Subject	Simple Future	Future Continuous	Future Perfect	Future Perfect Continuous
ami/amra	KorTam Pari KorTam naO Pari. KorTam Parini? KorTam Parinani?	KoraT thaKTam Pari KoraT thaKTam naO Pari KoraT thaKTam Parini? KoraT thaKTam Parinani?	KorTam ParTam KorTam ParTamnaay KorTam ParTamni? KorTam ParTamnaayni?	shoKal noyta Tone KoraT thaKTe ParTam shoKal noyta Tone KoraT thaKTe ParTamna shoKal noyta Tone KoraT thaKTe ParTamni? shoKal noyta Tone KorqT thaKTe ParTamnani?
aPne/aPnara Tain/Tara	KorTa Parioin KorTa naO Paroin. KorTa Paroinni? KorTa Paroinnani?	KoraT thaKTam Paroin KoraT thaKTam naO Paroin KoraT thaKTa Paroinni? KoraT thaKTa Paroinnai?	KorTam ParTa KorTa ParTanaay KorTa ParTani? KorTa ParTanaayni?	shoKal noyta Tone KoraT thaKTe ParTa shoKal noyta Tone KoraT thaKTe ParTana shoKal noyta Tone KoraT thaKTe ParTani? shoKal noyta Tone KoraT thaKTe ParTanani?
Tumi/TumiTain	KorTaay Pario KorTaay naO Paro. KorTaay Paroni? KorTaay Paronani?	KoraT thaKTaay Paro KoraT thaKTaay naO Paro KoraT thaKTaay Paroni? KoraT thaKTaay Paronani?	KorTaay ParTaay KorTaay ParTaaynaay KorTaay ParTaayni? KorTaay ParTaaynaayni?	shoKal noyta Tone KoraT thaKTe ParTaay shoKal noyta Tone KoraT thaKTe ParTaayna shoKal noyta Tone KoraT thaKTe ParTaayni? shoKal noyta Tone KoraT thaKTe ParTaaynani?
Tui/Tumra/Tura	KorTeParos KorTe naO Paros. KorTe Parosni? KorTe Parosnani?	KoraT thaKTe Paros KoraT thaKTe naO Paros KoraT thaKTe Parosni? KoraT thaKTe Parosnani?	KorTe ParTe KorTe ParTenaay KorTe ParTeyni? KorTe ParTenaayni?	shoKal noyta Tone KoraT thaKTe ParTe shoKal noyta Tone KoraT thaKTe ParTena shoKal noyta Tone KoraT thaKTe ParTeni? shoKal noyta Tone KoraT thaKTe ParTeynani?

Group A. ii

These verbs ends with a and aa as their verbal suffix. You take the root of the verbs and add the suffix to suit your need. zana: to know: zan+a. Now, add the necessary suffix depending on your tense form and subject of the sentence. Remember, the suffixes must be in line with the status of the subject. So ami zani and aPne zanoin but hE zane. I know, you know (you being aPne) and he knows (he being referred as Tui).

But unlike the other group here you add a noun before the verbs and they follow the same rules

To work	Kam Kora
To read a book	Boi PoYrha
To write a book	Boi lekha
To write a story	kichcha lekha
To have a bath	ghushol Kora
To shop	bazar Kora
To hold the door	Dorza dhora
To start speaking when one is not expected to speak	maath dhora
To learn Sylheti	Sylheti hIka
To touch one's hand	aT soaa
To call korim	korimre daaKa
To read well/with one's mind in it	mon Dia Porha

You now see the picture. Now try listing as many of these verbs you can make up from the list.

Present: bazar Kora-to shop

In the following table sentences are as follows
Positive sentence
Negagtive sentence
Positive question
Negative question
shoKal noyta Tone: since 9 in the morning
(shombar Tone: since Monday
Pac ghonta dhoria: for five hours
Pac Din dhoria: for five days
Pac mash dhoria: for five months
Pac bosor dhoria: for five years)

Subject	Simple Present	Present Continuous	Present Perfect	Present Perfect Continuous
ami/amra	bazar Kori. bazar Korna. bazar Korini? bazar Korinani?	bazar Koriar/Korram. bazar Koriarna/Korramna. bazar Koriarni?/Korramni? bazar Koriarnani?/Korramni?	bazar Korsi. bazar Korsina. bazar Korsini? bazar Korsinani?	shoKal noyta Tone bazar Koriar/Korram, shoKal nota Tone bazar Koriarna/Korramna shoKal noyta Tone bazar Koriarni/Korramni? shoKal noyta Tone bazar Koriarnani/Korramnani?
aPne/aPnara Tain/Tara	bazar Koroin. bazar Koroinna. bazar Koroinni? bazar Koroinnani?	bazar Korra bazar Korrana bazar Korrani? bazar Korranani?	bazar Korsoin bazar Korsoinna bazar Korsoinni? bazar Korsoinnani?	shoKal noyta Tone bazar Korra shoKal nota Tone bazar Korrana shoKal noyta Tone bazar Korrani shoKal noyta Tone bazar Korranani?
Tumi/TumiTain	bazar Koro bazar Korona. bazar Koroni? bazar Koronani?	bazar Korraay bazar Korraayna bazar Korrayni? bazar Korraaynani?	bazar Korso bazar Korsona bazar Korsoni? bazar Korsonani?	shoKal noyta Tone bazar Korraay shoKal nota Tone bazar Korraayna shoKal noyta Tone bazar Korraayni? shoKal noyta Tone bazar Korraaynani?
Tui/Tumra/Tura	bazar Koros bazar Korosna. bazar Korosni? bazar Korosnani?	bazar Korre bazar Korrena bazar Korreni? bazar Korrenani?	bazar KorsoT bazar KorsoTna bazar KorsoTni? bazar KorsoTnani?	shoKal noyta Tone bazar Korre shoKal nota Tone bazar Korrena shoKal noyta Tone bazar Korreni? shoKal noyta Tone bazar Korrenani?

Past: bazar Kora-to shop

In the following table sentences are as follows
Positive sentence
Negagtive sentence
Positive question
Negative question
shoKal noyta Tone: since 9 in the morning
(shombar Tone: since Monday
Pac ghonta dhoria: for five hours
Pac Din dhoria: for five days
Pac mash dhoria: for five months
Pac bosor dhoria: for five years)

Subject	Simple Past	Past Continuous	Past Perfect	Past Perfect Continuous
ami/amra	bazar Korlam bazar Korlamna. bazar Korlamni? bazar Korlamnani?	bazar KoraT aslam bazar KoraT aslamna bazar KoraT aslamni? bazar KoraT aslamnani?	bazar Korslam bazar Korslamna. bazar Korslamni? bazar Korslamnani?	shoKal noyta Tone bazar KoraT aslam shoKal nota Tone bazar KoraT aslamna shoKal noyta Tone bazar KoraT aslamni? shoKal noyta Tone bazar KoraT aslamnani?
aPne/aPnara Tain/Tara	Korla Korlana. Korlani? Korlanani?	KoraT asla KoraT aslana KoraT aslani? KoraT aslanani?	Korsla Korslana Korslani? Korslanani?	shoKal noyta Tone bazar KoraT asla shoKal nota Tone bazar KoraT aslana shoKal noyta Tone KoraT aslani? shoKal noyta Tone KoraT aslanani?
Tumi/TumiTain	bazar Korlaay bazar Korlaayna. bazar Korlaayni? bazar Korlaaynani?	bazar KoraT aslaay bazar KoraT aslaayna bazar KoraT aslaayni? bazar KoraT aslaaynani?	bazar Korslaay bazar Korslaayna bazar Korslaayni? bazar Korslaaynani?	shoKal noyta Tone bazar KoraT aslaay shoKal nota Tone bazar KoraT aslaayna shoKal noyta Tone bazar KoraT aslaayni? shoKal noyta Tone bazar KoraT aslaaynani?
Tui/Tumra/Tura	bazar Korle bazar Korlena. bazar Korleni? bazar Korlenanani?	bazar KoraT asle bazar KoraT aslena bazar KoraT asleni? bazar KoraT aslenani?	bazar Korsle bazar Korslena bazar Korsleni? bazar Korslenani?	shoKal noyta Tone bazar KoraT asle shoKal nota Tone bazar KoraT aslena shoKal noyta Tone bazar KoraT asleni? shoKal noyta Tone bazar KoraT aslenani?

Future: bazar Kora-to shop

In the following table sentences are as follows
Positive sentence
Negagtive sentence
Positive question
Negative question
shoKal noyta Tone: since 9 in the morning
(shombar Tone: since Monday
Pac ghonta dhoria: for five hours
Pac Din dhoria: for five days
Pac mash dhoria: for five months
Pac bosor dhoria: for five years)

Subject	Simple Future	Future Continuous	Future Perfect	Future Perfect Continuous
ami/amra	bazar Kormu bazar KorTamnaay. bazar Kormuni? bazar KorTamnaayni?	bazar KoraT thaKmu bazar KoraT thaKTamnaay bazar KoraT thaKmuni? bazar KoraT thaKTamnaayni?	bazar Koria harlam One bazar Koria harlam Onena. bazar Koria harlam Oneni? bazar Koria harlam Onenani?	shoKal noyta Tone bazar KoraT thaKlam One shoKal nota Tone bazar KoraT thaKlam Onena shoKal noyta Tone bazar KoraT thaKlam Oneni? shoKal noyta Tone bazar KoraT thaKlam Onenani?
aPne/aPnara Tain/Tara	bazar Korba bazar KorTanaay. bazar Korbani? bazar KorTanaayni?	bazar KoraT thaKba bazar KoraT thaKTanaay bazar KoraT thaKbani? bazar KoraT thaKTanaayni?	bazar Koria harla One bazar Koria harla Onena. bazar Koria harla Oneni? bazar Koria harla Onenani?	shoKal noyta Tone bazar KoraT thaKla One shoKal nota Tone bazar KoraT thaKla Onena shoKal noyta Tone bazar KoraT thaKla Oneni? shoKal noyta Tone bazar KoraT thaKla Onenani?
Tumi/TumiTain	bazar Korbaay bazar KorTaynaay. bazar Korbaayni? bazar KorTanaaynaayni?	bazar KoraT thaKbaay bazar KoraT thaKTaynaay bazar KoraT thaKbaayni? bazar KoraT thaKTaaynaayni?	bazar Koria harlaay One bazar Koria harlaay Onena. bazar Koria harlaay Oneni? bazar Koria harlaay Onenani?	shoKal noyta Tone bazar KoraT thaKlaay One shoKal nota Tone bazar KoraT thaKlaay Onena shoKal noyta Tone bazar KoraT thaKlaay Oneni? shoKal noyta Tone bazar KoraT thaKlaay Onenani?
Tui/Tumra/Tura	bazar Korbe bazar KorTenaay bazar KorTenaayni? bazar KorTenaayni?	bazar KoraT thaKbe bazar KoraT bazar thaKTenaay bazar KoraT thaKbeni? bazar KoraT thaKTenaayni?	bazar Koria harle One bazar Koria harle Onena bazar Koria harle Oneni? bazar Koria haarle Onenanni?	shoKal noyta Tone bazar KoraT thaKle One shoKal nota Tone bazar KoraT thaKle Onena shoKal noyta Tone bazar KoraT thaKle Onenni? shoKal noyta Tone bazar KoraT thaKle Onenani?

Conditional Present: bazar Kora-to shop

In the following table sentences are as follows
Positive sentence
Negagtive sentence
Positive question
Negative question
shoKal noyta Tone: since 9 in the morning
(shombar Tone: since Monday
Pac ghonta dhoria: for five hours
Pac Din dhoria: for five days
Pac mash dhoria: for five months
Pac bosor dhoria: for five years)

Subject	Simple Present	Continuous	Perfect	Perfect Continuous
ami/amra	bazar KorTe Pari bazar KorTe naO Pari. bazar KorTe Parini? bazar KorTe Parinani?	bazar KoraT thaKTe Pari bazar KoraT thaKTe naO Pari bazar KoraT thaKe Parini? bazar KoraT thaKe Parinani?	bazar Koria thaKe Pari bazar Koria thaKTe naO Pari. bazar Koria thaKTe Parini? bazar Koria thaKTe Parinani?	shoKal noyta Tone bazar Koria thaKTe Pari shoKal nota Tone bazar Koria thaKTe naO Pari shoKal noyta Tone bazar Koria thaKTe Parini? shoKal noyta Tone bazar Koria thaKTe Parinani?
aPne/aPnara Tain/Tara	bazar KorTa Paroin bazar KorTa naO Paroin. bazar KorTa Paroinni? bazar KorTa Paroinnani?	bazar KoraT thaKTa Paroin KoraT thaKTa naO Paroin bazar KoraT thaKa Paroinni? bazar KoraT thaKa Paroinnani?	bazar Koria thaKa Paroin bazar Koria thaKTa naO Paroin. bazar Koria thaKTa Paroini? bazar Koria thaKTa Paroinnani?	shoKal noyta Tone bazar Koria thaKTa Paroin shoKal nota Tone bazar Koria thaKTa naO Paroin shoKal noyta Tone bazar Koria thaKTa Paroinni? shoKal noyta Tone bazar Koria thaKTa Paroinnani?
Tumi/TumiTain	bazar KorTaay Paro bazar KorTaay naO Paro. bazar KorTaay Paroni? bazar KorTaay Paronani?	bazar KoraT thaKTaay Paro bazar KoraT thaKTaay naO Paro bazar KoraT thaKaay Paroini? bazar KoraT thaKaay Paronani?	bazar Koria thaKTaay Paro bazar Koria thaKTaay naO Paro. bazar Koria thaKTaay Paroni? bazar Koria thaKTaay Paronani?	shoKal noyta Tone bazar Koria thaKTaay Paro shoKal nota Tone bazar Koria thaKTaay naO Paro shoKal noyta Tone bazar Koria thaKTaay Paroni? shoKal noyta Tone bazar Koria thaKTaay Paronani?
Tui/Tumra/Tura	bazar KorTe Paros bazar KorTe naO Paros. bazar KorTe Parosni? bazar KorTe Parosnani?	bazar KoraT thaKTe Paros bazar KoraT thaKTe naO Paros bazar KoraT thaKe Parosni? bazar KoraT thaKe Parosnani?	bazar Koria thaKTe Paros bazar Koria thaKTe naO Paros. bazar Koria thaKTe Parosni? bazar Koria thaKTe Parosnani?	shoKal noyta Tone bazar Koria thaKTe Paros shoKal nota Tone bazar Koria thaKTe naO Paro shoKal noyta Tone bazar Koria thaKTe Parosni? shoKal noyta Tone bazar Koria thaKTe Parosnani?

Conditional Past: Kora-to do

In the following table sentences are as follows
Positive sentence
Negagtive sentence
Positive question
Negative question
shoKal noyta Tone: since 9 in the morning
(shombar Tone: since Monday
Pac ghonta dhoria: for five hours
Pac Din dhoria: for five days
Pac mash dhoria: for five months
Pac bosor dhoria: for five years)

Subject	Simple	continuous	Perfect	Perfect Continuous
ami/amra	KorTam ParTam KorTam naO ParTam. KorTam ParTamni? KorTam ParTamnaayni?	KoraT thaKTe ParTam KoraT thaKTe naO ParTam KoraT thaKTe ParTamni? KoraT thaKTe ParTam nani?	KoraT thaKlam One KoraT thaKTlam na One. KoraT thaKTlam Oneni? Koria thaKTlamna Oneni?	shoKal noyta Tone KoraT thaKTe ParTam shoKal nota Tone KoraT thaKTe naO ParTam shoKal noyta Tone KoraT thaKTe ParTamni? shoKal noyta Tone KoraT thaKTe ParTamnani?
aPne/aPnara Tain/Tara	KorTa Paroin KorTa naO Paroin. KorTa Paroinni? KorTa Paroinnani?	KoraT thaKTa Paroin KoraT thaKTa naO Paroin KoraT thaKa Paroinni? KoraT thaKa Paroinnani?	Koria thaKa Paroin Koria thaKTa naO Paroin. Koria thaKTa Paroini? Koria thaKTa Paroinnani?	shoKal noyta Tone Koria thaKTa Paroin shoKal nota Tone Koria thaKTa naO Paroin shoKal noyta Tone Koria thaKTa Paroinni? shoKal noyta Tone Koria thaKTa Paroinnani?
Tumi/TumiTain	KorTaay Paro KorTaay naO Paro. KorTaay Paroni? KorTaay Paronani?	KoraT thaKTaay Paro KoraT thaKTaay naO Paro KoraT thaKaay Paroini? KoraT thaKaay Paronani?	Koria thaKTaay Paro Koria thaKTaay naO Paro. Koria thaKTaay Paroni? Koria thaKTaay Paronani?	shoKal noyta Tone Koria thaKTaay Paro shoKal nota Tone Koria thaKTaay naO Paro shoKal noyta Tone Koria thaKTaay Paroni? shoKal noyta Tone Koria thaKTaay Paronani?
Tui/Tumra/Tura	KorTe Paros KorTe naO Paros. KorTe Parosni? KorTe Parosnani?	KoraT thaKTe Paros KoraT thaKTe naO Paros KoraT thaKe Parosni? KoraT thaKe Parosnani?	Koria thaKTe Paros Koria thaKTe naO Paros. Koria thaKTe Parosni? Koria thaKTe Parosnani?	shoKal noyta Tone Koria thaKTe Paros shoKal nota Tone Koria thaKTe naO Paro shoKal noyta Tone Koria thaKTe Parosni? shoKal noyta Tone Koria thaKTe Parosnani?

Conditional Future: Kora-to do

In the following table sentences are as follows
Positive sentence
Negagtive sentence
Positive question
Negative question
shoKal noyta Tone: since 9 in the morning
(shombar Tone: since Monday
Pac ghonta dhoria: for five hours
Pac Din dhoria: for five days
Pac mash dhoria: for five months
Pac bosor dhoria: for five years)

Subject	Simple Future	Future Continuous	Future Perfect	Future Perfect Continuous
ami/amra	KorTam Pari KorTam naO Pari. KorTam Parini? KorTam Parinani?	KoraT thaKTam Pari KoraT thaKTam naO Pari KoraT thaKTam Parini? KoraT thaKTam Parinani?	KorTam ParTam KorTam ParTamnaay KorTam ParTamni? KorTam ParTamnaayni?	shoKal noyta Tone KoraT thaKTe ParTam shoKal noyta Tone KoraT thaKTe ParTamna shoKal noyta Tone KoraT thaKTe ParTamni? shoKal noyta Tone KorqT thaKTe ParTamnani?
aPne/aPnara Tain/Tara	KorTa Parioin KorTa naO Paroin. KorTa Paroinni? KorTa Paroinnani?	KoraT thaKTam Paroin KoraT thaKTam naO Paroin KoraT thaKTa Paroinni? KoraT thaKTa Paroinnai?	KorTam ParTa KorTa ParTanaay KorTa ParTani? KorTa ParTanaayni?	shoKal noyta Tone KoraT thaKTe ParTa shoKal noyta Tone KoraT thaKTe ParTana shoKal noyta Tone KoraT thaKTe ParTani? shoKal noyta Tone KoraT thaKTe ParTanani?
Tumi/TumiTain	KorTaay Pario KorTaay naO Paro. KorTaay Paroni? KorTaay Paronani?	KoraT thaKTaay Paro KoraT thaKTaay naO Paro KoraT thaKTaay Paroni? KoraT thaKTaay Paronani?	KorTaay ParTaay KorTaay ParTaaynaay KorTaay ParTaayni? KorTaay ParTaaynaayni?	shoKal noyta Tone KoraT thaKTe ParTaay shoKal noyta Tone KoraT thaKTe ParTaayna shoKal noyta Tone KoraT thaKTe ParTaayni? shoKal noyta Tone KoraT thaKTe ParTaaynani?
Tui/Tumra/Tura	KorTeParos KorTe naO Paros. KorTe Parosni? KorTe Parosnani?	KoraT thaKTe Paros KoraT thaKTe naO Paros KoraT thaKTe Parosni? KoraT thaKTe Parosnani?	KorTe ParTe KorTe ParTenaay KorTe ParTeyni? KorTe ParTenaayni?	shoKal noyta Tone KoraT thaKTe ParTe shoKal noyta Tone KoraT thaKTe ParTena shoKal noyta Tone KoraT thaKTe ParTeni? shoKal noyta Tone KoraT thaKTe ParTeynani?

Group A. iii

These verbs ends with a and aa as their verbal suffix. You take the root of the verbs and add the suffix to suit your need. zana: to know: zan+a. Now, add the necessary suffix depending on your tense form and subject of the sentence. Remember, the suffixes must be in line with the status of the subject. So ami zani and aPne zanoin but he zane. I know, you know (you being aPne) and he knows (he being referred as Tui).

But unlike the other group here you add an adjective before the verbs that you have formed using a noun and they follow the same rules

To work well	Bala Kori/Koria Kam Kora
To read a book well	Bala Kori/Koria Boi PoYrha
To write a book well	Bala Kori/Koria Boi lekha
To write a story well	Bala Kori/Koria kichcha lekha
To have a bath well	Bala Kori/Koria ghushol Kora
To shop well	mon Dia bazar Kora
To hold the door well/strongly	shoKTo Kori/Koria Dorza dhora
To learn Sylheti slowly	asTe asTe Sylheti hIka
To touch one's hand softly	agla Kori/Koria aT soaa
To call korim loudly	zure/ zur Kori/Koria korimre daaKa

Group B. i

These verbs ends with owa as their verbal suffix. You drop the owa and add the suffix to suit your need. Aowa: to be. Now, add the necessary suffix depending on your tense form and subject of the sentence. Remember, the suffixes must be in line with the status of the subject. So ami Ai and aPne Ain but he Ay. I am (being), you are (you are being and referred as aPne) and hE Ay (he is being and referred as Tui).

To be	Aowa
To say	Kowa
To look	caowa
To put away	thowa
To take/to remove	neowa
To give	Deowa
To eat/drink	khaowa
To come	aowa
To go	zaowa
To stay	rowa
To wash	dhOwa
To sit	bOwa
To get/receive	Paowa
To sing	gaowa

khaowa-to eat/drink

In the following table sentences are as follows
Positive sentence
Negagtive sentence
Positive question
Negative question
shoKal noyta Tone: since 9 in the morning
(shombar Tone: since Monday
Pac ghonta dhoria: for five hours
Pac Din dhoria: for five days
Pac mash dhoria: for five months
Pac bosor dhoria: for five years)

Subject	Simple Present	Present Continuous	Present Perfect	Present Perfect Continuous
ami/amra	khai. khaina. khaini? Khainani?	Koriar/Korram. Koriarna/Korramna. Koriarni?/Korramni? Koriarnani?/Korramni?	Korsi. Korsina. Korsini? Korsinani?	shoKal noyta Tone Koriar/Korram, shoKal nota Tone Koriarna/Korramna shoKal noyta Tone Koriarni/Korramni? shoKal noyta Tone Koriarnani/Korramnani?
aPne/aPnara Tain/Tara	Koroin. Koroinna. Koroinni? Koroinnani?	Korra Korrana Korrani? Korranani?	Korsoin Korsoinna Korsoinni? Korsoinnani?	shoKal noyta Tone Korra shoKal nota Tone Korrana shoKal noyta Tone Korrani shoKal noyta Tone Korranani?
Tumi/TumiTain	Koro Korona. Koroni? Koronani?	Korraay Korraayna Korrayni? Korraaynani?	Korso Korsona Korsoni? Korsonani?	shoKal noyta Tone Korraay shoKal nota Tone Korraayna shoKal noyta Tone Korraayni? shoKal noyta Tone Korraaynani?
Tui/Tumra/Tura	Koros Korosna. Korosni? Korosnani?	Korre Korrena Korreni? Korrenani?	KorsoT KorsoTna KorsoTni? KorsoTnani?	shoKal noyta Tone Korre shoKal nota Tone Korrena shoKal noyta Tone Korreni? shoKal noyta Tone Korrenani?

Group B. ii

These verbs ends with owa as their verbal suffix. You drop the owa and add the suffix to suit your need. Aowa: to be. Now, add the necessary suffix depending on your tense form and subject of the sentence. Remember, the suffixes must be in line with the status of the subject. So ami Ai and aPne Ain but hE Ay. I am (being), you are (you are being and referred as aPne) and hE Ay (he is being and referred as Tui).

But unlike the other group here you add a noun before the verbs and they follow the same rules

To be a doctor	daKTor Aowa
To say the truth	hasa Kowa
To look up	uPreDi caowa
To put away on the table	tebulo thowa
To take/to remove the book	Boi neowa
To give money	teKa Deowa
To eat rice	BaT khaowa
To come home	barhiT aowa
To go to school	ishkulo zaowa
To wash one's hand	aT dhOwa
To sit on the ground	matiT bOwa
To get/receive money	teKa Paowa
To sing a song	gan gaowa

Group B. iii

These verbs ends with owa as their verbal suffix. You drop the owa and add the suffix to suit your need. Aowa: to be. Now, add the necessary suffix depending on your tense form and subject of the sentence. Remember, the suffixes must be in line with the status of the subject. So ami Ai and aPne Ain but he Ay. I am (being), you are (you are being and referred as aPne) and hE Ay (he is being and referred as Tui).

But unlike the other group here you add an adjective before the verbs and they follow the same rules

To be a doctor in proper way	Bala Kori/Koria daKTor Aowa
To say the truthwell	Bala Kori/Koria hasa Kowa
To look up well	Bala Kori/Koria uPreDi caowa
To put away on the table well	Bala Kori/Koria tebulo thowa
To take/to remove the book quickly	zolDi Kori/Koria Boi neowa
To give money quickly	TarhaTarhi teKa Deowa
To eat rice hot	gorom BaT khaowa
To come home quick	zolDi barhiT aowa
To go to school running	dourhaia ishkulo zaowa
To get/receive money soon	shigroU teKa Paowa
To sing a song well	Bala Kori/Koria gan gaowa

Group C. i

These verbs ends with ni as their verbal suffix. You drop the owa and add the suffix to suit your need. zanani: to let someone know/to notify. Now, add the necessary suffix depending on your tense form and subject of the sentence. Remember, the suffixes must be in line with the status of the subject. So, ami zanai and aPne zanain but hE zanaay. I notify, you notify (you as aPne) and he (he is Tui) notifies.

Let someone know/notify well	shuza zanani
To teach someone read/	PoYrhani
To teach	
To get some write	lekhani
To help one hold/to catch/to arrest	dhorani
To say hello to someone/	
or enable one to speak	maathani
To tell someone/	hunani
or get someone to listen	
To teach	hIkani
To walk a dog/child	atani
To help one understand	buzani
To cuase something to be done	Korani
To cause one to be hit	marani
To get something measured	maPani
To get something moved	hOrani
To show something to someone	Dekhani
To let someone touch something	sOowani
To cause something put away	thOwani
To get one to keep something	rakhani
To get one to call someone	daKani
To put on a dress on a child	PinDani
To cause someone to cry	KanDani
To get something cooked	randhani
To cause something to picked up	Tulani
To get something to rot	Pocani
To get something to ripe	PaKani
To go for a walk/visiting friends	PaKani
To get someone buy something	kinani
To get a child urinate	muthani
To get a child open the bowel	agaani

To cause something to move	lorhani
To run	Dourhani
To entertain people	khaowani

Group C. ii

These verbs ends with ni as their verbal suffix. You drop the owa and add the suffix to suit your need. zanani: to let someone know/to notify. Now, add the necessary suffix depending on your tense form and subject of the sentence. Remember, the suffixes must be in line with the status of the subject. So, ami zanai and aPne zanain but hE zanaay. I notify, you notify (you as aPne) and he (he is Tui) notifies.

But unlike the other group here you add a noun and pronoun before the verbs and they follow the same rules

To get some write a story	golPo lekhani
To help a child hold a pen	Kolom dhorani
To say hello to Korim	korimre maathani
To let him know	Tane hunani
To teach the time table	namoTa nhIkani
To help a child walk	baichchare atani
To help one understand a sum	Angko buzani
To cause way to be cleared	Poth Korani

Group B. iii

These verbs ends with owa as their verbal suffix. You drop the owa and add the suffix to suit your need. Aowa: to be. Now, add the necessary suffix depending on your tense form and subject of the sentence. Remember, the suffixes must be in line with the status of the subject. So ami Ai and aPne Ain but hE Ay. I am (being), you are (you are being and referred as aPne) and hE Ay (he is being and referred as Tui).

But unlike the other group here you add an adjective before the verbs and they follow the same rules

To get some write a story well	Bala Kori/Koria golPo lekhani
To help a child hold a pen properly	Bala Kori/Koria Kolom dhorani
To say hello to Korim properly	Bala Kori/Koria korimrre maathani
To let him know quickly	zolDi Tane hunani
To teach the time table quickly	TarhaTarhi namoTa hIkani
To help a child walk slowly	asTe asTe baichchare atani
To help one understand a sum well	Bala Kori/Koria Angko buzani
To cause way to be cleared nicely	shunDor Kori/Koria Poth Korani

Group D

To finish doing	Kori laowa
To finish talking	maathi laowa
To finish learning	hIki laowa
To finish eating/drinking	khai laowa
To finish washing	dhoi laowa
To finish listening	huni laowa
To finish cooking	randhi laowa
To finish tying up	banDi laowa

Group E

ghumai zaowa	to fall asleep
hori/horia zaowa	to move away
huni/hunia zaowa	to go after hearing
Dekhia zaowa	to go after seeing
boia zaowa	to go after siting/having a rest
khaia zaowa	to go after eating
thakia zaowa	to after staying
maathia zaowa	to after speaking
PoYrhia zaowa	to continue reading/to go after reading
Kam Koria zaowa	to continue working/to go after working
atia zaowa	to go by walking
base zaowa	to go by bus
ghariE zaowa	to go by car
PaowE zaowa	to go on foot
PoyDole zaowa	to go on foot
noukaay zaowa	to go by boat
treinE zaowa	to go by train
pleinE zaowa/bimanE zaowa	to go by plain
caia zaowa	to go looking
lekhia zaowa	to continue reading/to go after writing

Group F

Gorom laga	to feel hot
ţanda laga	to feel cold
Dukko laga	to feel sad/sympathy
Kosto laga	to feel pain/sympathy
Bala laga	to feel good/happy
baD laga	to feel bad
biroKTi/biroKTo laga	to feel bored/annoyed
kharaP laga	to feel bad
bOmi bOmi laga	to feel nausea/feel like vomitting
bish bish laga	to feel intolerable/unbearable
OicOi laga	trouble/shouting occurring
mair laga	fighting occurring
maramari laga	fighting occuring
BEzal laga	to feel sad
gondogul laga	feud/trouble occurring
foshaD laga	trouble/problem occurring
mita laga	to feel sweet
TiTTa laga	to feel bitter (taste of bitter things)
tenga laga	to feel sour
Benga laga	trouble occurring
randha laga	need to cook
norom laga	to feel soft (something feels soft)
shoKTo laga	to feel hard (something feels hard)
Qushi laga	to feel happy
Kotin laga	to feel difficult (something feels difficult)
shuza laga	to feel easy (something feels easy)

Group G

Kotha Deowa	to promise/give word
mathaa Deowa	to offer susbstantial support/stand by
maath Deowa	to speak up (in a meeting)
teKa Deowa	to give/lend money
Korzo Deowa	to lend
dhan Deowa	to give paddy
rin Deowa	to offer a loan
couk Deowa	to look at something and wish ill
dhaari Deowa	to warn someone (younger)
Bingri Deowa	to warn a young one with one's eyes
gail Deowa	to swear/call names
boKa Deowa	to tell off
aT Deowa	to give a hand/to help
Pas Deowa	to stand up/to stick up
BaT Deowa	to give rice/to give food
nac Deowa	to start dancing/start doing something without understanding it/getting excited without knowing why

Group H

ashmano uta	to get to the roof (as in showing off)
mathaaT uta	to take advange of someone for their weakness
KanDo uta	to take advange of someone for their weakness
KominDiT uta	to be profane
ghariT uta	to board a vehecle
baso uta	to board a bus
noukaT uta	to board a boat
saaTo uta	to climb to the ceiling
moiT uta	to get on a ladder
PoDo uta	to show off (on being spoilt)

208

Group I

Paglami Kora	to behave like an unreasonable person/Crazy like deed
Bala Kora	to do good
BaD Kora	to do bad
saf Kora	to clean/clear
moyla Kora	to make something dirty
suto Kora	to cause someone feel small/belittle
borho Kora	to cause someone feel big/proud
bazar Kora	to make someone sad/upset
bezal Kora	to create a problem
Kam Kora	to work
anchan Kora	to make a fuss
gundami Kora	to act as a thug/ruffian
shondami Kora	to act as a thug/ruffian
maTlami Kora	to be drunk
bisna Kora	to make bed
murubbiana Kora	to try acting like a leader where it is not accepted
bia Kora	to get married (a man marries)
bicar Kora	to judge
binash Kora	to destroy something
beTal Kora	to create a problem
shoyTani Kora	to be naughty
gusa Kora	to be angry/upset
rag Kora	to be angry
aga maatha Kora	to act as having no clue
noy soy Kora	to be unsure/hesitant
Pislami Kora	being slimy as in dishonest

Group J

begar khata	to work for nothing
mathaa khata	to get one's brain work
shoKTi khata	to get one's strength enaged
eKloge khata	to work together
milia khata	to work all together

Group K

zhEl Kata	to serve prison sentence
Kolla Kata	to cut off (head)
mathaa Kata	to cut off (head)
fiTa Kata	to cut of a ribbon
shiTa Kata	to part one's hair

Group L

matha khatani	to think
Poysha khatani	to invest
bebsha khatani	to invest capital
buDdhi khatani	to use brain/to invest brain
bicar khatani	to use judgement
aKol khatani	to use intelligence
zomin khatani	to use land
shoKTi khatani	to use strength

Group M

Koria aowa	to continue to do
Koria zaowa	to continue to do
Koria thoa	to keep having done
Koria rakha	to keep having done
Koria neowa	to take having done
Koria PaYlani	to get something done
Koria ana	to bring having something done

Group N

khaia zaowa	to go after eating
khaia aowa	to come after eating
khaia PaYlani	to finish eating/drinking
khaia ghumani	to sleep after eating
khaia gushol Kora	to bathe after eating

Group O

aile zaowa	to go (if someone else came)
gele aowa	to come (if someone else went)
hunle maatha	to speak (if one has heard)
Korle Deowa	to give (if someone else has done something)
Dile Kora	to dof (if someone has done something)
Dile Deowa	to give (if someone has diven something)
Paile Kora	to do (if someone has received something)
khaile khaowa	to eat/drink (if someone has eaten/drunk)
maathle huna	to speak (if one has heard)
ashle asha	to laugh/smile (if one has seen another smiles/laughs)
lagle lagani	to use if it is needed
utle zaowa	to go if others have got up
gele uta	to get up if others have gone
Parhle khaowa	to eat/drink if one can
Koraile Kora	to do if something is done
maathaile maatha	to sepeak with someone if he/she has spoken
maathaile maathani	to say hello to someone if he/she has said hello
khaowaile zomani	to gather if fed
zomaile khaowani	to feed if gathered
PoYrhaile hIkani	to teach if taught

Group P

Koria aowa	to continue doing
Dia aowa	to continue giving
maathia aowa	to continue speaking
Pitia aowa	to continue beating
hunaia aowa	to continue listening
shesh Koria aowa	to have come finishing something
mitaia aowa	to have come resolving something
gaia aowa	to have come singing
caia aowa	to have come having looked at something

Group Q

Koria zaowa	to carry on doing
Dia zaowa	to carry on giving
maathia zaowa	to carry on speaking
caia zaowa	to go having looked at something
shesh Koria zaowa	to go having completed something
mitaia zaowa	to go having resolved something
gaia aowa	to go having sung

Group R

With this group you treat the first part of the part zaowa+gi as the verb and add the verbal suffixes as necessary according to the status of the subjects and then add the gi at the end.

To be gone	zaowagi (irregular)
Go and eat	khai laowgi
Go and tell	Koi laowgi
Go and do	Kori laowgi
Go and hear	hunilaowgi
Go and speak	mathilaowgi
Go and read	PoYrhilaowgi
Go and draw	akilaowgi
Go and sing	gailaowgi
Go and catch	dhorilaowgi
Go and sleep	ghumailaogi
Go and cook	randhilaowgi
Go and tidy up	atailaowgi

ami/amra zaigi
I/We go.

aPne/aPnara/Tain/TainTain/Tara zaingi.
You/You all/He/She/They/They go.

Tumi/TumiTain/Tumra zaowgi
You/ You all go.

Tui/Tura/Tumra zasgi
You/You all go.

hE/Tai/oguE/hOguE/iguE/hIguE/era/hEra/iguinTe/hIguinTe/oguinTe/hOguin
Te/korime/lorene zaaygi.

He/She/He/She/He/She/they-near/they-far/they-here/they-far/they-here/they-
Far/korim/Lauren goes.

Present: Aowa-to be

In the following table sentences are as follows
Positive sentence
Negagtive sentence
Positive question
Negative question
shoKal noyta Tone: since 9 in the morning
(shombar Tone: since Monday
Pac ghonta dhoria: for five hours
Pac Din dhoria: for five days
Pac mash dhoria: for five months
Pac bosor dhoria: for five years)

Subject	Simple Present	Present Continuous	Present Perfect	Present Perfect Continuous
ami/amra	Ai. Aina. Aini? Ainani?	Aiar/Airam. Aiarna/Airamna. Aiarni?/Airamni? Aiarnani?/Airamnani?	Aisi. Aisina. Aisini? Aisinani?	shoKal noyta Tone Aiar/Airam, shoKal nota Tone Aiarna/Airamna shoKal noyta Tone Aiarni/Airamni? shoKal noyta Tone Aiarnani?/Airamnani?
aPne/aPnara Tain/Tara	Ain. Ainna. Ainni? Ainnani?	Aira Airana Airani? Airanani?	Aisoin Aisoinna. Aisoinni? Aisoinnani?	shoKal noyta Tone Aira shoKal nota Tone Airana shoKal noyta Tone Airani shoKal noyta Tone Airanani?
Tumi/TumiTain	Aow. Aowna. Aowni? Aownani?	Airaay Airaayna Airaayni? Airaaynani?	Aiso Aisona. Aisoni? Aisonani?	shoKal noyta Tone Airaar shoKal nota Tone Airaayna shoKal noyta Tone Airaayni shoKal noyta Tone Airaaynani?
Tui/Tumra/Tura	Aos. Aosna. Aosni? Aosnani?	Aire Airena Aireni? Airenani?	AisoT AisoTna. AisoTni? AisoTnani?	shoKal noyta Tone Aire shoKal nota Tone Airena shoKal noyta Tone Aireni shoKal noyta Tone Airenani?

Past: Aowa-to be

In the following table sentences are as follows
Positive sentence
Negagtive sentence
Positive question
Negative question
shoKal noyta Tone: since 9 in the morning
(shombar Tone: since Monday
Pac ghonta dhoria: for five hours
Pac Din dhoria: for five days
Pac mash dhoria: for five months
Pac bosor dhoria: for five years)

Subject	Simple Past	Past Continuous	Past Perfect	Past Perfect Continuous
ami/amra	Ailam. Ailamna. Ailamni? Ailamnani?	AowaT aslam AowaT aslamna AowaT aslamni? AowaT aslamnani?	Aislam Aislamna. Aislamni? Aislamnani?	shoKal noyta Tone AowaT aslam shoKal nota Tone AowaT aslamna shoKal noyta Tone AowaT aslamani? shoKal noyta Tone AowaT aslamnani?
aPne/aPnara Tain/Tara	Ailam. Ailamna. Ailamni? Ailamnani?	AowaT aslam AowaT aslamna AowaT aslamni? AowaT aslamnani?	Aislam Aislamna. Aislamni? Aislamnani?	shoKal noyta Tone AowaT aslam shoKal nota Tone AowaT aslamna shoKal noyta Tone AowaT aslamani? shoKal noyta Tone AowaT aslamnani?
Tumi/TumiTain	Ailaay Ailaayna. Ailaayni? Ailaaynani?	AowaT aslaay AowaT aslaayna AowaT aslaayni? AowaT aslaaynani?	Aislaay Aislaayna. Aislaayni? Aislaaynani?	shoKal noyta Tone AowaT aslaay shoKal nota Tone AowaT aslaayna shoKal noyta Tone AowaT aslaayni? shoKal noyta Tone AowaT aslaaynani?
Tui/Tumra/Tura	Aile Ailena. Aileni? Ailenani?	AowaT asle AowaT aslena AowaT asleni? AowaT aslenani?	Aisle Aislena. Aiseni? Aislenani?	shoKal noyta Tone AowaT asle shoKal nota Tone AowaT aslena shoKal noyta Tone AowaT asleni? shoKal noyta Tone AowaT aslenani?

Future: Aowa-to be

In the following table sentences are as follows
Positive sentence
Negagtive sentence
Positive question
Negative question
shoKal noyta Tone: since 9 in the morning
(shombar Tone: since Monday
Pac ghonta dhoria: for five hours
Pac Din dhoria: for five days
Pac mash dhoria: for five months
Pac bosor dhoria: for five years)

Subject	Simple Future	Future Continuous	Future Perfect	Future Perfect Continuous
ami/amra	Aimu. AiTamnaay. Aimuni? Aimunani?	AowaT thaKmu AowaT thaKTamnaay AowaT thaKmuni? AowaT thaKTamnaayni?	bazar Koria harlam One Aia harlam One Aia harlam Onena. Aia harlam Oneni? Aia harlam Onenani?	shoKal noyta Tone AowaT thaKlam One shoKal noyta Tone AowaT thaKlam Onena shoKal noyta Tone AowaT thaKlam Oneni? shoKal noyta Tone AowaT thaKlam Onenani?
aPne/aPnara Tain/Tara	Ailam. Ailamna. Ailamni? Ailamnani?	AowaT aslam AowaT aslamna AowaT aslamni? AowaT aslamnani?	Aia harla One Aia harla Onena. Aia harla Oneni? Aia harla Onenani?	shoKal noyta Tone AowaT thaKla One shoKal noyta Tone AowaT thaKla Onena shoKal noyta Tone AowaT thaKla Oneni? shoKal noyta Tone AowaT thaKla Onenani?
Tumi/TumiTain	Ailaay Ailaayna. Ailaayni? Ailaaynani?	AowaT aslaay AowaT aslaayna AowaT aslaayni? AowaT aslaaynani?	Aia harlaay One Aia harlaay Onena. Aia harlaay Oneni? Aia harlaay Onenani?	shoKal noyta Tone AowaT thaKlaay One shoKal noyta Tone AowaT thaKlaay Onena shoKal noyta Tone AowaT thaKlaay Oneni? shoKal noyta Tone AowaT thaKlaay Onenani?
Tui/Tumra/Tura	Aile Ailena. Aileni? Ailenani?	AowaT asle AowaT aslena AowaT asleni? AowaT aslenani?	Aia harle One Aia harle Onena. Aia harle Oneni? Aia harle Onenani?	shoKal noyta Tone AowaT thaKle One shoKal noyta Tone AowaT thaKle Onena shoKal noyta Tone AowaT thaKle Oneni? shoKal noyta Tone AowaT thaKle Onenani?

English to Sylheti

A

Aide by	mana/mania cola
Assume	mono Kora
Assumption	dhoria neowa/dhora
Animal	PoshuPaki/zibzonTu
And	ar/ebong
Arrow	Tir
Accumulation	zoma Aowa
Action	Kaz/Kormo
Aggrevation	zala/zonTrona/hoyrani
Alternative	bikolPo
Ant	PiPrha
Aeroplane	urhukkol/biman
Addition	zug
Alieanation	shamoz bichchinno
Alteration	boDlani
Another	Ainnozon (people)/AinnoTa (things)
Anyone/	ze Keu/zEsa
Anybody	
Acting	ABinoy Kora
All	shob/hoKol(people)/shobTa/hoKolTa (things)
Active	shokriO
Attractive	aKorshoniO/shunDor/Dekhar moTo
Air	baTash
Age	boysh/boyosh
Aged	boyshi/boyoshi/burha/briDdho
Angling	mas dhora/mas maraa
Angle	kun/kuna
Angel	firishTa/forishTa
Anger	raag/gUsa
Anti	biPoriT/ulta
Anarchy	bEsrinkola/bisrikolPonTa
Anarchic	bisrinkolabaDi/bisrinkolaPonTi
Allergy	biruP ProTikria
Abandon	Teaag Kora/ Palaia zaowa/ Palai Deowa
Abdomen	Petor Tola
Abduct	aPohoron/ dhoria loia zaowa
Abide	mana

Ability	zuiggoTa/shoKTi
Able	shokkom
Abode	bashosTan/thaKar zaga/barhi
Abort	baD Deowa (as in giving up)
About	bishoye/shongkranTo
Above	uPor
Abroad	biDesh/PorDesh/biDesh BiBui
Absent	AnuPosTiT
Absolute	curhanTo
Absorb	cUsha/cUshon Kora
Abstract	ADrishsho/ shukko
Absurd	acanoK/azobi/azgubi
Abundant	shimahin/prochur/zoTesto
Abuse	ATTacar
Accent	taana/taana Dia maatha (speaking with an accent)
Accept	grohon Kora
Access	probesh/ hamanir moTo/ duka
Accessory	logor zinish/shaijjoKari
Accident	Durghotona
Accompany	log/loge zaowa
Accomplice	shathi/logor manush
Accomplish	Arzon/Arzon Kora (as in achieving a great result)
Accord	cukTi
Account	hIshab/ekaunt/ bornona Kora
Accurate	tik/shotik
Accuse	ABizug Kora
Ache	bish/bEtha/beDna
Acknowledge	shikar Kora
Acquire	lowa/paowa/shoTTo neowa
Across	kunakuni
Actual	basToboTo
Adamant	Drirho Protiggo
Adapt	manaia lowa/manaia newa
Add	zug Kora/ milani
Addict	nishakur
Address	tikana/ shombuDon Kora
Adjust	milaia neowa
Admire	PoconDo Kora/ Bala Paowa
Admission	BorTi Aowa
Adopt	grohon Kora/ PalKa neowa

Advance	aguani/ aguail
Advantage	shubiDa
Advertising	biggaPon
Advice	uPoDesh/Poramish/Poramorsho
Affect	ProBab
After	baDe/Pore
Afternoon	maadhan

Aardvark: PiPrhakhaowra, afrikan prani zeKtaay PiPrha khaia bace.

Aback: buka boni zaowa (in shock/surprise), beakkol Ai zaowa (being dumbfounded), ashchorjo Aowa.

Abacus: abakas. gonar lagi shaijjoKari eKta Kator Toiri zontro ba zinish.

Abalone: shamuk zaTio eK shomuDDor prani.

Abandon: Teag Kora, Palai Deowa, PoriTTeag Kora, PoriTTeag, PaYlani.

Abase: biniTo Aowa, v, binoI, ad, Ahongkar na Kora, ad

Abashed: shorminDa, ad, shorom Paowa, v, shorminDa Aowa, v, lojja Paowa, v, lojjiTo Aowa, v, lojja Paowa, v

Abate: shoKTi Komi zaowa, v, norom Ai zaowa, v

Abattoir: Koshaikhana, n

Abbess: mohila Padri, n

Abbey: girza, n

Abbot: Padri, Purush Padri

Abbreviate: shobDo batti Kora,v, shobDo huru Kora, v, shobDo suto Kora, v
ABC: A-a, n, A-a Kora, v

Abdicate: shingashon Teag Kora, v, shingashon PoriTTeag Kora, v

Abdomen: Petor Tola, Petor nicor elaKa ba Angsho.

Abduct:

Aberration: aKTa Ashadharon PoriborTon ghota, v, hotaT AshaBabik PoriborTon ghota,

Abet: baD Kamo shaijjo Kora, v.

Abeyance: shamoikBabe biroTo thaKa, v, shamoikBabe raki Deowa, v

Abhor: ghinna, ghin, ghrina, n, ghinna/ghin/ghrina Kora, v

Abide: thaKa, bash Kora, boshobash Kora, rowa, v. boshobash, bash, n

Ability: zuiggoTa, khomoTa, DokkoTa, n.

Abject: AshomBob roKom kharaP, AshomBob roKom baD.

Abjure: Kosom khaia Ashshikar Kora, v.

Ablaze: zolonTo, ad, ze zinish zoler, ad,

Able: zuiggo, ad

Ablutions: ozu, n, ozu Kora,v.

Abnormal: AshshaBabik, niomor baire, ad

Aboard: uta, baso uta, ghariT uta, bimano uta, noukaT uta

Abode: barhi, ghor, ghorbarhi, bashosTan, grehosTali, nibash

Abolish: shesh Kora, shesh Kori laowa, biluPTo Kora

Abominable: ghriniTo, ghinnar zuiggo

Abomination: ghrina, ghinna

Aborigine: aDibashi, mul bashinDa

Abort: baD Deowa

Abortion: Pet Palani, gorBo nosto Kora

Abound: Bora, sheshhin, shesh nai, procure, zoTeshto

About: dhare Kace, nikote, KanDaT, pray.

Above: uPor, uPre, uPreDi

Abracadabra: zaDumonTro, abrakadabra.

Abrasion: camrha cEsi zaowa,

Abrasive: ABoDro, ABoDro beboar/bebohar

Abreast: zanashunar biTre, zana,

Abridge: suto Kora, batti Kora

Abroad: biDesh, biDesh BiBui, PorDesh, PoroDesh, probash

Abrogate: kuno cukTi ba shommoTi baTil Kora

Abrupt: aKTA, hoṭaT

Abs: petor nicor Anshor mangshoPeshi

Abscess: puz Aia fula

Abscond: Baga, Baga Deowa, Baga mara, Bagi zaowa, Polaia zaowa, Polani

Abseil: PorboT ba uca tilla Tone dorhi baia nama.

Absent: AnuPosTiT, gorazir, gorhazir, goyro

Absinthe: khub shoKshali kocua moD zaTio Panio

Absolute: curhanTo

Absolve: guna maP Aowa, maP Paowa

Absorb: Pani Tania neowa.

Abstain: biroTo thaKa

Abstract: bimurTo, maya

Abstruse: buzTe kotin

Absurd: azgubi, acanoK

Abundant: zothesto, AneK, procur

Abuse: ATTacar, Anacar, ATTacar Kora

Abysmal: BoyanoK, AshomBob kharaP/baD

Abyss: goBir khad/ghaT/Kua

Acacia: akashia, eKzaTor gac

Academy: ekademi, biDDaloy, skul, ishkul, shikkaproTishtan

Acanthus: eKzaTor gac

Accede: shommoTo Aowa, razi Aowa

Accelerate: (goTi) barhani, druTo Kora

Accent: taan, taana Deowa

Accentuate: guruTTo Deowa, pradhainno Deowa

Accept: grohon Kora, mania neowa, mani laowa

Access: probesh, hamani, dUka

Accession: shinggashono bowa, shinggashon grohon Kora

Accessory: Dorkari zinish

Accident: Durghotona, Aghotona, Aghoton

Acclaim: proshongsha, proshonghsha Kora

Acclimatize: abhaowar loge khap khaowani

Accolade: shomman, Purushkar, shommanona

Accommodate: manaia neowa, milia neowa, zaga Kora

Accompany: loge zaowa, shathe zaowa

Accomplice: shohozugi, shaijjoKari

Accomplish: kuno zinish Koria shesh Kori laowa, shesh Kori laowa, shesh Kora, Arjon, shofol (as in accomplished man)

Accord: cukTi

Accordance: mil thaKa

According: Anushare

Accordion: ekordion, eKta ganor zonTro

Account: ekaunt, hIshab

Accounting: hIshab biDDa, hIshab Kora, hIshabPoTro

Accredited: AnumoDiTo

Accretion: dhire dhire borho Aowa

Accrue: asTe asTe barha, zoma Aowa

Accumulate: zoma Aowa

Accurate: shotik, tik

Accursed: ABishoPTo

Accusative: ABizugor lakhan

Accuse: ABizug Kora

Accustom: PoriciTo Aowa

Acerbic: TiTTa, Amoshrin, shoKTo

Acetate: esetik acidor Tone Aowa lobon

Acetic: esidor lakhan

Ache: beDna, bish,

Achieve: Arzon, Arzon Kora

Achromatic: ronghin, rong sarha, rong nai

Acid: esid, khar

Acknowledge: shikar Kora,

Acme: Arzonor uchchoTomo curha

Acne: ekni, Dag, guti, fUri

Acquaint: PoriciTo Koraia Deowa, Poricoy Koria Deowa, cinaia Deowa

Acquiesce: eKmoT Aowa, razi Aowa, shommoTo Aowa, shommoTi Deowa, moT Deowa

Acquire: Paowa, grohon Kora, ana

Acre: eKor

Acrimonious: bibaDPurno, shoTruTaPurno

Across: mazeDi, shuza, shorashori

Act: ghotona, Kaz, Kora, ABinoy Kora, ABinoy

Action: Kaz, Kam, ghotona
Active: shokrio, Kamo

Actual: hasa, hasa hasa, shoTTiKar, basToboTo
Acupuncture: akupankcar

Acute: kotin, shoKTishali, maraTToK, Qub beshi

Adagio: dhirogoTir shongiT, shongiTor dhirogoTiaala Aungsho

Adamant: DirhoproTiggo, mathabandha, Ahongkari

Adapt: khaP khaowani, khaP khaowaia neowa

Add: zug Kora, milani, milai laowa

Addendum: sheshe lagaia Deowa, ze zinish sheshe lagaia Deowa Ay

Addict: ashoKTo

Addition: zug, zug Kora, zurha Deowa

Address: t̲ikana, nibash, abash, abash nibash, bashosTan

Adequate: zoTesto, PorzaPTo

Adhere: mania cola, mania neowa, Anushoron Kora

Adhesive: at̲aa, at̲aalo

ad hoc: AsTaI, sTaI nay

adieu: biDaay, biDaay neowa, biDaay Deowa, biDaay lowa

adjacent: nikote, nikot, KanDaT, dharo

adjective: gunbacoK shobDo, gunbacoK

adjoin: zurha Deowa, zurha lagaini

adjourn: mulTobi, mulTobi Kora

adjudicate: edzuket, edjukeit, bicaroK

adjust: milaia neowa, milmish Kora, milani

admin: proshashonik, proshasongoTo
administer: Poricalona Kora, calani

administrate: Poricalona Kora, calani, calaia neowa

administration: proshashon

administrative: proshashonik

admiral: edmiral, shenaPoTi

admire: Bala Paowa, PosonDo Kora

admissible: grohonzuiggo, grohon Korar moTo

admission: BorTi, BorTi Kora, BorTi Aowa, BorTi Korani

admit: shikar Kora, BorTi Kora

ado: cillacilli, hoicoi, aalla cilla

adolescence: selebela, seleKal, baillo boyosh
adopt: PaloK neowa, PalKa neowa
adore: Bala Paowa, maya Kora
adorn: PinDa

adrift: Baasha, Baashan, BaashanTo, BaashonTo

adsorb: tani laowa, shUshi laowa, shUsha

adult: praPTo boyoshko, borho, Purno boyoshko
adultery: AboiDo shomPorko

advance: aguani, agam, agam Deowa, agam caowa

advantage: shubiDa

advent: shomoy shima, DinOKlor eKta Pokko

adventure: ABizan, edvenchar

adverb: zeshob shobDoOKle KambuDoK shobDoOKlor beaPare kichchu Koy

adversary: shoTru, biruDDobaDi, biruDDo Pokko

adverse: biruP

advert: biggaPon

advertise: biggaPon Deowa

advice: uPoDesh

adviser: uPoDeshDaTa

advocate: edBuket, ukil

aerial: ashmon Tone nice Dia Dekha, Pakir Drishti

aerodynamics: baTashor colacolor PoDDoTi

aerogram: erogram, earmeil, eameilor citi

aeronautics: bimanbiDDa

aeroplane: biman, urhuzaaz

aerospace: mohaaashman

aesthetic: shounDDoirzo, shunDoroTa, shunDorbishoyok

afar: Dur, Duroi, Dure

affair: bishoy, beaPar, Kelenkari

affect: ProBab

affection: sneho, sheno momoTa, momoTa, aDor, maya, maya momoTa

affianced: bia ţik Aowa

affidavit: efidebit, holoPnama, biboroni

affiliate: zorhiTo, miliTo, shomporkiTo

affinity: shomanmon, shomanmonmanshikoTa, shomomona

affirm: PunoukkTo Kora, Punoraay shikar Kora

affix: lagani

affluent: dhoni

afford: kinar zuiggoTa, kinar khomoTa

affray: mair, maramari, zogrha, zoghrazhati, mairdhorbar

Afghan: afgan zaTi, afgani

Aflame: zonlonTo

Afloat: Baasha, Baashan, BaashanTo, BaashonTo

Afoot: coler, Aor, Aowa

Aforesaid: age za Kowa Aise

Aforethought: age cinTa Koria

Afraid: Boy, dor, KHof

Afresh: TorTaza, Taza

African: afrika bishoyok, afrikar

Afrikaans: afrikan, afrikan manush, afrikar manush

After: bade, Pore, sheshe

Afterbirth: zonmor Pore

Aftercare: baDor sheba shushusha, baDor shebazoTno

Aftereffect: baDor PoTikria

Afterglow: baDor uzlani

Afterlife: Poror zonmo, Porozonom, PoroKal

Aftermath: baDor folafol, sheshfol

Afternoon: DuiPor

Afterthought: baDe mono Aowa, baDe cinTa Kora, baDor cinTa

Afterwards: baDe, heshe, sheshe, Pore

Again: abar, hirbar, hiribar, Punoraay, Punorbar

Against: biruDDe, biPokke

Age: boyosh, Kal, zug

Agency: shongoton, proTishtan

Agenda: alaPor bishoy, bishoy, ezenda

Agent: Dalal, proTiniDi

agent provocateur: guPon Dalal, guenDa

aggrandize: borho Koria Dekhani

aggravate: baD Kora, uTTeziTo Kora, biroP proTikria dhorani

aggregate: gorh, gorhe, gorhPorhTa

aggression: shohishoTa, shohishroTa

aggrieved: ahoTo Aowa, shohingshoTar shika

agile: goTishil, shushaisToshomponno

agitate: uTTeziTo Korani

agnostic: shonDehobaDi

ago: age, agor, Purana Dinor, Purana Kalor

agony: Koshto, Dukko, bearam

ate: khail laowa

atheism: nasTikkobaD

athlete: khelowarh

atmosphere: Porimondol

atom: Poromanu,

atomic: anobik

atomize: AnuTe Bag Kora

atomizer: ze zinishre Tar AnuTe Bag Kore ba Bange

atop: uPore, uPor

atrium: riDoyor ba zanor kutar eKta Kamra ba kuta ba kokko.

Manshor zanor kutar maze aro biBinno suto kokko ase. In human heart there are other small atria.

atrocious: maraTTok, Dojjal

Mashuk Ailo eKta maraTTok manush. Mashuk is an atrocious man. Korimor bou Ailo eK Dojjal(Dojjalni). Karim's wife is atrocious.

attach: lagani
tebulor Paow cairota abo lagaisoinnani? Have you not got the four legs of the table attached yet?

attack: akromon, akromon Kora, akromon Korani
bina uskaniTe he salamoTre akromon Korse. He has attacked Salamot without any provocation. shoTrur KamUTo Ailo akromon Kora. It is the job of the enemy to attack. zoshime Tar kuTTa Dia Korimre akromon Korase. Zashim has got his dot attack Karim.

attain: Arzon Kora, laB Kora, zoy Kora
Bala Koria Kam Korle Bala fol Arzon Kora zaay. If (one) works hard (one) can achieve great results. shofoloTa laB KorTe Aile Koshto Kora lagbo. In order to attain success (one) has to suffer (work hard for it). Kichchu zoy KorTe Aile Porishrom Kora lagbo. In order to attain something (one has to) work hard.

attempt: cesta, uDDug, procesta, cesta Kora
cesta na Korle kunTa AiTonaay. Without any attempts nothing will happen. Bala Koria cesta Koroukka: Try harder. Maya's ishkultare Bala Koria calaibar lagi Qub Bala uDDug nisoin: to run the school properly Maya has taken great attempts.

attend: uPosTiT, aazir, aazir Aowa, aazira Deowa, aazir Kora, aazira Deowani
Maya ikano uPosTiT: Maya is present here. Maya aazrini?: Is Maya present? Maya aazir Aisoinni? Has Maya made her appearance (at a court or a class or meeting). Maya klaso aazira Dise. Maya has been present at the class. aPnar mokkelre aDaloTo ania aazir Kora aPnar DayiTTo: It is your duty to ensure your client is present at the court. Pulishe ashamire aDaloTo aazira Deowaise: The Police have presented the accused to the Court.

attest: shoiTTayon, shoiTTayon Korani, etest, etest Kora, etest Koria Deowa, etest Korani
pasPurtor lagi aPnar sobi shoiTTayon Korani lagbo: you will have to get your photos attested for your passport. ami alamoTor sobi shoiTTayon Koria Disi: I have attested Alamot's photos, Tumar fotu etest Koraisoni? Have you got your photos attested?

attic: uPror rum, uPror kuta, etik

attire: Pushak, PushaK ashak

attitude: khaishloT, monoBab, monor goTi

attorney: ainbiD, ainzibi, ukil

attract: akorshon, akorshon Kora

aubergine: bainggon, begun

auburn: Kanor dharor khula cul

auction: nilam

audacious: birat, borho dhoronor, borhoroKomor, DushshaOshmuluk, DushshaOshi

audience: Dorshok-shruTa/Dorshok, shruTa, Adiens
audio: hunar zuiggo

audit: Porjobekkon, Adit, hIshab khoTaia Dekha

audition: Pator lagi Porikka (Pat being a part of a performance of something)

auditorium: Aditoriam, milon kenDro, milar zaga, milar KenDro

auditory: huna bishoyok, shrobon bishoyok

aught: Kora uciT, KorToibbor zuiggo, KorToibbo

August: agost, agost mash

unt: fufu(paternal), moi/khala(maternal)

au pair: shechchamononiTo Poribarik shebaDanKari/shebika

aura: aDdhaTTik coKro ba ruP

au revoir: biDaay/khuDa hafiz, nomoshkar/assalamualaikum

B

Bad	baD/kharaP
Bet	zua
Bent	beak
Bed	bisna/Palong
Bat	bet
Better	Bala (ikta hIkta Tone Bala)
But	kinTu
Berry	boroi
Bank	benk
Bill	bil
Building	bilding
Big	borho/muta
Bigger	aro borho
Bite	Kamorh
Beat	KaPa/dhoKdhoki Kora
Button	guTam/buTam
Butter	ghI
Basket	zhurhi/kholoi
Black	Kala

Bug	ulosh (bed bug), kIt, kit PoTongo
Bark	khal
Blue	nilua/nil
Book	Boi
Bull	boloD/deKa
Bark	daKa
Bee	mouPuk
Bird	Paki
Bind	bandha
Blind	blaind
Bear	Balluk
Bang	zure daKa
Buy	kina/loa
Boy	Pua
Buyer	kinra/lowra
Bond	bond
Ball	futbol
Break	Banga
Broken	Banga
Brick	It

Back	Kor/Pic/Pit
Background	PotoBumi
Base	BiT/BiTTi
Basket	kholoi/basket
Bat	baDur
Bathe	gushol Kora
Bath	gusholkhana
Battle	zuDdho
Bay	shagor/uPoshagor
Beard	Darhi
Bear	Balluk
Beer	moD
Beautiful	shunDor
Beef	gorur manghsho
Bag	tholi/beg
Before	age
Behind	Kor/Pic
Believe	bishshash Kora
Bell	ghonta/ghonti
Berry	zam

Belt	belt
Bend	beak
Best	shob thaki Bala/shobceYE Bala
Better	iktar thaki Bala/ en Tone Bala (as in better than this one or better than him)
Bird	Paki
Black	Kala
Blanket	KaaYTa
Blizzard	Tusharzhorh
Blood	roKTo
Blunt	BuTa
Boast	futani Kora/ futani Dekhani
Body	shoril/goTor/goTTor
Boil	Una/Una Deowa
Bone	aaddi/haaddi
Boost	barhTi
Boss	menezar
Bowel	Pet
Boy	Pua/selE
Bridge	Pul/sheTu/haKom
Broadcast	procar/procar Kora

Broken	Banga
Broke	Deulia (bankrupt)
Brother	Bai (addressings: Baiaa/Baisaab)
Brown	baDami
Browse	Dekha

C

Cat	bilai/mekur/billi
Can	Para/ken (drink can)
Call	daK/daKa
Cup	kaP, Piaala, PEaala
Cute	shunDor
Chirst	jishu kristo, jishu khristo
Cut	Kata
Coat	kut
Catastrophe	shorbonash
Carrot	gazor
Combe	ciroin
Car	garhi
Classic	Puran/ Qub Bala
Class	shreni/klas/kelas
Cable	Taar
Catch	dhora
Cake	kek
Calculate	hIshab Kora
Calf	gurur baichcha

Cow	gai/gaBi
Cattle	goru
Call	daK/daKa *dew*
Come	aowa
Camel	Ut
Camoflouge	lukani/mukush
Cancel	baTil/baTil Kora
Candle	mombaTTi/mombaTi
Candy	misti
Cannabis	ganja
Cannabis-user	gangjakur/ganjakhaowra
Cannon	Kaman
Canoe	nouka/dingi
Capable	shokkom
Capital	muldhon/rajdhani
City	shOr/shohor/taun
Capture	Dokhol Kora/Dokhol lowa/ Dokhol neowa/dhora
Card (for the game)	Tash
Card games	Tash khela
Career	caKri

Careless	hushbuDdhi sarha Kam Kora
Carpet	galica/karPet/karPit
Carrier	bOwra
Cart	garhi/tEla/tElagarhi
Castle	rajproshaD/rajprashaD
Cave	guha
Cause	Karon
Cease	shesh Aowa/shomaPTi
Centre	KenDro/mazkhan
Chair — same	chear
Challenge	cheleinj Kora/ cheleinj Deowa/ daKa/DaK Deowa
Change	boDla/boDol/PoriborTon
Chaos	bisrinkola
Cheat	tOga
Cheek	gal
Chicken	murug
Chick	murgir baichcha
Chef	baburci
Chief	prodhan
Child	baichcha/PuT

Chilli	moric
Chin	Kota/thutha
Choire	ganor Dol
Cheese	Ponir
Choice	PoconDo
Cinnamon	dailchini/dalchini
Clear	Porishkar/Porichchonno
Click	ṭiPa Deowa
Climb	baowa/ baia uta
Coin	Poysha/BangTi Poysha/Korhi
Collect	zomani
Colour	rong
Comedy	aashir natoK
Command	aDesh (positive) nisheD (negative)
Compare	Tulona/ Tulona Kora
Complete	Purno Kora/shesh Kora
Compose	lekha/banda (poem: lekha/ song: banDa)
Concrete	kongkrit/ItPaTTor
Condition	AbosTa
Confirm	nishchiT Koria Kowa

Confident	aTTobishshash
Connect	zugazug
Cardigan	angorkha/jampar/zampar

Note: all woollen wear in modern Sylheit is jampar or zampar! However, angorkha is truly a Sylheit word for cardigan which I heard my mother use! Even than, I used to tease her for using such a word for no one else used it even in her time. She proably used it to remember my grandmother who used to use it. And here it is my way of remembering my mother!

D

Dad, daddy: abba, baba, abbu

Daft: bukami, arhuami

Daffodil: defodil ful

Dagger: cakku, sUri

Dahlia: dalia

Day: Din

Daily: Doinik, DinDin, PorTekDin, PorTiDin, ProTiDin, PoiTTeKDin

Dainty: ruchishommoTo, ruciPurno, shuruchiPurno,

Dairy: gualbarhi, gualabarhi

Dale: Toli, gram, Tola

Dam: bandh

Dame: mohila, beti manush, beti

Damn: dhur! dhurza! dhuroza! maileneowra!

Damp: Biza, cEPa, cEPcEPa, sheTsheTe

Damsel: Purhi, bala, bali, balika

Dance: nac, naca, nriTTo, NiTTo (rarely used in folk songs)

Dadruff: baowfa, khoir

Danger: biPoD, aPoD, biPoD aPoD

Dank: KHiTKHiTe

Dare: beta Aile/beti Aile Kora, shaosh thaKle Kora

Dark: andhair, AndhoKar, Kala

Darling: shuna, shunanu, babu, ma, mai, baba (depending on contexts)

Data: ToiTTo, ToTTo

Date: Tarik

Daze: comoKlaga, cokuT dhanDa laga

Dazzle: matha ghurai laowa, matha ghurai zaowa

Dawn: Bur, BurraiT

Dead: mora

Death: mriTTu, moioT, moron

Deadly: biPoDzonoK

Deaf: Kala, ze Kane hunena

Deal: cukTi, becakinar shommoTi

Dear: prio, mayar, momoTar

Debate: Torko, TorkobiTorko, zukTiTorko

Debonair: shuruchipurno, coloia, shunDormona

Debt: rin, Koroz, Korzo, dhaar, dhaarKorzo

Decade: Dosh bosor, DoshoK

Decease: mriTo, mori zaowa, mriTTu boron Kora, moioT Aowa

Decay: Poci zaowa, Poca, Poca dhora, baD Aowa, baD Ai zaowa

Decide: ṭik Kora, shidhanTo neowa

Decision: shiDdhanTo, mon tik Kora

Decimal: Doshomik, Doshor eK

Declare: ghushona Kora, Kowa, shikar Kora

Decline: baD Aowa, Komzuri Aowa, AdhogoTi Aowa

Decode: Banga, milani

Decompose: Poca, Poci zaowa

Decorate: shazani, hazani

Decoy: ruPboDlani, boDlaruP

Deep: gohin, goIn, goBir

Deer: Aring, Arin, horin, Arin

Defect: shomoshsha ala, Duish ala

Defence: proTirokka, aTTorokka

Defend: aTTorokka Kora

Defender: rokkaKari, bacaowra, bacaneowala

Defiance: shaosh loia kharhani,

Define: bornona Deowa, bornona Kora, buzaia Deowa

Demise: dhonsho Aowa, dhongsho Ai zaowa, shesh Aowa, shesh Ai zaowa

Demon: shoyTan, azazil, zinBUT

Dental: DaTor beaPar, DaTor beaParor

Deny: Ashshikar Kora, Ashshikar zaowa

Dog: kukur/kuTTa (kuTTa is rather derogatory)

Do: Kora

Dig: QuDa

Dark: andhair

Den: gaaT

Dare: shaOsh

Duck: aash

Duck: aai

Drake: aaowa

Day: Din

Dull: monDa/mondo

Dip: zubani/zubai laowa

E

Egg	dim/boiDa
End	shesh
Err	Bul
Error	Bul
Emergency	zoruri
Enquiry	khobor lowa/Quz khobor lowa
Energy	shoKTi
Eager	besTo (though it's main meaning is busy)
Eagle	cIl
Empty	khali, shuinno, huDa
Empathy	shohomotmiTa, monomil, monormil
Entity	zinish, bosTu, kunTa, eKta zinish

F

Fan	fen
Fart	PaaYD
For	Karon/Daay
Fine	zorimana/norom/shunDor
Father	baP
Far	Duroi
Fun	moza
Fund	mul dhon/Poysha
Fate	KoPal/Baaiggo
Finish	shesh Kora/finIsh Kora
Find	Paowa, Quza, Tukani, Talash, Talash Kora
Found	Paowa zaowa, Paowa gese
Fond	Bala Paowa
Fin	masor danKa
Finland	suomea, finlend, finOKlor Desh
Finn	suomalainen, finlendor manush, fInish
Finnish	suomalainen, finlendor manush, fInish, fIn
Finnish	suomi, fInish, fInish Basha, fInish zoban, suomi zoban
Fan	Pakha, fen

Fan	baTash Kora
Feed	khaowani
Fed up	biroKTo Aowa
Fight	mair, mair Kora, maramari Kora
Figure	shoril
Figure	shoinka, hishab
Far	DUr, Duroi
Further	barhTi, beshi, ATirikTo
Farther	aguani, Agroshor Aowa
From	Tone, AiTe
Form	forom
Farm	kheT, khamar
Firm	shoKTo, mozbuT
Fire	aguin, agun
Friday	shukkurbar
Fence	bEYrha
Foam	fena
Force	shoKTi
Force	bahini (armed force)
Fit	laga (dress fitting)

Fall	Porha
File	fail
Feel	AnuBob Kora
Fell	(gas) Kata
Foal	baichcha
Faul	faul (faul in football)
Faul	unacceptable/ talking rubbish
Finance	arTik, ArthoniTik, PoyshaKorhi bishoyok
Financial	arTik
Find	Danob
Pharaoh	Feraun
Four	cair
Fol	fruit, result
Folmul	fruits
Folafol	results

G

Gamble	zua, zua khela
Gell	jel
Gun	bonDuk
Goat	sagol
Goal	loikko, uDDeishsh, goUl
Goal keeper	gouli
Get	paowa
Go	zaowa
god	Deb/Debi/murTi
God	allaa/God
Good	Bala
Goods	malamal/malPoTro/mal
Gap	faaYK (beware, how you pronounce it for it does not sound anything like the word you are thinking of!)
Ghost	BUT, PreT, FeroT, BUTpreT, BUTPeroT, Ashoriri aTTa
Ghostly	BUthurhe, BUTla
Gas	gesh
Gram	geram, gram, gau
Gear	ghiar

H

Hand	aaT
Harp	harp, arp
Happy	Qushi, ashiQushi, Qushibashi, Qushbash, anonDiTo
Happiness	Qushi, anonDo
Hat	tuPi
Hate	ghin, ghinna, ghrina
Hatred	ghinnna, ghin, ghrina
Hall	hol, milonayoTon, KenDro
Hallmark	cin, cinno
Hard	Kotin, shoKTo
Her	Tan, Tanor, Tair
His	Tan, Tanor, Tar
Hurt	agaT, Duk, Dukko
Hurtle	surhia mara, ita mara, zure ghuria zaowa/aowa
Hurdle	badha, shomoishsha
Hunt	shikar, shikar Kora
Haunted	BUTurhe
Hold	dhora

Hand over	Deowa, prodhan Kora
High	Uca
Hide	lukani
Hire	Barha/Barha newa/lowa/Deowa
Hope	asha
Hill	tilla, tila, PaYrh
Hilly	PaYrhia, Paharhi
Hind	Pic, Kor, Pison
Hook	kukrha borIr lakhan
Housing	ghorbarhi bishoyok, ghorbarhi
Hint	ishara, ishara Deowa
Hip	Komor

I

I: ami

Iberian: aiberiar manush, aiberia

Ice: borof, boraf

Icicle: borofor tukra

Icon: sobi, cInno

Idea: dharona, monoBab

Ideal: BabmurTi, BammurTir sobi, uDDeishsho, nikTi

Identical: shoman, eKlakhan DekhTe, doppelganger, shoman DekhTe

Identify: Poricoy, PoriciTi

Ideology: moTobaD

Idiocy: bukami, arhuami, abDul hashimi (col)

Idiosyncrasy: Paglami, arhuami, bukami

Idiot: buka, arhua

Idle: beKama, sTir, Kam Korena, Alosh

Idol: murTi

If: zuDi, zoDi, zoDina, zuDina, zoDichoy, zuDichoy

Igloo: borofor ghor, iglu

Ignite: zalani, aguin dhorani, calani

Ignition: calani, calu Kora

Ignominy: Ashomman, APoman

Ignorant: anPorh, gIanhin, AshikkiTo

Ignore: Abohela Kora, Ela Kora, PaTTa na Deowa, guruTTo na Deowa

Ill: bemar, AshusTo, Ashuk, Ashukbishuk, bemar azar

Illegal: beaini, aninor baira

Illegible: PoYrha zaay na emon aTor lekha

Illegitimate: AboiDo

Illicit: AboiDo

Illiterate: AshikkiTo, anPoYrh

Illogical: AzukTik

Illuminate: ujjol Kora

Illusion: AbasTob, cokur Bibrom, Bibrom, maya

Illustrate: bisTariTo Koria bornona Korra, sobi akia bornona Kora

Image: sobi, fotu, proTikriTi

Imagine: KolPona Kora, mono Kora

Imam: imam

Imbalance: Barshaimmohin

Imbecile: arhua, nabuzra, buka, arhua

Imitate: AnukriTi Kora, Dekia PunorabriTTi Kora

Immature: ApraPTo manoshikoTa

Immediate: shigroU

Immense: birat

Immigration: ATibashon, Adhibashon

Imminent: AchireU Aibo emon

Immobile: Acol

Immoderate: curhanTobaDi, kottorPonTi

Immoral: AnoiTik

Immortal: moioThin, mriTTuhin, moronsarha

Immune: aTTorokka bebosTa (sharirik)

Immunodeficiency: shoriror aTTorokka bebosTar DurboloTa

Immunology: shoriror aTTorokka bishoyok biggan

Impact: proBab, proTikria

Impair: Banga, Bangi zaiwa, Kam na Kora, khoTi Aowa

Impala: AYring zaTio prani

Impale: shoril Kana Koria hamani

Impart: Deowa

Impartial: niroPekko

Impassable: ATikrom Korar moTo naay

Impasse: badha, atki zaowa, atka
Impatient: AsTir, Adhir, dhoirzo na thaKa

Impeach: curhanTo AnasTar prosTab

Impeccable: BulTrutihin, Qub shunDor, PoriPurno

Imperative: AboishshoI Kora uciT, Kora zoruri

Imperfect: za purnango ba Trutihin naay

Imperial: uponibeshik

Impersonal: beKTigoTo naay, AbeKTigoTo

Impetus: TagiD, TagDa

Imply: buzani

Import: amDani

Important: zoruri, DorKari, proyozonio

Impose: caPaia Deowa

Impossible: AshomBob, beshomBob, zeKta AiTo Pare na

Imposter: uPre Porha, eKzone aroKzonor Abinoy Kora

Impoverish: gorib, DoriDro

Impress: monor uPre Dag Kata

Impressive: Dekhar moTo

Imprison: zhElo zaowa, bonDi Aowa

Improbable: shomBabonar bairre

Impromptu: loge loge, aKTa, Porikolpona sarahU

Improper: ṯik naay, beṯik, Aṯik, Bul

Improve:unnoTi, AgrogoTi, aguani, Bala Aowa

Impulse: zeta mono Ailo Akta Kora

Impure: khati naay, BEzal, BEzale Bora, Akhati

In: BiTre, BiTTor

Inability: AkkomoTa, DurboloTa

Inaccurate: Bul, ţik naay

Inadequate: zoTesto naay

Incalculable: hIshabor baire, hIshab Kora zaiTo naay emon

Incapable: Akkom

Inch: inchi

Incidence: ghotona, Durghotona

Incident: ghotona, Durghotona

Incidental: ghotonar loge shomporkiTo

Incinerate: zalani, Purhani

Incite: uTTeziTo Kora

Include: hIshabo dhora, shorik Kora

Incoherent: AbuiDDo

Income: aay

Incoming: ar

Increase: barha, barhani

Incredible: Abishshaishsho

Increment: beTon barha, asTe asTe barha

Incriminate: nizor khoTi Kora (ainor cokuT)

Incur: zoma Kora

Incurable: Bala Kora zaiTo naay emon bemar

Indebted: rini, ringrosTo

Indecent: Ashlil, khraP, ABoDro

Indefinite: AnirDisto

Independent: shadhin

in-depth: goBir, Bala Koria, goBiBabe

indescribable: bornona Kora zaiTo naay emon

index: Talika

Indian: BaroTio, BaroTor, Indian

Indicate: buzani, Dekhaia Deowa

Indict: Abizug Kora

Indignity: Ashomman, ApmanbuD

Indigo: nil, lilua rong

Indirect: shorashori naay, ghuraia

Indiscreet: Qulamela, lukail naay

Individual: beKTi

Indo-European: inDo-Iuropian, inDoIuropio

Indoor: ghoror BiTre, BiTre

Inertia: beQial, Qialhin, AshoceTonoTa

Infamous: kukkeaTo, kukkaTo

Infect: akranTo Aowa

Infernal: DuzoKor lakhan

Inferno: DuzoK, zuzoK

Infidel: Abishshashi, ze allaaT bishsha Korena

Infidelity: Abishshashi Acoron Kora (bour ba zamair loge)

Infinite: Ashim, sheshhin, shimahin

Infirm: Akkom, Acol, burha, briDDo

Inflame: zolonTo, zoli zar, aguino Purher

Inflammable: zoli zaiTo Pare

Inflate: Fulani

Inflation: muDrasfiTi

Inform: zanani

Infuse: mishani, milani, shongmisron Kora

Ingest: shorilo dukani, injekshon Deowa

Inhale: shash neowa

Inherent: eKebare miliTo, alaDa Korar moTo naay

Inherit: Paowa, uTToradhikar hIshabe Paowa, owarishi Arzon Kora

Inhibit: bash Kora, boshobash Kora

Inhuman: Amanushik, Amanobik

Inhumane: Amanobik, Amanushik

Iniquity: ToDonTo

Initial: prathomik, Poyla

Initiate: shuru Kora

Initiative: uDDug neowa

Injunction: aingoTo badha, aDaloTor Deowa badhanisheD, injangshon

Injure: ahoTo Aowa

Injustice: Abicar, Annaay

Ink: Kali, cIaai

in-laws: bour Pokkor kutum

inmate: zhElia

inner: BiTToror, BiTri

innocent: nishPaP, niroPoradh

J

Jab: tika

Jackal: hIal

Jacket: zeket, jeket

Jackpot: zekPot, borho purushkar, shob thaki borho Purushkar

Jade: Panna

Jagged: TerhabeKa

Jaguar: bag zaTio, bag

Jail: jEl, zEl, Karagar, Karaghor

Jam: zem, zam, caTni zaTio

Jamboree: zamburi

Janitor: suipar

January: zanoari, zanuari

Japan: zapan

Jar: buTol

Jargon: Acina shobDo, DaTBanga shobDo

Jasmine: caPa ful, Iasmin

Jaundice: Almi, Almi rug, zondis

Jaw: daTor bandh

Jazz: zEz shongiT, zEz gan

Jealous: Irsha, zola, gaaT zola

Jeans: Jins, zins, zinsor KaPorh, jinsor KaPorh

Jeep: jip, zip

Jeer: cirhani

Jell: zeli, norom khanir zinish

Jelly: zeli

Jellyfish: zeli mas, zelifish

Jenny: jeni, zeni

Jeopardy: shomoishsha Aowa, biPoD Aowa, Bondul Aowa

Jerk: dhakka khaowa, dhakka mara

Jersey: zarsi, urDi

Jest: agroho, uTTezona

Jet: biman, plein

Jetty: zaaYz ghat

Jew: ihuDi

Jewel: moni, moni manik, moni manikko

Jibe: galiani, galagali, galagali Kora, cirhani

jiggery-pokery: AshoT acoron, curami, curami Kora

Jigsaw: zigso

Jihad: zehaD, jehaD, jihad

Jilt: nisturBabe Teag Kora (lover)

Jingle: ghontar shobDo

Job: Kam, KamKaz, KazKam, Kormo

Jog: asTe asTe Dourhani

Join: zug Deowa, shorik Aowa

Joke: Tamasha, Tamsha, mozak, mozak Kora

Jolly: ashi Qushi,

Jostle: ṯElaadhakka, ṯElaateli, dhakkadhakki

Journal: Kagoz, zarnal, dayri, megazin, shamoyiki

Journey: Bromon

Journeyman: BromonKari

Joy: anonDo, Qushi, ashi Qushi

Jubilant: anonDiTo, uTshobmukhor

Jubilee: bieshesh borshoPurTi, bishesh barshiki

Judaism: ihuDi dhormo

Judge: bicaroK, zaaz, jaaj

Judicial: aingoTo, aini

Judiciary: ain Bibag, aino bishoyok

Judicious: neaaybicari, nayshongoTo, neaay Porayon

Jug: zog, jog

Juggle: KoyeKta zinish eKloge loia zaowar cesta Kora

Juice: shira, rosh, zUs, zUsh

July: zulai, julai

Jumble: mishail

Jumbo: zambo, borho, birat

Jump: fal, fal Deowa, laf, lafalafi

Jumper: zampar, jampar

Junction: zangshon, zongshon

Juncture: uDDug, uDDzug

June: zun, jun

Jungle: jongol, bon

Junior: huru, junior, zunior

Junk: baDacaaDa, bezaal, aborzona

Junta: zanTa, janTa

Jurisdiction: ainor shimana, ainor Poridhi, ainor elaKa

Jurisprudence: ainshasro, ain biDDa

Jurist: ain bisheshoggo

Jury: zuri, aam bicaroK (lay judge)

Just: neaay shongoTo, neaay, bicarPurno

Justice: bicar, neaay, neaay bicar

Justify: (kuno zinish ba bishoyre shomorTon Kora

Jute: PaYt

Juvenile: huruTa, baichchain, selemanush

Juxtapose: eKtar uPore aroKta rakha

K

Kaffir: Kafir, non believer, faithless, heartless, cruel

Kaftan: KaPTan

Kalashnikov: kalashnikoB

Kaleidoscope: biciTro, bohuronga

Kangaroo: Kengaru

Karate: kerati

Karma: Kam, Kormofol, Baiggo

Kayak: dingi, dingi nouka, huru naow, huru nouka

Kebab: Kobab, Kebab, Kabab

Kedgeree: KHicurhi

Keen: agrohi

Keep: rakha

Kelvin: kelvin, selsias

Kennel: kukuror thaKar zaga, kukuror ghor

Kept: rakha, rokkiTa

Kerb: rasTar gala

Kerchief: rumal

Kerosene: Keroshin, Keres, KeresTel

Ketchup: kechap, KecaP

Kettle: KeTli

Key: cabi

Keyboard: kibourd

Keyhole: cabir Kana

Keynote: mul zinish, mul boKTiTa (keynote speech)

Kg: Kezi, keji, kilogram

KGB: kejibi, Kezibi, rashian guenDa shongsTa, rashiar guenDa bahini

Khaki: khaki

Kick: laaT, laaTiani, laaTTi, laaTT mara, laaTTi mara

Kid: baichcha, huruTa, selemeye, huru

Kidnap: APohoron, Apohoron, sinaia neowa

Kidney: Kolza

Kill: mara, mari laowa, Qun, Qun Kora, Qun Kori laowa

Kilo: kilo, kilogram, Kezi, keji

Kilogram: kilogram (could be said as sher the traditional unit)

Kilometre: kilomitar (could be said as mile)

Kilowatt: kilo owat

Kin: shomPorkiTo, roKTo shomporkiTo, aTio

Kind: Doyaban, Doyalu, Doyamoy, zaT, zaTi, shreni, guTro

Kindergarten: kindar garden ishkul, narsari, huru baichchainTor ishkul

Kinetic: goTi bishoyok, goTishiloTa

King: raza

Kingfisher: gaangcil

Kiosk: stol

Kismet: kishmoT, Baiggo

Kiss: cumu, cumaa, cumbon, maya, maya Deowa

Kitchen: randha ghor, ranna ghor, roshoi, roshoi ghor

Kite: ghurhi, gUddi

Kitten: bilair baichcha, bilai baichcha

Kiwi: kiuI fol

Km: kilomitar

Knackered: hoyran, heran, zanshesh

Knee: atU

Kneel: noTo Aowa

Knew: zanTam

Knife: sUri, cakku

Knight: nait

Knit: shelai Kora

Knob: Dorzar aaTol

Knock: t̲uka, t̲uka mara

Knot: gait

Know: zana

Knowledge: gIan

Koala: Koala

Koran: kuraan, kur aan, al kuraan, kiTab kuraan

Kosher: halal

Kremlin: kremlin,

kung fu: kongfu

276

L

Label: lebel, namfolok

Labour: Porisrom, Kosto, baichcha Aibar beDna/bIsh, lebar

Laboratory: gobeshonagaar, leb, leboretri, gobeshonakenDro

Laborious: Porisromi

Labor Party: sromik Dol, lebar

Labrador: lebrador, eK zaTio kukur

Labyrinth: lebirinT, zotil zamiTik akriTir ghor ba sTapona

Lace: fITa, zuTar fITa

Lack: ABab, sholPoTa, KomTi, Kom

Lackadaisical: pranshoKTihin, AloshmonoBabala, alshia shoBabor

Lad: Pua, zuboK, zuanPua, baloK

Ladder: moI

Laden: buzhaai, Bora, Poripurno

Lady: mohila, nari, beti, beti manush, BoDromohila, zuboTi nari

Lake: bil, aOr, zhil

Lamb: BErhi, BErha, mErha, mErhi

Lame: aTur

Lament: Dukko Kora, maTom Kora, maTTom Kora

Laminate: lemineit Kora, lemineiting Kora

Lamp: baTTi, lem

Land: zomin, zaaga, zaagazomin, zaayga, Bumi, mati

Landlord: malik, zomir malik, ghoror malik, zominDar(old use), zomiDar (old use)

Landmark: cInnoT, cInPoricoyor zinish

Lane: rasTa, Poth, lein, shorhoK

Language: Basha, buli, zoman, Kotha

Lap: kur

lapis lazuli: ghono nil rong, eK zaTio muilloban PaTTor

large: borho, birat, prokando

lariat: golar faashor Dorhi, goru, sagol bar kukuror golar ze Dorhi Dia bandha Ay AKta kukuror golaT faash lagaia ki laB? What's the point putting lariat on the dog?

Lark: lark, eK zaTio Paki.
Tumi kiTa shara raiT larkor lakhan gan gaibaay na kiTa? Are you going to sing all night like a lark?

Larynx: gola, lerinks

Lasagne: lasania, eK zaTor iTalio khani

Laser: sutoroKom, khuDroTor, lezar (printer)

Lash: Dorhi, banDa, shoKTo Koria banDa

Lashings: beT mara, mara, dhUra Deowa, Pita

Lass: Purhi, zuboTi, nari, mohila, nari, bala
bala Koia zaow Tumar ki nam. Lass, do tell me what your name is before you go.

Lassitude: heran Aowa, heran laga, hoyran, hoyran AbosTa, zan Tanaa Ai zaowa

Last: shesh, hEsh, baaD, bade, hEshe

Late: Deri, Deri Kora, Deri Aowa, proyaTo (dead)

Lateral: AnuBumik, Bumir shomanToral

Latex: robar zaTio zinish

Latin: letin, letin Basha

Latitude: shadhinoBabe thaKar moTo PorisTiTi, norhacorha Korar AbosTa, Bougolik PorimaPor eKta bebosTa

Latrine: Paykhana, toilet, letting, lettrin

Latter: bade, baaD, baaDor, sheshor, hEshor, hEsher

Lattice: berha, zulonTo berha, zaal, caaYng, macaang, macaan

Laugh: aashaa, aashi, hashi, aashaaaashi

Launch: shuru Kora, calu Kora, Qula, Quli laowa

Laureate: shommaniTo, shommanuiggo
Laurel: Purushkar, shomman

Lavatory: Paykhana, toilet, Paykhanar ghor, lettrin, letting

Lavish: zaKzhomokpurno, zaKzhomoK Koria, shane showkoTe

Law: ain

Lawn: utan, angon, angina, Angon

Lawyer: ukil, ainbiD, ainjibi, edBuket

Lay: hUTa, bowa, Porhi thaKa

Layer: sTor, Porzaay, PoroT

Lazy: Alosh, alshIa, ailsha

Lead: neTriTTo Deowa, Poricalona Kora, calani

Leader: neTa, neTri, murobbi, garjian

Leaf: PaTa, PoTro

Leaflet: liflet

League: lIg, Dol, jUt

Leak: Pani Porha, gesh bar Aowa, Tel Porha, cUia Porha, cUa.

Lean: aaYla

Leap: fal, fal Deowa

Learn: hika, shika, hiki, hikoin, hiko, hikos, hike, hiker

Lease: bonDoK, bonDoK Deowa, bonDoK neowa, lIz

Leash: Dorhi, roshi

Least: shob Thaki baaDe

Leather: camrha

Leave: zaowa, biDaay lowa, suti, sutti

Lecherous: bishshash ghaTokoTapurno

Lecture: boKTiTa, boKTriTa, boKTiTa Deowa, PoYrhani

Lecturer: AiDdhaPok, ADdhaPok, shikkok, mastor, lekcharar, profesarshab (col), povesarshab (col)

Ledger: khoTian, hIshabor Boi, lejar

Leech: zhUk

Left: bam, bau

Left: zaowa, gelo, gela, gelam

Leftover: baDa, barhTi zinish thaKa

Leg: Paow

Legacy: uTToradhikar, owarishana

Legal: ainoTo, ainI, aingoTo, ain bishoyok

Legend: kingboDonTi, nozirbihin kahini, misaal

Legible: PoYrhar moTo, PoYrhar zuiggo

Legion: Dol, shoinikOKlor eKta Dol ba Tim

Legislate: ain faash Kora, ain Kora, ain banani

Legislation: ain

Legitimate: aini, aingoTo, ain shommoTo, boiDo

Leisure: Abshor, nicinTa

Lemon: lemBu, lebu

Lend: Korzo, Korzo Deowa, Korzo neowa, Korzo caowa, Korzo lowa, dhar, dhar Kora, rin Deowa

Length: lamba, Doirgo

Lenient: khomashil

Lens: lens

Lent: lent, ruza, ruza rakha, ruza thaKa

Lentil: dail

Leopard: lepard, ciTa, zaTio

Lesson: Paat, Klas, leson

Let: Korte Deowa, Barha, Barha Deowa

Lethal: maraTTok, Boyanok, Boyonkor, shorbonashi

Lethargy: shoKTir ABab

Letter: Akkor, citi, PhoTro

Lettuce: letus

Leukaemia: roKTor, kensar, lIukomia

Level: sTor, porzaay

Liable: DaaYI

Liaise: shomozuTa, zugazug

Liar: misa mathra, beiman, miTTuk, miTTabaDi

Libel: Apoman, Ashomman, Apomanzonok, Ashommanzonok

Liberal: uDarPonTi, uDarmona, uDarmonor

Liberate: shadhin, shadhin Kora, shadhin Aowa

Libertarian: Adhikar shomorTonkari, uDarPhonti

Liberty: nizshadhin, mukTi, shadhinoTa,

Library: laiberi, laibreri, gronTagar, PusTokagar

Lice: ukoin

2

Licence: laisens, aingoTo AnumoTiPoTro, aini AnumoTiPoTro

Lick: cUa, cUia khaowa, cUsha

Lid: daKna, horaa, shoraa

Lie: misa, misa math, miTTa, miTTe, hUDa, hUDa math

Lieu: PoriborT, boDla

Lieutenant: leftenent

Life: zibon, zinDegi, zinDegani, Dom

Lift: Tula, Tuli laowa, Tulia lowa, lift (of a building)

Ligament: rog, manghoPeshi, Peshi

Light: alo, baTTi, rushni, rushnai, roshshi, lem, moshal

Light: PaTla, halKa, halka

Lighter: laitar, baTTi, Diasholoi, mEs, mech

Lightning: bozroPaT

Like: lakhan, shoman, shoman shoman, Olakhan, hOlakhan, Ilakhan, hIlakhan

Like: PosonDo, PosonDo Kora, Bala Paowa, khaish Kora

Likely: shomBoboTo, shomBaibbo, Aowa shomBod

Lilliputian: kutimuti, sutomuto, huru, liliputian

Lily: lili ful

Limb: aT Paow

Limbo: zulonTo

Lime: lebu, lembu

Limerick: limerik, limerik zaTio sorha

Limit: shima, shimana

Limousine: limozin garhi

Limp: Qurhaia ataa

Line: lain, rekha, taan

Lineage: dhara, bongshodhara, couDDogusti, roKTodhara

lingua franca: mul Basha, zaTio zoban, manshor zoban

linguist: BashabiD, BashaTaTTik

link: zugazug, zugsuTro, shomporko, shomporkiTo

lion: shinggo, shingho

lip: tUt

liqueur: moD, moD zaTio Torol PoDarTo

liquid: Torol, Torol PoDarTo

lira: lira, iTalir zaTio tEKa (age asil, ekhon nay)

list: Talika, Talika Kora, list, list Kora

listen: huna, shuna

literacy: PoYrha zanra, PoYrhTe Para

literal: Akkore Akkore, zEla Kowa Ola Kora,

literary: shaiTTobishoyok, shaiTTo shomporkiTo
literature: shaiTTo, kichchakahini

litre: litar

litter: baDa, moyla, aborzona

little: suto, huru, kuti, kutimuti, hurumuru, sutokhato, QuDro, TiTkina, AToguni, Titkini

live: baca, bash Kora, bacia thaKa, zibiTo thaKa, ziTa, thaKa

livelihood: zibika

liver: Kolza

livestock: gorubasur, zibzonTo, grihoPaliTo zibzonTu

living: baca, bacia thaKa

lizard: lizard

llama: lama Dokkin amerikar eK

load: bUzha, Baar

loaf: luf, louf, ruti, bred, bered

loam: fena

loan: rin, Korzo, dhaar, dhaarKorz, Paowna, Deowna

loathe: ghInna, ghInna Kora, ghInPiT

lobster: golDa cingrhi, borho cingrhi, borho ica

local: sTanio, sTan, KanDar elaKa

locate: baro Kora, cinniTo Kora, ṭiK Kora

loch: lokh, bil

lock: Tala

lock: bandh

locum: AsTaI

locust: Pukor zhOrh

lodge: loz, loj, bangle

loft: cilekuta

log: khaarha, khaarhi, goDa

logarithm: lOgariDom eK zaTio Ankshasro

logic: zukTi, zukTibiDDa

loiter: ghurghur Kora, ghuraghuri Kora

lone: eKla, eKlaguli, eKaki

long: lamba, lomba, Dirgo

longevity: zibonKal

longitude: Bougolik PorimaPor PoDDoTi, longIchuD

loo: Paykhana, toylet

look: Dekha, caowa

loony: Pagol, mathaaT Duish, srkudila

loose: shoKTo naay, Qula, Quchra

lord: malik, proBu, rob, allaa (in English sense Lords would be zominDar, zomiDar)
lore: lukoshaiTTo, lukogatha, lukoKotha, lukokahini

lorry: lori, traK

lost: aara, aarai zaowa, aari zaowa

lot: zinish, shara zinish
lotion: lushon

lottery: lotari

lotus: PoDDo, PoDDoful

loud: zure mathaa, uca shobDe mathaa

louse: ukoin

love: maya, maya momoTa, Balobasha, piar, prem, priTi, Anurag

low: nicu, nic, nica, namani

lower: nicani, namani

loyal: bishshosTo, bishshashBazon, bishshashzuiggo

lubricate: ataalo Kora

luck: Baiggo, KoPal

lucrative: akorshonio

ludicrous: ashchoirjozonok, azgubi

luggage: malPoTro, zinishPoTro, lageiz, lagez

lukewarm: umgorom umli

lull: khali, shuinno, bina, biroTi

lullaby: ghumParhani gan, ghumParhania gan

luminous: zhikimikipurno, ujjol, ujjol Aia zola

lump: caKa, tukra, guta

lunar: canDor, canD bishoyok

lunatic: Pagol, boDDo unmaD

lunch: maDani belar khaowa, lanch
lung: fushfush

lure: Bulaia neowa

Luscious: mozaDar, ruchikor

Lush: zibonTo, zanBora, shunDor

Lust: lUB, lalsha, lalos

Luxury: aramDayok, aramor, arampurno

Lying: hUTa, hUTi thaKa

Lyric: giTimoy KobiTa, aTTomoy KobiTa, beKTimoy KobiTa

M

Ma: ma, amma, ammu, maa

MA: eme digri, eme fash, maastars digri
Ma'am: zonaba, BoDromohila, mem, mem shaheb (old use)

Machine: meshin, mishin, zonTro, KolKobza

Mad: Pagol, unmaD, mathaaT Duish, mathaaT dhora, mathaaT godogul

Madam: zonaba, BoDromohila

Made: banail, banana, Toiri, Toiari

Mademoiselle: maDamozel, mis, musammoT

Madrigal: gan, shongiT, gozol

Mafia: mafia, dragor Karbari, neshar Karbari, neshar Kalobazri

Magazine: megazin, shamoiki, shamoik PoTro, shamoik PoTrika

Magic: zaDu, azob zinish, azgubi Kando,

Magistrate: majistreit, bicaroK, bicarPoTi

Magnanimous: mohoTriDoyor, mohan

Magpie: Doirol, Doirol Paki, Duel, Duel Paki

Mahout: maYuT, mahuT (elephant jokey)

Maid: Kamla, Kamla beti, Kamla Purhi, Kamor beti, Kazor Purhi

Maiden: nari, mohila, zuboTi, Puri, bala, balika.

Mail: meil, daK, Poust, citiPoTro

Main: mul, ashol, proDan

Maintain: bozaay rakha, bohal rakha, calai zaowa

Maisonette: mesonet, DuiTala ghor

Majesty: razokio

Major: borho, birat, mejor (army), prodhan (E major etc)

Majority: shoikagorist, beshi shoingkok

Make: banana, Toiri Kora

Maladjusted: ze khaP khaowaiTo Parena, bekhappa

Maladministration: Aproshashon, proshashonik AshongoTi, proshashonik DurniTi

Malaria: meleria, meleria zor/Tap

Malcontent: Ashuki, naQush, bezar

Male: Purush, Purush manush

Malfunction: Kam Korena emon zinish,

Malpractice: DurniTi, Apoproyog

Man: manush, Purush manush, beta, beta manush

Manage: bebosTa Kora, calaia neowa, Poricalona Kora, bebosTaPona Kora

Manager: bebosTaPoK, menezar

Mandarin: cIna, cIn bishoyok, mendarin Basha

Mandate: AnumoTi Deowa, gono AnumoTi, mendeit

Manger: bebosTaPok, Poricalok, calowra

Mango: am

Mangrove: amor bagan, am bagan, amor bagica

Manila: menila, filipainor razdhani

Manipulate: calani, kubuDdhi Deowa, APothe neowa, nionTron Kora

Manner: acoron, beboar, acarbeboar

Manpower: zonoshoKTi

Manqué: canDoa

Mansion: menshon

Manslaughter: hoTTa, Qun (zekhano Purbo Porikolpona sarha Qun Kora Aise)

Mantra: monTro

Manual: biboroni Boi, menual

Manufacturer: banaowra, prosTuTKarok, Toiri Korra

Manuscript: PanduliPi, Pandulipi

Many: AneK, beshi, KoyeKta, KoYta, koyta, BouT, BouTTa

Maori: maori zaTir manush

Map: mEP, manciTro

Marble: marbel

March: Dourh

March: Dourhani

March: march mash

Mare: ghurhi

Margin: lain, shimana

Marijuana: marijuana, ganza

Marine: shamuDrik

Maritime: shamuDrik shomoy

Mark: cin, cinno, cinnoT

Market: bazaar, haat, aat

Marquee: canDoa

Marry: aashiQushi Kora, anonDo Kora, moza Kora, furTi Kora

Marsh: zoloi, zola, zolaBumi

Martyr: shohiD

Marvel: couk Boria Dekha

Marxism: marksbaD

Mask: mukush, muQush

Massacre: gonohoTTa, gononiDon

Message: barTa, khobor, shongbaD, shombaD

Master: mastor, malik, shikkok, shikaowra, tichar

Mat: PaPush

Match: milani, mil, miliaowa

Mate: shathi, bonDu, Iar, shongishathi

Material: bosTu, zinish, shamogri

Mathematics: goniT, Anko, Ankoshasro, AnkobiDDa

Maths: Anko

Matriarch: Poribaror mohila murobbi

Matrimony: bia, bibaho, biabiDi, biashaDi

Matrix: lekhociTrozaTio, TrimaTrik lekhociTro

Matron: shebika, nars, DaiTToPraPTo mohila Kormi

Matter: zinish, beaPar, bishoy

Mature: PraPToboyoshko

Maxim: niTi

May: hoyTo, AuTo, AiTo Pare

May: me mash

Maybe: hoyTo, hoyToba, AyTo, AiTo Pare

Mayday: me Dibosh, me Din, Mer Din, shromik Dibosh

Mayhem: ujzhat, haangama, zhamela, zoyzhonjhat

Mayor: meor

Meadow: bonD, maat, kheT, bagan, bicra

Meal: khabar, khaiDDo

Mean: shongkirnomona, shongkirno

Meantime: iTToboshore, iTimoiDDe

Meat: gusT, gusto, mangsho

Mecca: mokka

Mechanic: mekanik

Mechanism: PoDDoTi, bebosTa

Media: maiDDom, gonomaiDDom, PoTroPoTrika

Mediaeval: moiDDozugio, moiDDozugor

Medic: daKTori bishoyok Kormi, DakTor, cikiTshok

Medical: cikiTsha biggan, cikiTsha bishoyok

Medicine: cikiTsha biggan, cikiTsha bishoyok biggan, oushoD, oshuD

Medieval: moiDDozug

Mediocre: sutokhato, guruTTohin, Tuchcho, Tuichcho

Meditate: moiDDoborTiTa, moiDDoborTiTa Kora

Medium: maiDDom, uPaay

Meet: mila, milmish, misha, Dekha Kora

Melancholy: eKakiTTo, noishongo, nishshogoTa, nishshongoTabuD, niralamonoBab, niralaciTTo

Melody: shongiT, gan, shur

Melon: Tormuz

Melt: gOlaa, gOli zaowa

Member: shoDoishsho

Membrane: camrha

Memento: sriTicinno

Memo: memo, ofishial citi

Memoir: aTTosriTimulok zibon kahini

Memorable: mono rakhar moTo, shoronio

Memory: IaD, sriTi

Men: manush, Purush, Purush manush

Mend: tik Kora

Menstruation: riTu, riTu Aowa

Mental: manushik, monor BiTror

Mention: ullekh Kora, Kowa

Merchant: bebshaI, beboshaI

Mercy: khoma, KHoma, maaf

Merge: mili zoawa, mila, mishi zaowa

Merger: ekhano Aowa, eK Aowa

Meridian: mul lain, meridian

Merit: zuiggoTa

Merry: bia Kora, bia Aowa, bia bowa

Mess: baDa, aborzona, moyla, BEzal

Metabolism: shorilor BiTre khaiDDoshoKTir beboaror prokria

Metal: dhaaTu, dhaaTu zaTio

Metamorphosis: zonmanTor, eK zinish Tone aroK zinisho boDli zaowa

Metaphor: uPoma, Tulona

Methinks: mono Koy, mono Aowa, cinTa Kora, AnuBob Kora

Method: PoDDoTi, uPaay, bebosTa

Metropolis: shohor, shOr

Metropolitan: shOr bishoyok, shohure

Mice: unDur, iDur

Micro: QuDro, suto

Mid: maz, maze, moiDDe, moiDDoborTi, mazkhano

Midday: maDan, moiDDoDin

Middle: mazkhan, moiDDo

Might: shoKTi, zur

Migraine: maigren, mathaar bish

Migrate: Desh sarhia zoawa, Ainno Desho zaowa, biDesho zaowa

Mild: norom, halka

Mile: mail

Milk: Dudh

Mill: mIl, Karkhana

Millennium: azar bosor

Million: lokko, loikko

Mime: maim, mukaBinoy, AngoBongi Dia ABynoy Kora

Mimic: cirhani, AnuruP zinish Kora

Minaret: minar

Mince: kima, mangshor kima

Mind: mon, manosh, AnTor, BiTTor

Mine: amar, mor, nizor

Mine: main boma

Mineral: Bibinno roshayonik bosTor Torol ruP zegula manshor roKToT ba PaniT Paowa zaay, minarel

Minestrone: maIlcInno, maIlfolok, maIl foloK

Mingle: misha, milamisha, milamisha Kora

Mini: suto, huru, mini

Miniature: suto akaror khelna ba shilopoKola

Minibus: minibas

Minicab: minikeb

Minimum: shob thaki Kom

Minister: monTri

Minor: sutokhato, ATo guruTTopurno nay, huru

Minus: biyog, Komani, shorani, horani

Minute: minit

Miracle: allaar azob lila

Mirage: moricIka

Mirror: ayna

Misappropriate: betik, Azuiggo

Miscarriage: ainor beaghaT, ainor dhara Annaay ghota

Miscellaneous: benami, biBinno, namhin

Mischief: Dustami, Dustumi, shoyTani

Misconduct: Durbeboar,Durbebohar

Miserable: Ashuki, naQush

Misfit: fit Ayna, lagena, milena, Amil

Misfortune: DurBaiggo, baD KoPal, KoPalor monDo

Misgiving: shonDeho, DurBabna, DurBabna

Misguided: bePothe cola, bePothu

Mislead: Bul Pothe calani, Bul Pothe loia zaowa

Misplace: Bul zaagaT thowa

Misprint: muDronor Bul, saafar Bul

Miss: mis Aowa, uDDeishoT na laga

Missile: misail

Mission: uDdeishsho, mishon

Mist: kuasha, Quasha, dhuasha

Mistake: Bul, Atik

Mistrust: Abishshash, bishshash na Kora

Misunderstand: Bul buza

Misuse: Apobeboar Kora

Mix: mishani, mishail

MM: merilin monro: MM, Michael Madhusudan Dutta

MM is one of the most profound and successful poets of Bangla Language and Literature of all time. He wrote in English and later in life in Bangla. He is known as the Bangaali epic poet, particularly, famous for shaping the modernism of Bangla Language and Literature long before its time, translating the Greek epics Iliad and Odessey into Bangla and writing the frist Bangla epics, most famous of which is titled, The Fall of Meghonad. MM is credited for the Bangla Renessance and for introducing Blank Verse and Sonnets in Bangla Language. His friends affectionately called him MM for short and thus, he is still referred as MM.

mm: mili mitar

Moan: Kostor shobDo Kora, ABizug Kora

Mobile: colacolor zuiggo, mobail fon

Mobilize: sTananTor Kora, shorani, horani

Mode: uPaay, PoDDoTi

Model: boDlaruP, shomanruP, model

Modem: kompiutaror/ promanobor modem, promanobor modem ba grohonkari zonTro

Moderate: ze ba zara progoTishil monmanoshikoTa pushon Koroin

Modern: adhunik, aizkailkur, borToman zomanar, borToman zobanar

Modest: Ahongkarhin, nirohonkari

Modify: unnoyon Kora, unnoTi Kora, boDlani

Module: kuno shonzukTo zinishor eKta Angsho

modus operandi: Poricalonar ba calanir mul zinish

mogul: mugol

moist: Biza, sheTsheTe, PEcPEca

molasses: gurh

molecule: Anu

moment: muhurTo, KHon

momentous: gurTTopurno

momentum: goTishiloTa, curhanTo goTishiloTa

monarch: raza, rani

Mnastery: dhormoshala, dhormaloy, dhormoproTistan

Monday: shombar

Monetary: arTik, ArToshonkranTo, ArTobishoyok

Money: taKa, tEKa, taKaPoysha, ArTo

Mongol: mongol

Monitor: Dekhra, Porzobekkok, minitar (kompiutar)

Monk: shadhu

Monkey: banDor, banor, banDra

Monogamy: eK bia bebosTa

Monologue: eKoK shonglaP, eKla KothabarTa, eKla eKla maatha

Monopoly: eKcetia khomoTaban bebsha ProTistan

Monotheism: ekeshshorbaD, eK sritiKorTaT bishshash Korar moTobaD

Monsoon: bristiKal, meghor Din, meghor Kal

Monster: DoiTTo, Danob, DoiTToDanob

Month: mash

Monument: shoronsTomBo, shriTiminar, sriTir minar

Mood: monor AbosTa, monmanoshikoTa

Moon: canD, caD

Moral: noiTik, niTi, noiTikoTa, ṭik, shoṭik
Morale: monobol

Morbid: gumra, monbezar

More: beshi, besh, ATirikTo, aro

Morgue: morg, lashKata ghor

Morn: shoKal, Bian

Morning: sobalibala, sobal, shoKal, Bian

Morphine: morfin

Mortal: mriTTushil, moronshil, moiTmoy

Moslem: musolman, muslim, islam dhormabolomBi

Mosque: mosiD, moshziD, moshjiD, nomazor ghor, allaar ghor

Mosquito: mosha

Most: shob thaki beshi

Motel: hotel, Otol

Mother: maTa, ma, maa, amma

Motion: goTi, colonTo

Motive: uDDeishsho

Motor: motor, garhir injin

Mound: tilla

Mountain: PaYrh, PorboT

Mourn: Dukko, Dukko Kora

Mouse: unDur

Moustache: muc, guf
Mouth: muk

Move: cola, shora, hora

Movie: sinema

MP: empi, shongshoD shoDoishsho, shangshoD

Much: AneK, aro, besh, beshi, Qub

Mucus: Puz

Mud: PEK

Muddle: gondogul, BEzal

Muezzin: muajjin, azan Deowra

Mug: mog

Mullah: mulla

Multi: AneK, bohu

Multiple: AneK, bohu, bohumuki, bohuzaTio

Multiply: Puron Kora, gun Kora, zonmo Deowa, shoingka barhani

Mum: ma, maa, amma, ammu

Murder: Qun, hoTTa, hoTTKando

Murmur: zhirizhiri shobDo Kora

Muscle: Peshi

Muse: manoshi, manushi, monor manobi, monomiTro, aTTashathi

Museum: zaDugor, miuziam

Mushroom: mashrum, bengor saTTi

Music: shongiT, gan, ganbazna
Muslim: musolman, islam dhormabolomBi

Muslin: moshlin, moshlin KaPorh

Must: Aboishsho, AboishshoI

Mustang: boinno prani shikar Kora ba dhora

Mustard: lai, shorisha, shorsha

Mutation: eKta Tone aroKtaT PoriborTiTo Aowa

Mute: buba, ze mathTo Parena, shobDohin

Mutiny: biDruho, shena biDruho

Mutton: mangsho, gust

Mutual: Paroshparik, uBoyPokkor lagi

Myself: niz, nize

Mystery: rohoishsho

Myth: Purakahini

N

Nan: nan, nan ruti

Nail: nouk

Naked: lemta (whole body bare), uDla (only the top is bare used for men)

Name: nam

Napkin: napkin, tishu, rumal

Nappy: nepi

Narcissism: ATToprem, nizor ruPe mugDo, nizor ruPor Pagol

Narrate: bornona Kora, bisTariTo Kowa

Narrative: bornona Kora, golPo, Kahini, kichcha, boKToibbo

Narrow: shoru, atail, shongkirno

Nasal: nakua, naKeDia

Nasty: Dushto, kharaP, shoyTan

Nation: zaTi

National: zaTio

Nationalism: zaTioTabaD

Nationality: zaTioTa

Nationalize: zaTiKoron

Native: mul bashinDa, mul nagorik, Deshor manush

NATO: neto, neto zhut

Natural: prakriTik, shaBabik

Nature: prokriTi, shoBab

Naught: shuinno, shuinnoTa, ghurhar dim, ghurhar enda

Naughty: Dushto, Dushtu, shoyTan

Nausea: bomi bomi Bab

Naval: nou bishoyok, shomuDro bishoyok

Navigate: calani, Poricalona Kora

Navvy: nou bahini

Nazi: naTsi, bornobaDi

Near: KanDaT, Kase, dhare, dharo, dhareKase, nikot, nikote

Neat: Porichchonno

Necessary: Dorkari, proyozonio

Neck: gola

Nectar: modhu, mou

Need: DorKar, proyojon

Needle: shui

Negate: na Kora, na Kori Deowa

Negative: neTibacoK

Neglect: Abohela, Ela

Negligence: Ela, ghafloTi, beQial, beQialPona

Negligible: Tuchcho, Tuchcho Korar moTo

Negotiate: shomozuTa, shomozuTa Kora, alaP alucona Kora

Negro: nigro zaTi, nigro zaTio, Kala manush, Kalo zaTio manush, krishnango manush. siletiT Kala manushre Keu borToman Kalo 'nigro' KoiTo naay. Kala manush ba sheTango Ailo mul shobDo za shochorachor beboar Kora Aia thaKe.

Neighbour: Porhshi, ParhaPorhshi, ProTibeshi, KanDar manush

Neither: kunotaU nay

Nemesis: shoTru

Nephew: BaTiza, BaTiuza, Bagna, Baigna, BaiPuT, BoinPuT

Nepotism: shozonpriTi, DurniTi, khomoTar Apobeboar Koria nizor aTio shozonre shaijjo Kora

Nerve: snayu, snayu TonTro, narB

Nervous: uTTeziTo, AshosTigrosTo, AshanTo, DushchinTagrosTo

Nest: baDaa, basha

Net: zaal
Network: zugazugkenDro, netowark

Neurology: moshTishkobiggan, mogozbiggan

Neutral: niroPekko, kuno PokkoT nay

Never: kuno shomoyU nay, kokhono nay

New: noya, noTun

News: PaTTa, khobor, shombaD, shongbaD, QuzTalash, Quzkhobor

Next: baaD, baaDe, PoroborTiTe

Nib: Kolomor niP, Kolmor nib

Nice: Bala, shunDor

Nickname: daK nam

Niece: BaTizi, BaTiuzi, Bagni, Baigni, Boinzhi, Baizhi

Night: raiT, raT, raTri

Nil: shuinno

Nine: noy

Nineteen: unnish

Ninety: nobboi

Nirvana: nirban
Nitrogen: naitrojen gesh

No: na

Nobble: Balo bongshor, Balo manush, shomBranTo, shomBranTo ghoror manush

Nobel Prize: noBel Purushkar

Nobody: keu naay, Keu na, kunozon naay

Nocturnal: raiTzibi, raiTkurcor, raiTcor

Noise: shobDo, Kesormesor

Nominate: prosTab Kora, mononoyon Deowa, mononoyon Kora

None: Keu na, Keu nay

Nonsense: bukami, maninai

Noon: maDan

Nor: ba, noyToba

Nordic: noruE bishoyok

Norm: procholiTo, zeta coler

Normal: shaBabik

North: uTTor

Nose: naK

Nostalgia: agor zibon ba shomoyor gun gaowa

Not: naay

Notable: shoron rakhar moTo, mono rakha

Notary: notary

Note: nout

Nothing: kunTa naay, emneU

Notice: nutish, nutish Kora, nozoro Porha

Notify: zanani

Notion: dharona

Notorious: kukkaTo, kukkheaTo

Noun: nam buzaowra shobDo, namshobDo, namPoD

Nourishment: Pushti

Novel: uPonnash, uPoinnash, golPo, kahini, kichcha

November: noBembor mash

Novice: saTro, shikra, noya zugi

Now: ebla, ekhon

Nowhere: kunokhano naay

Nuclear: paromanobik

Nucleus: kenDro

Nugget: tukra. Tumi amar zanor tukra. You are a nugget of my heart.

Nuisance: zonTrona, shomoishsha, zhamela

Number: shoingka

Numerical: shoingka Anushare

Numerous: AneK, zothesto

Nurse: shebika, nars

Nursery: narsari, huru baichchaTor ishkul
Nurture: Tushto Kora, Pushto Kora, Poricorcha Kora

Nut: baDam

Nutrient: Pushti

Nutriment: Pusti zaTio, Pustikor

Nutrition: Pushti

Nylon: lailon, nailon

Nymph: Purano borniTo Amanob zaTio shunDor nari

O

Oar: biota, logi, Darh

Oasis: BEsTor lakhan, shanTir bagan, shanTir khoni

Oath: shoPoT, shoPoT Kora, shoPoT neowa, ProTigga, ProTigga Kora, kira Kora, Kira, Kosom, Kosom Kora, Kosom Kata, Kosom khaowa

Obedient: baiDDo, baiDDogoTo, Kotha hunra

Obese: AshomBob muta, beshi muta

Obey: mana, mainnoTa, mainnogoinno Kora, kotha huna

Object: badha Deowa, biruDiTa Kora, aPoTTi, aPoTTi Kora/Tula

Object: baikkor Kormo (object of a sentence), buzar zinish (object of understanding)

Objective: AbekTik ba AbekTigoTo, beKTigoTo nay emon

Oblige: baiDDo, baiDDo Aowa/thaKa

Obliterate: dhongsho Kora, shesh Kori laowa, Bangi laowa

Oblivious: monBula, Bulmona

Obscene: Ashlil, AruchiKor, ruchihin

Obscure: APorishkar, Porishkar naay emon zinish, AporiciTo, Acena Azana, nam nishana nai

Observe: Dekha, Porzobekko Kora, loikko Kora

Observer: Porzobekkok

Obstacle: badha, shomoishsha, proTikuloTa

Obstruct: badha Deowa, badha sristi Kora

Obtain: Paowa, Arzon Kora

Obvious: DrishshoTo, couke Dekha zar emon

Ocarina: okarina, eKta shongiTor zonTro

Occasion: Anustan

Occupant: bashinDa

Occupation: Pesha, zibika, Dokhol,DokhoDariTTo

Occupy: Dokhol Kora

Occur: Aowa, sristi Aowa

Ocean: shagor, shomuDro

o'clock: ghonta, ta (eKta, Duita etc)

October: Aktobor

Octagon: at Dikala akar, AstoBuz

Octopus: Aktupas, Aktopas

Odour: gondho, Durgondho

Odyssey: Bromon Kahini, berhanir Kahini, Desh Bromonor Kahini ba kichcha

Offend: ApomaniTo Kora, ain Amainno Kora

Offender: ainBongoKari

Offer: prosTab

Office: ofish, afish, Kamor zaaga, karjaloy

Officer: ofisar, Kormi, KormoKorTa

Official: ofishial, ofish bishoyok, ofish shongkranTo

officious: amlaTanTrik, amlaTonTri, nizor guruTTo shomporke shocheTon

off-licence: moDor Dukan, shurar Dukan

offside: Dekhar baire, DristishoKTir baire

offspring: shonTan, seleshonTan, baichchaKaichchain, baichchaKaichcha

often: prayU, shob shomoy, AneK shomoy

ogle: benozore caowa, kunozore caowa

oh: O, aha, haayre, haay

oil: Tel

ointment: molom, ointment

O.K: aichcha, oke, ṭik ase, Ay

Okra: bindi

Old: Purana, Puran, agor, agor Dinor

Olive: belPoi, zolPoi

Ombudsman: AdhiKorTa, uchchoToro ToDonToKari

Omelette: dim Baza, dim Bazi, enda Bazi, enda Baza, boiDa Baza

Omen: kulokkon, baD lokkon, kharaP lokkon

Omit: Bul Kora, Bul Porha, Bulia baD Deowa

Omnibus: omonibash, shomogro, shoKolTa, hOKolTa, sharaTa

Omnipotent: shorboshoKTiman, allaa, khoDa, khuDa, Bogoban, ishshor

Omnipresent: shorboTro birazoman

Omnivorous: shorboBuk, shobTa khaowra

On: thaKa, ase, roise

Once: eKbar

Oncoming: shamne Tone aowa, shamne Tone ar, shamne Tone aowar

One: eK, eKta

Onerous: Kotin, biroKTiKor, bUzha

Ongoing: coler, colonTo, colia aowa, colia ar

Onion: Piaz, Piaiz

Onlooker: Dorshok, Dekhra
Only: eKmaTro

Onset: shuru Aowa, shuru howa, shuru,

Onslaught: akromon, shuru

Onto: uPre

Onward: shamne, shamneDi

Ooze: bar Aowa

Opaque: Aporishkar, Porishkar nay

Open: Qula

Opera: opera

Operate: calani, poricalona Kora, opareshon Kora (on a patient)

Ophthalmic: couk bishoyok

Opiate: afim zaTio

Opinion: moT, moTamoT, dharona

Opium: afim

Opponent: biruDdhobaDi, biPokko, biruDdhe

Opportunity: shuzug

Oppose: birudhiTa, birudhiTa Kora

Opposite: biPoriT, ulta

Oppress: saTani, Kosto Deowa, dushshashon Kora, Durbeboar Kora

Optic: alo bishoyok, alo shomporkiTo

Optician: cokur cikiTshok ba DaKTor, optishian

Optimism: ashabaD, asha Kora
Optimum: shorbochcho, shob thaki beshi

Option: PosonDo Korar zinish ba PonTa

Opulent: dhoni, riDdho, shomriDdho

Opus: borho Kaz, borho Kormo, borho lekha, shob thaki muilloban lekha (kuno lekhokor)

Or: Athoba, ba

Oracle: BobishshoT bani

Oral: moukik, muke muke

Orange: Komla, Komla rong

Orang-utan: urangutaan

Orator: boKTa, mathra

Oratorio: boKTiTa bishoyok

Orb: alur rushni, alor ujjol binDu

Orbit: gularKar Poth, briTTakar Poth

Orchard: bagan, bagicha

Orchestra: orkestra, uchchoToro shongiTor baDoKDol, shongiTbaiDDoDol

Orchid: orkid

Ordain: nirDeshona Paowa, nirDeshona lowa

Ordeal: DurBug, Kosto

Order: aDesh, nirDesh, ordar

Ordinance: zonomoT, zongon bishoyok

Ordinary: shadharon, guruTTohin, guruTTosarha

Organ: Angsho (shoriror Angsho)

Organize: shongotiTo Kora, ayozon Kora

Orient: ashia bishoyok

Origami: Kazog Dia Bibinno zinish banana

Origin: mul, shuru, shuchona, uTsho

Ornament: Alongkar, zEOr, zEOrPaTi, ghoyna, ghoynaPoTro, ghoynaPaTi

Orphan: eTim

Orthodox: Purano, agor Dinor, PuranaPonTi

Other: Ainno, AinnoTa, Ainnozon, Ainno zinish

Ottoman: ottoman, Turki, Turki bishoyok

Ouch: maigo! Babago! allaago! Iallaa!

Ought: uciT, KorToibbo

Our: amrar, amaDer

Out: bair, baira, baire

Outbreak: shuru Aowa

Outburst: ciTkar Kora, cillani, gorzani

Outcast: nicu zaTor, KomzaTor, shomazor baire, shomazor baira

Outcome: folafol, fol

Outdoors: baira, bahir, bar

Outfit: KaPorth, KaPorhcuPorh

Outgrow: borho Ai zaowa

Outhouse: bairor ghor, bair barhi
Outlaw: ain Tone Bagra, ferari ashami, ferari

Outlet: uPaay

Outline: bairor shima

Outlook: DrishtiBongi

Outpatient: bair Tone aowra rugi

Outpost: bairor couki

Outpouring: bair Aowa, nirgoTo Aowa

Output: shorbomut folon, folon, folafol

Outrage: gonoAkrush, gonoceTonabirudhi

Outset: sharbikBabe, niTigoToBabe

Outside: baira, bahir, bara

Oval: gul, gulaKar

Oven: sUla, oBen

Over: shesh Aowa, oBar (a cricket over)

Overall: sharbik

Overboard: Porhi zaowa

Overcast: shomaz bohirBuTo, shomazor baire

Overcome: ATikrom Kora, Par Aiwa aowa

Overdo: beshi Kora, besh besh Kora, besh Kora

Overdose: beshi oushoD khai laowa

Overdraft: oBardraft

Overdraw: beshi Poysha Tuli laowa
Overdrawn: beshi Poysha Tula

Overdue: shomoy Par Ai zaowa

Overgrown: beshi baarhi zaowa

Overhaul: purnangoBabe shongskar Kora

Overhead: uPre, mathaar uPre

Overhear: hunTe Pare, Dur Tone hunTe Para

Overjoyed: Qub Qushi Aowa, Qub anonDiTo Aowa

Overland: Bumir uPror, zominor uPre

Overlap: eKtar loge aroKtar miliTo Aowa, eKtar loge aroKtar KataKati

Overlook: DekhTe na Para, na Dekha

Overnight: shara raiT, asTa RaT

Overpower: Komzuri Kori laowa, niyonTrono ana/ ani laowa

Overrule: (abeDon) baTil ba khariz Kori Deowa

Overseas: biDesh

Oversee: Dekha, loikko rakha

Overstay: beshi Din thaKa

Overtake: oBarteik Kora

Overthrow: Palai Deowa, APoshariTo Kora, APosharon Kora

Overtime: beshi shomoy, nirDishto shomoyor baire

Owe: Deowna, rin, dhaar, Korzo

Owl: PeYca

Own: nizor, aPon
Ox: sharh, deKa, boloD

Oxygen: oksijen

Oxymoron: biPoriT, boiPoriTTo, biruDhomukiTa

Oyster: shamuk zaTio

Ozone: ozon gesh

P

Pace: atar goTi, Paycari Kora

Pacifist: hoTashabaDi, nirash manush, nirashabaDi, noiraishshbaDi

Pacify: Tush Kora, TriPo Kora

Pack: bosTa, Toli, ghattibuska, buska, Pek

Package: Pekeiz, Peket

Packet: Peket

Pact: cukTi, shommoTi

Paddy: dhan

paddy field: dhan kheT, dhanor zomin, dhanor bond

padre: PaDri

paediatrics: shishu cikiTshok, shishur daKTor, huruTar daKTor

page: PaTa, prista

Pagoda: Pegoda

Paid: Poysha Deowa, beTon Deowa, Deowa, mara

Pain: bIsh, beDna, Kosto, dhora (caP-pressure)

Paint: rong, Peint

Painter: ciTrokor, ciTroshilpi

Pair: zurha

Palace: razproshaD, razBobon, razbarhi

Pale: rongmora

Palm: aTor gaTa

Palmistry: aTor rekha Dekha

Panda: Panda

Pandemic: mohamari, morhoK

Pane: zanalar dhaar, KHirhkir dhaar ba KanDa

Panic: Beushi Kora

Papaya: KoPol, Koyfol, pepe

Paper: Kagoz

Papyrus: pepiras, puraTon kagoz

Paradise: BEsT, shorgo, zannaT, Aloka, behesT

Paradox: biruDdhomuki, boiPoriTTomulok, boiPoriTTo

Parallel: shomanToral

Paralysis: Ardhango rug, shoril Abosh Ai zoawa

Pardon: khoma, maaYf

Parent: ma baba, maTafiTa, fiTamaTa, ma baf

Parity: Dol

Q

Quake: KaPa, Kompon, Bumikompo, Boical, Buical

Qualify: fash Kora, kriTokairzo Aowa, shofol Aowa, zuiggo

Quality: man, gun

Quantify: nirDishto Koria Kowa, shoingka nishchiT Koria Kowa

Quantity: Poriman

Quantum: biraT, borho, kuantam (as in Quantum Physics)

Quarrel: zhogrha, bibaD, zhogrha bibaD, maramari, Dorbar, Kazia, Dorbar kazia

Quarter: cair Bagor eK Bag, eK anaa

Queen: rani, razrani

Quench: Tishna mitani

Quest: ABizhan

Question: proshno, soal, ziggasha

Queue: lain, kiU

Quick: zolDi, DruTo, TarhaTarhi, urhaurhi

Quid: tEKa

Quiet: nirai, nishshobDo, nishchuP

Quit: baD Deowa, sarhi Deowa

R

Race: borno, zaTi

Race: Dourh, Dourhani

Radar: rada, redar

Radial: abar dayel Kora

Radiant: ujjol, cIKmik Kora, zhikzhik Kora

Radiate: nisriTo Aowa, bair Aowa, nirzhoriTo Aowa, bikiriTo Aowa

Radiation: rashayonik bikiron

Radical: DurDanTo

Radio: redio, beTar

Radioactive: Torongoshokrio, redioektiB

Radish: mula

Radium: rediam

Rage: rag, ghusha

Rail: rel, berha, rel lain

Rain: megh, bristi

Raj: raj, british raj, rajokio

Raja: raza

Ramadan: romzan, ruza, ruza mash

Ramifications: proTikria, folosruTi, fol

Rampant: usrikkol, niyonTronor baire

Rampart: proTirokka buhu, proTirokkar Deowal

Random: hoṭaT, maze maze

Range: shima

Rank: PoD

Ransack: TOcnoc Kora

Ransom: aPohoronkarir DabiDaowa

Rape: boloTkar, boloTkariTa, dhorshon

Rapid: DruTo, TarhaTarhi

Rare: DurloB

Rastafarian: rasTafarian

Rat: cIka

Rate: shuDor har

Ratio: AnuPaT

Ration: reshon

Rational: zukTishongoTo, zuKTizukTo, zuKTiPurno

Raw: Kaca, randha nay

Ray: alor rushni, alor roshshi

Reach: Pouca

React: proTikria

Read: PoYrha

Reader: PatoK, PoYrra

Ready: prosTuT, Toiri, Toiar

Real: ashol, hasa, basTob, basToboTa

Realistic: basTob shommoTo, basTobor lakhan

Realize: AnuBob Kora, buzTe Para, buza

Realm: raijjo, Dunia

Rear: Kor, Pic

Reason: Karon, hETu

Rebel: biDruhi

Recipient: Paowra

Recite: muke muke Kowa, aBriTTi Kora

Recognize: cInTe Para, cIna

Recollect: mono Kora, shoron Kora

Recommend: Koia Patani

Record: Dolil, KagozPoTro

Recover: uDDar Kora

re-create: abar sristi Kora

recreation: binoDonmuloK

rectify: t̲ik Kora, Bul shuDrani

red: lal

rent: Barha

Regalia: razokio PushaK PorichchoD

Regina: rani

S

Sabbath: ihuDi manshor/zaTir dhormio uTshob, ihuDi sabaT

Sabotage: PonDo Kora, BOndul Kora, khoTi Kora, aPoghaT Kora, nosto Kora

Saccharin: sEKarin, roshayonikBabe banail cini

Sachet: PuTli, suto PEket

Sack: beg, tholi, bOsTa

Sack: (caKri Tone) borkhasTo Kora/ Aowa

Sacred: PobiTTro, Paak, Paak PobiTro

Sacrifice: Teag, bishorjon

Sacrilege: dhormo biruDdho, dhormo burudhi, Adhormor Kam

Sad: Dukko, bezar, AQushi

Saddle: ghurhar uPre bowar ashon ba sIt.

Sadism: DukkobaD

Safe: niraPoD

Safeguard: niraPoTTa, nishchiT niraPoTTar uPaay.

Safety: niraPoTTa

Sag: zhulonTo, lotKail, lotKi thaKa

Said: from Kowa, to say, simple past Koilam, Koila Koilaay, Koile, Koilo etc

Sail: Paal Paal Tula

Saint: Pir, allaar Oli, allaaia manush, allaadhari manush

Sake: lagia, lagi, Karone, Daay

Salaam: greetings by Muslim people.

Salad: salaT, salad, salaT, chaTni, chatni

Salary: beTon, mozuri, Parisromik, Kamor Poysha

Sale: biki, becakina, kinabeca, bikri, bikri Kora, sEil (as in Sale at a shop)

Saline: selaain

Saliva: lob, lof, sef

Salmon: salmon mas

Salmonella: salmonela, Petor bearam

Saloon: shelun, naPiTor Dukan, naPiTghor

Salt: nun, lobon

Salutary: shombuDonmulok, salam alki

Salute: sEliUt, sEliUt Kora, salam, salam Kora

Salvage: bacani, rokka Kora

Salvation: aTTo uDdhar, aTTo prayoshchiTTo, khoma, khoma laB Kora

Samaritan: shaijjoKari, aTTonirbaciTo/aTTomononiTo shechchasheboK, BalaKamor Kormi, Balar Kormi

Same: shoman, lakhan, moTo, eKlakhan, eKroKom, shoman shoman

Samovar: rashian somoBar

Sampan: Sampan, dingi, saampanor nouka

Sample: nomuna, sempul

Sanatorium: ashPaTal ba shaisTo bishoyoK proTistan

Sanctify: allaar shanTi borshiTo Aise emon AbosTa, PobiTro Kora

Sanction: nisheD, baDa proDan, baron Kora

Sanctuary: asroyor zaaga, asroy, niraPoD zaaga

Sanctum: niraPoD o PobiTro zaaga, like a mosque or temple or church

Sand: balu, bali

Sandal: sendel, choPol, choppol

Sandwich: senduich

Sane: Bala, Pagol nay, shusTo mathaar, shusToshobol, shusTo

Sang: from gaowa, to sing, gailam, gaila, gailaay, gaile, gailo

Sanitary: beKTigoTo shaisTo bishoyok
Sank: from duba, to sink, Dulo, dubi gelo
Sanskrit: shongskriT, shangskriT

Sapphire: safaiar, moni, eK zaTor muilloban PaTTor

Sarcasm: Tikkno roshikoTa, shukko roshobuD, shukko roshobuD zaTo Poriaash/Porihaash

Sarcophagus: sarkofegas, kofin

Sardine: sardin mas

Sardonic: Poriaashmulok, Porihaashmulok, shleshaTTok

Sari: sharhi, sharhi KaPorh, sari

Sat: from to sit, bowa, boilam, boila, boilaay, boile, boilo etc

Satan: shoyTan

Satellite: uPogroho, setElait

Satin: silkzaTio, satin

Satire: prohoshon, prohoshonmulok

Satisfy: Tust Kora, PoriTriPTo Kora

Saturday: shonibar

Saturn: shoni groho

Sauce: shira, zhul

Sauna: Sona, sauna

Savage: guhabashi, nistur, pashan, pashondo

Savannah: pranTor, moyDan, maat

Save: bacani, zomani, zoma Kora

Saviour: uDdharKari, uDdharKorTa, uDdhar Korra

Saw: from Dekha, to see Dekhlam, Dekhla, Dekhlaay, Dekhle, Dekhlo etc

Saw: aarI, cIra, cIrani, aarakhoshi

Saxon: sekson

Saxophone: seksofon

Say: Kowa, maatha, bola

Scald: gorom PaniT/Telo zola/zoli zaowa, gorom PaniT/Telo PurhI zaowa

Scale: Pallaa, nikTi, DarhiPallaa

Scam: AshoT PonTaa, AshoTBabe manshore ṭOgani/ṭOga

Scan: sken, sken Kora, sobir/fotor lakhan koPi Kora

Scandal: Kelenkari, boDnam, Durnam, skendal

Scapegoat: AinnaayBabe Dushi banana, AinnaayBabe Dush Dowa

Scar: Daag

Scarce: ABab, KomTi, gharhTi

Scare: dor, dOrai zaowa, dOr laga, dOr

Scarf: skarf, maflar

Scarlet: ghono lal, abir, abir ronga

Scathing: kotorBabe aKromon Kora, kotorBabe shomalochona Kora

Scatter: sItaia Palani, sItai laowa, sItaia mara

Scene: Drishsho

Scent: ghran, sent

Schedule: Kormoshuchi, Kormobiboroni, Kormo Talika

Scheme: Kormo PorikolPona

Schizophrenia: skiTsofrenia, eKdhoroner manushik Ashuk zar fole rugiE mone Kore Tar mathaar BiTre Tone Keu Tar loge mather. All kinds of mental illness is referred as manushik AshusToTa ba Ashuk. mathaaT Duish is another expression that might mean anything to do with mental illness of some kind. However, these are the official terms relating to mental illness:

Pagol: mad, metanly ill. However, Pagol is used in every day life the way crazy or mad is used in every day speech in every life by every day people to mean exciting or exhilarating or eccentric etc

mono bikar: that is sever mental illness or psychotic or suffering from some form of psychosis or sever mental break down as a result of muptiple illness.

manushik AshusToTa/Ashuk: means general mental illness including depression etc

monorug: mental illness of generalised nature would include mild symptoms such as anxiety disorders, mild depression etc

manushik sTobiroTa: this is the official name of depression which literally translate as mental sluggingness or tiredness or lack of interest (in life and reality).

bohubEKTiruPi manushik beaDi/rug: multiple personality disorders etc

sriTiBibrom: dementia

scholar: gIani, boiPoTror manush, PoYrhua, PoYrhua manush, shikkiTo manush, biDDan, biDDan manush

school: ishkul, biDDaloy, Paatshala, Paashshala

sciatica: sayatika

science: biggan

scissors: Kaanchi

scold: boKa, shashon Kora, couk rangani

scooter: skutar, motor shaikel

score: skoUr, goUl

scorn: ghInna, biDDesh

scorpion: skorpion, bishaKTo eKta suto kIt

Scot: skot, skotish manush, skotlendor manush

Scoundrel: skaundrel, boDmash, Dushto, shoyTan

Scout: skaut, iskaut

Scratch: Dag, Dag laga, Dag Porha, Dag lagi zaowa

Scream: cIllani, cIkmara, cIkani, cITkar, cITkar Parha, cIk Deowa

Screen: PorDa

Screw: iskru, skru

Script: Pandulipi, skript

Scripture: dhormio bani

Scroll: taana

Sea: shagor, shomuDro

Seal: sil mas

Seal: shil

Seamstress: mohila Dorzi, shelai Korri

Search: Tukani, Quza, Talash Kora, Tallash Kora

Season: wriTu, Kaal, bosror Bibinno Kaal

Seat: zaaga, sIt, sTan

Second: sekend

Second: DiTio, Dui nombor

Secondary: DiTioTo, Duinombori, uchcho biDDaloy, hai skul, hai ishkul

Secret: guPon, lukail

Secretariat: sekretariet, monTronaloy, shochobaloy

Secretary: shochib, shadharon shompaDok, sekretari

Secrete: nisriTo Aowa, bar Aowa, Porha

Sect: Dol, guTro

Section: shakha

Sector: sektor, elaKa

Secular: dhormo niroPekko

Secure: nishchiTBabe rakha, shurokkiTo

See: Dekha

Seed: bici, biz, cEra

Seek: Quza, Takani

Seem: laga, mono Aowa

seen: Dekhar moTo, Dekhar zuiggo

seesaw: uPrenice utauti, sIsO

T

Tabla: Tobla, Tobola.

Table: Tebul

Tablet: tablet, gulli, oushoDor gulli, borhi

Tact: koushol

Tactics: koushol

Tail: lenjurh, lezurh

Tailor: Dorzi, teilar

Take: neowa

Tale: golPo, kichcha, kahini, kahani

Talent: medha

Talisman: Tabiz, Tabiz Koboz

Talk: math, maatha, Kotha, KothabarTa

Tall: uca, lomba

Tame: Pusha, shanTosisto, shanTosristo

Tamper: monor Abosta (tempar is used to mean rag, ghusha or volatile behaviour etc)

Tandoori: Tanduri

Tangible: AnuBobor zuiggo, pray nagal zuiggo

Tank: tenk

Tantrum: cITkar Koria KanDa, aTPaowa curhia mara

Tape: tep, teip, teP

Tapestry: shelair Kaz, noKsha

Target: loikko, uDDeishsho

Task: Kaz, Kam

Taste: shaD neowa, zacai Kora, ruci

Taught: shikail

Tautology: mukosTobiDDa

Tax: Kor, rajoshsho, khazna

Taxi: teksi

Tea: caY, caYPani

Teach: shikka Deowa, PoYrhani, shikani

Teacher: shikkok, mastor, tichar, shikaowra

Team: Dol, Tim

Tear: sirha, farha, fara

Tear: coukor Pani, cokur Pani, KanDa

Tease: moza Kora, mozak Kora, dOng Kora

Technology: prozukTi

Tedious: klanTikor, biroKTikor

Teenager: utTiboyish, utTiboyoshi, utTiboyshi, zuboK zuboTi

Telecommunications: Tar zugazug

Telegram: Tar, teligram, Teli

Telepathy: mone mone mil, monor mil, manushik zugazug

Telephone: telifon, fon

Television: teliBishon

Tell: Kowa, bola

Temperature: TaPmaTra, TaPPorimaP, ṭanda gorom bishoyok

Temple: uPashonar zaaga, monDir

Temporary: AsTaI

Ten: Dosh

Tenant: Barhatia, Barhate

Tender: norom, Komol, kumol

Tendon: rog

Tenement: shariboDDo ghorbarhi

Tense: Kal

Tense: uTTeziTo, AsTiroTa, AsTir

Tension: DushciTagrosTo

Tent: Tabu

Tentative: eKmoTa, praTomikBabe

Term: shomoy shima

Terminal: shesh, mriTTuborTi, mriTTur nikotborTi, terminal (airport)
Terminate: shesh Kora, Kati laowa, shesh Kori laowa, baTil Kora/ Kori laowa

Terminology: shobDomala, beboriTo shobDor shomabesh

The: ta

Theatre: natoK, thIetar

Theft: curi

Their: Tarar

Them: Tara

Then: Tar bade, er bade, sheshe, Pore

Theory: ToiTTo, ToTTo

There: hOno, hOkhano, hOkhan, hIno

These: Oguin, Iguin, ITa

Those: hOgula, hIgula, hoTa, hITa

Thesis: ToTTo bishoyoK prosTabona, thIsis

They: Tara

Thick: gaari

Thief: cur

Thigh: uraT

Thin: PaTla

Thing: zinish, bosTu, mal, malamal

Think: cinTa, cinTa Kora, Baba

Thirst: Trishna, Teshta, Tishna

Thirteen: Tero

Thirty: Tish, Trish, Tirish

This: OKta, ikta, ita

Thorn: Kata, gosa

Thought: cinTa, Babna, dharona

Thousand: azar

Tiara: mukut, mathaar mukut

Tide: zuar

Tiger: bag

Tight: atail, shoKto

Timber: Kat, lakhri

Time: shomoy, Kal, bela, beil, bala

Toady: aiz, aizku

Toast: toust

Tobacco: shaaDa, tubako

Together: eK loge, eK shathe

Toil: Porisrom, Kosto

Toilet: Paykhana, Paykhanaghor, Paykhanarghor, toilet, letrin, lettin

Tolerate: shoijjo Kora, mania lowa, mania neowa

Tomato: bilaTi Baingoin, tometu, tomato
Tomorrow: Kail, agami Kail, aibo Kail

Tonight: aiz raiT

Too: O (amiO- me too)

U

Udder: uloin

Ugly: AshunDor, bisri, kuTshiT, zinnaTor lakhan

Ukulele: Iukelili

Umbrella: saTTi, saTa

Umpire: ampayar, kriket khelar bicaroK ba refari

UN: zaTishongo

Unaccountable: hIshabhin, hIshab nai, behIshab

Unanimous: oikkomoT, eKmoT

Unarmed: Asrohin, beAsro

Unaware: bekheal, AshabDan

Unbearable: shoijjor baira, Ashoijjo, shoijjo Korar moTo nay

Unbeknown: Azana, nazana, azana

Uncle: caca, mama

Unclean: Aporishkar, APorichchonno

Uncomfortable: AshosTiPurno, shosTihin

Uncommon: zekta beshi Paowa ba Dekha zaay na

Unconscious: AcETon, cETonahin

Uncover: Qula, adaaKa

Undecided: shiDdhanTohin

Undeniable: Ashshikar Korar moTo nay

Under: nice, Tole

Underage: Kom boyoshi, ApraPToboyoshko

Understand: buza

Undertake: Kora, KorTe razi Aowa, KorTe zaowa

Undo: Bango: Korso, ebla Bango. You have done it now undo it (break the doing)

Undoubted: shonDehohin

Uneasy: AshosTikor

Unemployed: bekar, Kamhin, Kamkaz nai

Unequivocal: spostoTo, PorishkarBabe, nishchiT Koria

Unfit: Azuiggo

Unfold: Abola, AKowa, naKowa

Unforgettable: Bular moTo nay

Unfortunate: Dukkozonok

V

Vacant: khali, shuinno, faaKa

Vacate: khali Kora, ghor sarhia zoawa

Vaccinate: tika Deowa. Tika na Dibar fole PoiTTeK bosor aazar aazar huruTa behuDa mara zaay. As a result of not vaccinating thousands of children die pointlessly every year.

Vacuous: shuinno, khali, faaKa

Vacuum: faaka, khali, shuinno

Vagabond: Boboghure, beKama, BEgabond

Vagina: sTri Ango, zuni, zounango. Pun, PunD (these two words are not used in social circumstances).

Vague: Aporishkar, Porishkar nay

Vain: aTTopremik, nizor shomporke fapa ba suinno dharona

Vainglorious: fapa aTTomorzaDabuD

Vale: gram, elaKa, bonani, bond

Valentine: BElentain

Valiant: shaOshi, biroTTpurno, morzaDashomponno

Valid: bohal, boaal, KairzoTo

Valley: PorboTor nicoborTi elaKa

Valour: biroTTpurno

Value: muillo, Dam, morzaDa

Vampire: roKTocusha

Van: Ben, Bengarhi

Vandal: Dustoluk, APoKormi

Vanguard: Agroshor shoinik, Agroshor shena, agor rokki

Vanish: milai zaowa

Vanity: aTTopremik, nizor shomporke fapa ba suinno dharona
Vanquish

vapour: bashPo, dhua, dhuma

variable: PoriborTonshil, poriborTonshil Porimaippo

variant: PoriborTiT Angsho

variation: beTikrom, beTikrom zoniT fol

variety: biBinnoTa

various: biBinno

varnish: Baarnish, Baarnish Deowa

vary: boDla, PoriborTon

vascular: roKTor shira bishoyok

vase: fulDani

vasectomy: Besektomi

Vaseline: Beselin

Vast: birat, prokando

Vatican: Batikan

Vector: BeKtor

Vegan: shobjiBugi, anazBugi

Vegetable: shakshobji, TarKari

Vegetarian: shobjiBugi, anazBugi

Vegetation: kheT kheTali

Vehement: Drirho ProTiggo

Vehicle: zanbahon, garhi ghurha
Veil: ghumta, mukush

Vein: shiraa, shirauposhiraa, roKTonali

Velocity: goTi
Vendetta: rushbandha, ProTihInghshaPorayon, rish bandha, rish dhora, proTishuD
Porayon

Vengeance: proTishuD

Venison: AYringor mangsho, AYringor gUsT

Venom: bIsh

Venous: bIshaKTo, bIshal, bIshaala

Ventilate: baTash aowa zaowar bebosTa Kora, baTash colacolor bebosTa Kora

Venture: uDDug, uDDzug

Venue: zaaga, sTan

Verandah: baranDa

Verb: Kam buzaowar shobDo

Verdict: raay, aDesh
Verify: shonaKTo Kora, shoTTaiTo Kora

Vermicelli: shemai

Vermin: cIka

Vernacular: mul Basha, KoiTTo Basha, colTi Basha

Versatile: cOloia, shorbozonin, sharbozonin, bishshmoy

Verse: sorhaa, KobiTa, PoiDDo

Version: PoTranTor

Versus: biruDDe, biPokke, loge, shathe

Vertical: uPormuki

Very: AiTTanoTo, Qub, beshi, Anek, biBinnoTa, boDla

Vessel: zanbahon, garhi, nouka, zaaYz

Vest: genji

Vet: Porikka Kora, Tolaia Dekha, Quz khobor loa.

Veteran: probin, Purana, agor, AbshorpraPTo shoinik

Veterinary: Poshu biggan bishoyok, Poshubishoyok

Veto: birudhiTa Kora, biruDdhe BUt Deowa, BEtu Deowa

Via: maiDDome, maz Dia, maze Dia

Viable: shomBaibbo, shomBabonaPurno

Vibe: AnToror goTi

Vibrant: zibonTo, zanBora, zan aala

Vibrate: KaPa

Vic: Biktoria

Vicar: PaDri

Vicarious: shomporkiTo DaITTo ba KorToibbo

Vice: baD AiBBash, Duish, bEkhaishloT

Vice: shohoKari, shoho, uPo. shohoKari prodhan shikkok, assistant head teacher, uPo prodhan zela proshashok: deputy district commissioner

Vice/Vice Chancellor: Baais as in Vice Chancellor of a University

Viceroy: Baaisroy, laat, laatshab

vice versa: iTTaDi, iTTaDi iTTaDi

vicinity: nikotborTi, dhareKase, KanDaT, bazuT, KanDaKasaT

Vicious: Pashobik, Poshur lakhan, hayenar lakhan

Victim: shikar

Victor: bizoI, zoI

Victoria Cross: Biktoria Kros

Victorian: Biktorian, rani Biktorian shomoyor manush, rani Biktoriar shashon amolor ba shashon amol bishoyok

Victory: zoy, bizoy

Vicuña: AYring zaTio

Video: Vidio

Video cassette: Bidio keset

Video tape: Bidio tep, Bidior tep

View: Drishsho, Dekhar shimana

Vigil: shanTi misil, shanTi shomabesh, shanTir lagi PoDozaTra

Vigilante: ainor baire khoborDari Korra

Vigour: pranshoKTi, monor bol, TEz

Vile: Poca, BaD, kharaP, boDDu, boDe Bora

Vilify: ninDa Kora, shomman nosto Kora, giboT Kora, giboT gaowa

Villa: Bila

Village: gram, gaU, Pur, Paarha, moholla, elaKa

Villain: khol, kholo, kholo nayok

Vindicate: shoiTTo promaniTo Aowa, nirDush promaniTo Aowa, shotik promaniTo Aowa

Vine: loTa, anguror loTa ba gaas

Violate: ATikrom Kora, lOngon Kora, APomaniTo Kora, AsroDDa Dekhani

Violence: shonTrash, roKToPaT, maramari

Violet: baingoni, baingon rongia, beguni

Violin: bElaa, Baiolin, behala, beala

VIP: Biaaipi, guruTTopurno manush ba beKTi

Viper: shaaP, haaP

Virgin: shoTi, nishPaP, niroPoraD

Virology: Bairasbiggan

Virtual: AnubasTob, basTobruPi, basTobor lakhan

Virtue: gun

Virtuoso: proTiBaban

Virus: Bairas, ADrishsho zibanu

Visa: Bisaa

Visage: ruP, Kaya

Visible: Dekhar moTo, Dekhar zuiggo, Drishsho zuiggo

Vision: Dristi, coukor Dekha

Visit: DekhaT zaowa, Dekha Kora, Bromon, Bromono zaowa, berhaani, berhaniT zaowa, zaowa

Visual: Drishshor BiTre, Dekhar moTo

Vital: Qub Dorkari, Qub proyozonio, Qub zoruri

Vitamin: Baitamin, Bitamin

Viva: zoy, joy, zinDabaD

Vivacious: ashiQushi, zibonTo, zibonBora

viva voce: Baiba Bosi, baiOdata, shongkiPTo aTToziboni,

vivid: biciTro, boiciTroPurno

vocabulary: shobDoTalika, shobDormala, shobDolara

vocation: Kam, Peshaa, zibika

Vogue: feshonDurosTo

Voice: Konto, gola

Void: khali, baTil, shuinno

Volatile: AsTir, AsTiTishil

Volcano: BOlkano, Agnigiri, agunor khoni

Volume: ghonoTTo, beaPoKoTa

Voluntary: shechchamulok, nizor ichchaay

Volunteer: shechchashebok

Vomit: bomI Kora, bomI

Voodoo: zaDutuna

Vortex: ghurni, ghurni cokro

Vote: BUt, BUt Deowa

Vouch: shakki Deowa, Pokke mathaa, shomorTon Kora

Voucher: BaUchar

Vow: shoPoT Kora, shoPoT, proTigga, proTigga Kora, kira, kira Kora

Vowel: shorborno

Voyage: Bromon

Vulgar: Ashlil, muta maathar, Aruchishil, AruchiPurno

Vulnerable: Durbol, Komzur, Ashoaay, Ashohaay

Vulture: hokum, shokun

W

Water: Pani, zol, jol. Pani shaisTor lagi QubI zoruri zinish. Water is very necessary for health.

Waffle: aProyzonio math, beKama math

Waft: baTasho Bashia aowa, baTashor loge aowa

Wage: Parisromik, Porisromik, beTon (salary)

Wager: bazi dhora

Waggle: lorha, hora, zolDi horia zaowa

Wagon: owagon, garhi

Waif: eTim-esir, basTuhin, grihohin, tukai

Wail: beDnaay cillani

Waist: Pet, Komoror uPor

Wait: APekka, APekka Kora, ubani, Darhani, kharhani, dhoirzo, dhoirzo dhora, sobor, sobor Kora

Waive: kunu niom Palon Kora Tone biroTo thaKa.

Waiver: Dabi Teag Kora, Dabi PoriTTeag Kora

Wake: hozag, hozag thaKa, hozag Aowa, uṭa, ghum Tone uṭa

Walk: ataa

Wall: Deowal, owal

Wallaby: owalabi

Wallet: manibeg, owalet

Wallow: PeKor maze gorhagorhi zaowa/khaowa, aTTokoruna, nizor proTi Koruna

Waltz: eK dhoronor nac, shaBabik o aTTobishshashi acoron

Wand: KaYti (zaDur KaYti)

Wander: Anmona, anmonaBabe ataa

Want: cahiDa, caowa, DorKar, proyozon

Wanton: AKaron dhongshaTTok acoron

War: zuDdho

Ward: oward, elaKa

Warden: PeaDa

Wardrobe: Deraz

Ware: bashonPoTro, zinishPoTro, malPoTro

Warm: groom, Um, Umgorom

Warn: shabdhan, shabdhan Kora, shoTorko, shoTorko Kora

Warrant: Dabi Kora, grefTari Porwana, owarint, owarent

Warrior: zuDdha, bir

Was: asil, silo, also

Wash: dhowa

Wasp: eK dhoronor Puka

Waste: aPocoy Kora, nosto Kora, Abeboar Kora

Watch: nozor rakha, PaaYra Deowa, ghorhi

Water: Pani

Wave: d̲eU

Wax: mom

Way: Poth, shorhok, rasTa

Wayward: shaneDia, shamneDi, AgrogoTi

We: amra, mOraaY

Weak: Durbol, shoKTihin, Komzur, láaYzur

Wealth: dhon, dhonshomPoD, shomPoD, shomPoTTi

Weapon: Asro, AsTro

Wear: PinDa, Poron Kora

Weather: abhaowa, PorisTiTi, AbosTa

Weave: shelai Kora, banana

Web: zal, internet, Ueb

Wed: bia, bia Kora, bia Deowa, bia bowa

Wednesday: buDbar

Wee: huru, suto, sutomuto

Weed: zOngla

Week: shaPTa, haPTa, hoPTa, shoPTa

Weep: KaanDa

Weigh: uzon Kora

Weight: uzon

Weighting: bishesh BaTa (London Weighting)

Weird: biciTro, acanoK, azob, azgubi

Welcome: shagoTom, shagoTo zanani

Welfare: Bala, Bala Kora, Bala caowa, Bala Korani

Well: Bala, aichcha

Wellbeing: shusToTa, shusTo shaisTo

Well-meaning: Bala caowa

Well-spoken: Bala mathra

Well-worn: Bala PinDa

Welsh: uelsh

Went: gese, gesoin, gesi, geslam, gelam

Were: aslam, asil, also

West: Pocim, Poshchim

Wet: Biza

Whack: thaba mara, thaba Deowa, dhakka mara

Whale: Timi, Timi mas

What: ki, kiTa

Wheat: gom

Wheel: caKa, cakka, chakka

When: kun bala, kun shomoy, kokhon, kun Din

Where: Koi, kunkhano, kunano, kuano, kubai, kubaay, keano

Whether: ni na, ki na

Which: kunta, kungu

While: ermaze, iTimoiDDe

Whisper: caPashore matha

Whistle: huisol, Uisol, huishel

White: shaDa, dhOla

Whitewash: shaDa rong Kora/Deowa

Who: Ke (singular) Ke Ke (plural), Kegu (singular), Kegu Kegu (plural), Keta, Keta Keta

Whole: shara, shomosTo, hoKolTa, shoKolTa, shobTa

Wholesale: paikari becakina

Wholesome: poripurno

Whom: Kar/zar

Whore: beshsha, maagi

Whose: Kar

Why: Kene, KiTar lagi, KiTar Daay, KiTallagi, ki Karone, kisher Daay, ki hETu

Wicked: shoyTan, Dushto

Wide: melaa, bisTar, bisTriTo

Widow: larhi, larhi beti

Width: bisTar, BEr

Wife: bou, sTri, ginni, bibi (rarely used as wife and young children sometime call their grandmother as bibi). bou: father and mother in laws call their daughter in law as bou shortened from son's wife Puar bou.

Wild: boinno, zongli,

Wilderness: boinno poribesh, bonbonani

Wildlife: boinno poshuprani, boinno zibzonTu

Wilful: ichchakriTo, shoichchaay

Will: ichcha, ichcha shoKTi, beKTiceTona, beKTiTTo

Will: Kormu, Korba, Korbaay, Korbe

Willy-nilly: zEla ichcha Ola

Win: zoy, zoy Kora, ziTa

Wind: baTash, baaiU

Window: zanala, zanla, KHikrhi, KHirhki

Wine: moD, moD zaTio Panio

Wing: dana, dankha, Pakha, Pakhna

Wink: couk mara

Winter: shiT, shiTor Din, shiTKal, tandar Din, EOT, EOTKal

Wipe: musaa, Pusaa, musi laowa, Pusi laowa

Wire: Tar

Wireless: Tarhin, Tarsarha, beTar, redio

Wisdom: gianbuDdhi, aKol,

Wise: gIani, shomozDar, shaibbosTor manush

Wish: asha Kora, ichcha Kora, bashona Kora, shaadh Kora, shokh Kora

Wit: buDdhimoTTa

Witch: PETni

With: shaTe, loge, loge loge, shonge

Withdraw: proTTahar Kora, Tula, Tuli laowa

Withhold: sTogiT Kora, bondho Kori laowa

Withstand: shoijjo Kora, dhoria rakhTe shokkom

Witness: shakki

Witty: coTurmona,

Wizard: zaDugor

Wolf: KHekrhe shIal

Woman: mohila, beti, beti manush, nari

Womb: gorBo, Pet

Wonder: cinTa Kora, Baba, Babna

Wood: lakhrhi, KaYt, cEli

Wool: ul

Word: shobDo

Work: Kam, Kaz, KamKaz, kormo, Kormo

World: Dunia, priTibi

Worm: Kecu

Worn: sIrha

Worry: DushcinTa, cinTa

Worse: aro/AneK/besh kharaP, aro/AneK/besh baD

Worship: Puza, prarTona, nomaz, Doydhormo Kora

Worth: muillo, morzaDa, guruTTo

Wound: zoKom, Kataa, ghaa

Wrath: rag, gUsa, rag gUsa

Wreath: fulor mala

Wreck: nosto Kora, Bangi laowa

Wriggle: murani, muramuri

Wrinkle: mukor Dag

Wrist: aTor Kobzi/Kobza. Tain aTor KobzaT Duk Paisoin. He/she got hurt in the wrist.

Writ: rit, aDaloTor bishesh nirDesh (nirDesh-direction nor sentence (as in a case)

Write: lekha. Kolom Dia lekha Ay. Writing is done by the pen. lekhok: writer/author, lekhra: one who write, copy writer. lkhani: to get someone write/ get written

Writhe: TerhabeKa Koria cola, shaPor lakhan cola. shaP cole TerhabeKa Pothe. Snake moves in a writhing way.

Wrong: Bul, Aṯik, beṯik.

X

X-ray: eksre (to do an X-ray is eksre Kora). daKTore bukor eksre Korbar lagi Koison. The doctor has asked for the chest x-ray. I betar eksrer couk. This man had x-ray eyes/vision.

Xeroxing: fotukopi/fotukopi Kora. PasPutor fotukopi Kora lagbo. The passport needs to be photocopied/reroxed.

Xenon: gondho o bornohin eKzaTor gesh zeKta baTashor maze shamainno Porimane uPosTiT ase. zenon eKzaTor gesh.

Xenophobia: biDeshi biDDeshi, bornobaDi (racist), aPoriciTo azana biDshi manushor proTi gInna Pushon Kora. biDeshi biDDesh zinishta Qub kharaP zinish. Xenophobia is a very bad thing.

Xerox: fotokopi mishin, fotokopi Kora, kopi Kora. Dukanor fotokopi mishin nosto Ai gese. The shop's Xerox has broken down.

Xmas: krismas, eksmas, borhoDin. borhoDin Ailo disembor mashor Pochchish Tarik. Christmas is on the 25th of December.

Xylophone: zailofon. silet Keu zailofon bazaay na. No one plays xylophone in Sylhet.

Y

Year: bosor/bochchor

Year (2000): shaal/shOn

Yearly: bosri/bosor bosor/bosre bosre)

Yard: goz (five yards)

Yard: utaan

Yearn: zano Koc Koci Kora

Ya: Ay

Yacht: bilash Tori, bilashor nouka, bilashor naow

Yak: PorboTor goru, Iaak

Yam: matir alu, matia alu

Yankee: amerikan, Iaanki

Yap: BoKorBoKor Kora, BErBEr Kora, PErPEr Kora, BeKuaani (Barking)

Yard: goz, goj

Yard: utaan, Angon, angon, angina

Yarn: shuTa

Yawn: aamuaani

Year: bosor, bochchor, boros

Yearn: biroho, (premikar lagi) zano kiTA Kora

Yell: cillaani

Yellow: AlDia, AlDi, AloiD, holuD, holDia

Yes: jI Ay (formal), jI (formal), Ay, aichcha

Yesterday: goToKail, geseKail, geloKail

Yet: aabo

Yield: folon Deowa, fol dhora, folon

Yob: gunda, gunda zuan, shanda

Yoga: zug shadhona, zugcorca

Yogurt: DoI

Yoke: dimor kum, dimor kushum, boiDar Kum, boiDar kushum

Yolk: zual, Baar, bUza, DashoTTo

Yonder: hOno, hObaayDi, hOUkhano, hOkhano

You: aPne (singular/formal), aPnara (plural/formal), Tumi (friendly/familiar), Tui (informal/for children that are known closely to one or between close friends)

Young: zubok, zuan

Your: aPnar/aPnarar, Tumar/TumaTanor, Tor/Turar/Tumrar

Youth: zoubon, zuani

yo-yo: ghurghuri, Io-Io

Z

Zeal: pranshoKTi

Zing: agrohozonoK, akorshonio

Zebra: zebra

Zenith: curha

Zero: shuinno/enda/ghurhar dim

Zigzag: beKatErha/aKabaKa

Zionism: ihuDibaD

Zodiac: Baiggocokro

Zone: elaKa

Zoo: cirhiakhana

Zoology: pranibiggan

Zombie: BuT, morar lakhan

Zero: shuinno, binDu, gullaa

Zest: uTTezona, uTTezonaPurno, anonDomoy, QushiBora

Zinc: DosTa

Zing: KaKaPi shobDo Kora, bonDukor BUletor shobDo, agrohozonok, zibonTo, zibonBora

Zionism: ihuDibaD, zaayonbaD (negative connotation and can not be used in a positive way). To mean of development or theology or theosophy of Judaism one should use ihuDi dhormo or ihuDi dhormobaD

Zip: zip

Zodiac: Baiggocokro

Zoom: zUm, zUm Kora. zum kheT is a particular way of farming that the peoples (tribes as Khashia) living on the hills and mountains use.

Zulu: zulu zaTi.

Zygote: zaigot, zonombinDu, gEDakush,

Subject-wise Dictionar
Sylheti-English

ami ar amar amiTTo II I and Myself

Beyond I II amar baire

My Body, Mind and Soul II amar shoril, mon ar aTTa

My Family II amar Poribar

My Numbers II amar shoingka

my questions II amar proshno

my days II amar Din

my months II amar mash

my seasons II amar rITu

my dates and times II amar Tarik o shomoy

my place my direction II amar zaaga amar DIk

my colours II amar rong

my shapes and sizes II amar aKar ar aKriTi

my opposites II amar biPoriT

my subjects II amar bishoy

my food and drink II amar khani o PaniO

sylheti fishes II sileti mas

my kitchen II amar randhaghor

my home II amar barhi

my children II amar baichchain

my emotions II amar mongoTi

my life II amar zinDegi

charity II Bala Kam

Education II shikka

Social Services II shomaz sheba bIBag

Medicine II DaKTori biggan

Housing Services II ghorbarhir bIBag

General   II shadharon

my garden II amar bagan

my society II amar shomaz

my festivals II amar uTshob

my politics II amar razniTi

my economics II amar ArToniTi

my london II amar bilaT

my england II amar inglend

my uk II amar Iuke

my sylhet II amar silet

My Bangladesh II amar banglaDesh

my europe II amar iUruP

My World II amar PrithIbi

My Universe II amar mohaDunia

God's World II allar Dunia

My Body, Mind and Soul II amar shoril, mon ar aTTa

shoril	body/health
goTor	body
shaisTo	health
shusTo	well being, health
shusToTa	well being
mon	mind
mono	in the mind
mathaa	head
mogoz	brain. mosTishko, gIlu
cul	hair
couk	eye. chouk, chukh, noyon, noyonTera
coukor PaTa	eye lid. Cokur PaTa
Buru	eye brow
coukor PuTli	pupil. cokur PuTli
coukor Pani	tear/natural water of the eyes. cokur Pani
muk	face. cEraa.
KoPal	forehead/fate/destiny/luck. ToKDir
Kan	ear
gola	neck, throat. golar BiTTor
KanYD	shoulder
bUYk	chest/breast as in when a mother feed the Baby from her breast
bUni	breast. sthon
camrha	skin
aT	hand/arm
aTor PaTa	palm
angul	finger
nOuk	nail
Kobzi	wrist
Koni	elbow
PIt	back
Komor	hip
Paow	leg
Paor PaTa	foot
Paor angul	toes
atu	knee
ghurhali	ankle

zurha	joint
haddi/aaddi	bone
meruDondo	backbone
roKTo	blood. loU
bukor Pinjira	ribcage
angot /Pinzor	skeleton
Purushango	Pennis(non sexual description)
Boga	Pennis (sexual description and can be very offensive and should not be used in social forums)
sTriOngo	Vegina (non sexual description)
PUnD	Vegina (sexual description and can be very offensive and should not be used in social forums)
aTTa	soul
aTTar	of the soul
manoshik	mental/emotional. manushik, monor BiTror

My Family II amar Poribar

Poribar	family
ma	mother
baP	father
amma/ammu/mai/maizi/ ma	mummy
abba/abbu/abbi/baba/ baP/baPzan	daddy
DaDa	paternal grand father
DaDi	paternal grand mother
nana	maternal grand father
nani	maternal grand mother
caca	paternal uncle
caci	wife of paternal uncle
fufu	paternal aunt
fufa	husband of paternal aunt
khala/mOi/khalamma	maternal aunt
khalu	husband of maternal aunt
mama/mamu	maternal uncle
mami/mamani	wife of maternal uncle
Bai	brother
Baia/Baisab	addressing to elder brothers
Boin	sister
aPa/apu/buaai	addressing to elder sisters
Pua	son/boy. sele
Purhi	daughter/girl. meye
BaiPuT/BaaTiza/ BaaTiuza	nephew (sons of one's brothers)
BaizhI	nieces (daughters one's of brothers)
BoinPuT	nephew (sons of one's sisters)
BoinzhI/Bagni	nieces (daughters of one's sisters)
Bair Bou	brother's wife
Baabi	addressing for brother's wife
naTinaTni	grandchildren
naTi	grandchild (male)
naTin	grandchildren (female)
Puar ghoror naTinaTni	grandchildren from son's
Purhir ghoror naTinaTni	grandchildren from daughters

Beai	father in laws of one's children
Beain	mother in laws of one's children
hOur	father in law
hOrhi	mother in law
PuTra	sons of one's "beai and beain"
zhIari	daughters of one's "beai and beain"
aTio/kutum	relation
roKTor kutum	blood relations
kutum	relations (social or by law)
aTioTa	in laws' relations

My Numbers II amar shoingka

0	shuinno. ghurhar dim. gullaa
1	eK
2	Dui
3	Tin
4	cair
5	Pac
6	soy
7	shaT/haaT
8	at
9	noy
10	Dosh
11	eggaro
12	baro
13	Tero
14	couDDo
15	Pondo
16	Shullo
17	shoTro
18	ataro
19	unnish
20	bish
21	ekkuish
22	baish
23	Teish
24	cobbish
25	Pochchish
26	Sabbish
27	shaTTaish
28	attaish
29	unTish
30	Tish/Tirish
31	eKTish
32	boTTish
33	TeTTish

34	couTish
35	PayTish
36	soyTish
37	sharhTish
38	atTish
39	uncallish
40	callish
41	eKcallish
42	beaallish
43	TeTallish
44	coucallish
45	Pachchallish
46	soycallish
47	shaTcallish
48	atcallish
49	unuPonchash
50	Ponchash
51	eKanno
52	baayanno
53	Teppanno
54	couanno
55	Ponchanno
56	sappanno
57	shaTanno
58	ataanno
59	unushait
60	shait
61	eKshotti
62	bashotti
63	Teshotti
64	coushotti
65	Poyshotti
66	soyshotti
67	shashotti
68	ashotti
69	unushoTToir
70	shoTToir

71	eKoTToir
72	baoTToir
73	TeoTToir
74	couoTToir
75	PosoTToir
76	sioTToir
77	shaToTToir
78	atoTToir
79	unuashi
80	ashi
81	eKashi
82	birashi
83	Tirashi
84	Courashi
85	Pocashi
86	siashi
87	shaTashi
88	atashi/Astoashi/Astashi
89	ununobboi
90	nobboi
91	eKannobboi
92	birannoi
93	Tirannobboi
94	Courannobboi
95	Pocannobboi
96	siannobboi
97	shaTannobboi
98	atannobboi
99	nirannobboi
100	eKsho
200	Duisho
300	Tinsho
500	Pacsho
1000	eK azar
2000	Dui azar
100000	eK lakh

| 1000000 | Dosh lakh |
| 10000000 | ek kuti |

my questions II amar proshno

KiTa	what
Ke	who (singular)
KeKe	who (plural)

Kegu   who (only if the person involved should be addressed as Tui)
Koi/kunkhano/kuno/
kuai/kubaay/kiano

kunnano	where
kila	how
kunDin	what/which day
kunbala	what time
kunshomoy	
kunmash	which month
kunshaPTa	which week
kunzon	which one (for people other than children)

kungu which one (if it is an object/animal or child)

KiTar Daay	what for
kiTar lagi	what for
kiTallagi	
kunta	which one (objects/animals)

my days II amar Din

shombar	Monday
mongolbar	Tuesday
budhbar	Wednesday
biroshoiTbar	Thursday
shukkurbar/zummabar	Friday
shonibar	Saturday
robibar/roibbar	Sunday
Din	Day
shoKal/Bian	Morning
shoKalibala/Bianibala	Morning Time
bikal/bIal	evening
bikalibala/bIalibala	evening time
madhan/DuiPor	midday
raiT	night

my months II amar mash

In Sylhet people would use both Bangla and English calendar and Sylhet has six seasons.

Sylheti Months

boishag/boishakh mash	First Month of the year
zoit/zet/zoisto mash	Second Month
aarh/aasharh mash	Third
haaOn mash	Fourth
BaaDo/BaaDro mash	Fifth
ashin mash	Sixth
KaTTi/KarTik mash	Seventh
Agon mash	eighth
Push/Poush mash	Ninth
Magh mash	Tenth
Falgun mash	Eleventh
coiT/coiTro mash	Twelfth

ingrezi months in Sylheti

zanoari	January
febroari/februari	February
march	March
epril	April
mE	May
jun	June
julai	July
agost	August
septembor	September
octobor	October
noBembor	November
disembor	December

my seasons II amar rITu/Kal

gormor Din	Summer
barshar/barishar/meghor Din	Monsoon
shoroTor Din	Early Autumn
hemonTor Din	Autumn
shiTor Din/EOTor Din	Winter
boshonTor Din	Spring
rITu/Din/	season
rITu	menstrual cycle as well

my dates and times II amar Tarik o shomoy

shomoy/bela/beil/bala	time
Din	day. Dibosh
raiT	night. raT
Dinor bela	day time
raiTor/raiTkur bela	night time
madhani bela/bala	noon time
Bianibela/bala	morning time
shoKalibela/bala	morning time
Tarik	date
Bosor/bochchor	year
shaPTa/haPTa	week
mash	month
Dosh bosor	Decade
eKsho bosor	century
Bala shomoy	good time
baD shomoy	bad time
eK Tarik	1st of any month
Dui Tarik	2nd
Tin Tarik	3rd and so on
aiz	today
aizku	(on) today
aizkur	(of) today
Kail	day (in both past and future)
agami Kail	tomorrow
goTo Kail	yesterday
Porshu	day after/before
goTo Porshu	day before yesterday
agami Porshu	day after tomorrow
IDaning	recently
ghonta	hour
minit	minute
sekend	second
eKta	one o'clock

Duita	two o'clock
Tinta	three o'clock
cairta	four o'clock and so on
Derhta/Detta	half past one
arhaita	half past two
sharhe Tinta	half past three and like so in all the other half past hours
shoa eKta	quarter past one and like so in all the other quarter past hours
Pone eKta	quarter to one and like so in all the Other quarter to
maz raiT	midnight
Din nai raiT nai	to mean there is no respect for routine time
uDan nai madhan nai	to mean there is no respect for routine or time
ebla/ekhon	now
hebla/Tokhon	than

my place my direction II amar zaaga amar DIk

Ino/ono/okhano/Ikano	here
hIno/hono/hokhano/hIkano	there
kunkhano/Kunano/kuai/kubai	where
obay/obayDi/Ibay/IbayDi	this way
hobay/hobayDi/hIbay/hIbayDi	that way
Dain	right
Daine	on the right
DaineDi	towards the right
bau/bam	left
bauE	on the left
bauEDi	towards the left
uPor	up
uPre	when something is on the up
uPreDi	upward
Tol/nic	bellow/bottom
Tole/nice	under/beneath
ToleDi/niceDi	downhill/downward
shamna	front
shamne	in front
shamneDi	towards the front
Kor/Pic	back
Kore/Pice	at the back
KoreDi/PiceDi	towards the back
uTTor	north
uTTre	in the north
uTToreDi/uTTomuka	towards north
Dokkin	south
Dokne	in the south
DoKneDi/Dokinmuka	towards south
Pub	east
Pube	in the east
PubeDi/Pubmuka	towards east
Pocim	west
Poicme	in the west
PoicmeDi/Pocimmuka	towards west

KanDaT	near
KanDabaayDi	quite close by
Dur	far
Duroi	far
Duroir	from far
nIkot	near
nIkote	situated near by
shuza	straight
beKa/Terha	not staright/bent
ghura	turn round

my colours II amar rong

rong	colour. borno
rongdhonnuk	rainbow
beguni/baingoni	purple
nil/nilua/lilua	blue
ashmani	turquoise
Kocua/shobuz	green
Oloid/OlDia	yellow
Komla	orange
lal	red
matia rong/khaki	grey
baDami	brown
gulabi/gulapi	pink/rose
dhola/shaDa	white
Kala	black
ruPali	silver
shunali/shuna rong	gold

my shapes and sizes II amar aKar ar aKriTi

aKar	size
aKriTi	shape
binDu	dot
shuza lain/rekha	straight line
beKa lain	curved line
TirBUz/Tinkuni	triangle
cairkuni	rectangle
gulaKar/briTTo	round/circle
borho	big
sUto/huru/kuti/kutimuti	small
mazari	medium
Packuni	pentagon
Soykuni	hexagon
atkuni	octagon
goBir	deep
AgoBir	shallow
beshi	more
Kom/Turha	little
aro beshi	little more
aro Kom	little less
ayoTon	area
goBiroTa	volume
muillo	value
PaTro	container

my opposites II amar biPoriT

Din (day)	raiT (night)
shoKal (morning)	biKal (evening)
halka/PaTla (light)	Baari (heavy)
uPor (up)	nic (down)
ashman (sky)	zomin (land)
thama (stop)	cola (move)
dain (right)	bau (left)
Pub (east)	Pocim (west)
Dokkin (south)	uTTor (north)
alomoy (lit)	andhair (dark)
ghum (sleep)	hozag (awake)
dhola (white)	Kala (black)
tenga (sour)	mita (sweet)
TiTTa (bitter)	mita (sweet)
Biza (wet)	hukna (dry)
nari (woman)	Purush (man)
beta manush (man)	beti manush (woman)
Pua (boy)	Purhi (girl)
megh (cloudy/rainy)	roiD (sunny)
Qula (open)	bondho (closed)
ashaa (laugh)	KanDa (cry)
KanYDaT (near)	Duroi (distant)
maatha (speak)	namaatha (not speaking)
Qushi (happy)	bezar (sad)
besTo (busy)	Alosh (lazy)

my subjects II amar bishoy

BashabiDDa	linguistics
Angko	mathematics
ITiaash	history
Bugol	geography
shilpo	art
Basha	language
gan	songs/music
razniTi biggan	political science
shomaz biggan	social science
PouroniTi	civics
ain	law
shongbiDan	constitution
biggan	science
zamiTi	geometry
Pati goniT	arithmetic
elzabra	Algebra
PoDarTo biggan	physics
roshayon biggan	chemistry
shaiTTo	literature
KobiTa	poetry
golPo/kichcha	story
kichchakahini	novel
natoK	play
huru golPo	shortstory
TiTna golPo	microstory
mazari kahini	novella
ArToniTi	Economics
borhoDristi ArToniTi	Macro Economics
TiTkinaDristi ArToniTi	Micro Economics

my food and drink II amar khani o PaniO

khani/	food
khaibar zinish/	
khaowar zinish	
PaniO	drink
Pani	water
BaT	cooked rice
caYul	rice
dhan	paddy
mas	fish
hUtki/shUtki	dry fish
shagshobzi	vegetables
shag/haag	spinach
saalom/TorKari	curry
TorKari	vegetable added to the curry
Baazi	dry vegetable dishes
caaTni	a dry dish made of fish/dry fish/vegetable
tenga	sour dishes
zhaal	hot
mita	sweet
TiTTa	sour
Uri	green beans
Uri bici	beans
moric	chilli
Kaca moric	green chilli
hukna moric	dry chilli
PaKna moric	ripe chilli
somosa	samosa
denga	a vegetable. data
laiPaTa	mustard leaf
lai	mustard
lubi/lubi Uri	long green beans
Kola	banana
boroi	sour berry
Komla	orange
belPoi/zolPoi	olive
ayfol/apol/apel	apple
am	mango

KoYfol/Koyfol	papaya
shoPri	guava
nairhkol	coconut
bel	a hard shelled fruit that has yellow creamy soft fruit inside
Tal	palm fruit
KaYtol	jackfruit
loTa	a green root vegetable
muki	muki, a root vegetable
tometu/bilaTi baingon	tomato
baingon	aubergine
mula	muli, a white root vegetable
Kaac Kola	green banana eaten as vegetable
PaKna Kola	ripe banana
lEcu	lychee
mangsho/gusT	meat
gurur manghso	beef
murgor mangsho	chicken
sagolor mangsho	goat meat
khoshir/khashir mangsho	goat meat (from he goat)
Paatar mangsho	goat meat (from un castrated he goat)
nasTa	breakfast
madhanor khani	lunch/food eaten at lunch time
raiTkur khani	supper
caYPani	tea and snacks
shuPari	beetle nuts and Pan eaten with "cun"
cun/cuna	soft paste of lime stone used with beetle nuts and Pan
mula	raddish
muki/muki alu/Biki/Biki alu	A potatoe like vegetable except it is sticky when cooked

sylheti fishes II sileti mas

rou mas	
gual/bual mas	
ilish/ilisha mas	
gozar mas	
baUsh mash	
cITol mas	
Kangla mas	
Baag mas	
KOi mas	
GuTum/buTum mas	
ceng mas	
PUti mas	
tEngra mas	
hIngi/shingi/shing mas	
magur mas	cat fish
Darhkina/TiTna/TiTkina mas	
Pona mas	
hUga/caPila mas	
BEDa/BErha mas	
shutki/hutki	dry fish
chingrhi/Isa mas	pranws
golDa chingri	king prawns

my kitchen II amar randhaghor

randhuni	female cook in the family kitchen
randhra	male cook in the family kitchen
baburci	chef at a restaurant or a wedding
randha	to cook
degdeKci	cooking utensils
deg/haandi	saucepan
TaYowa	frying pan
caYmoc	spoon
sUri	knife
aDaa	ginger
OloiD	turmeric
roUn/roshun	garlic
Piaz	onion
moshla	spice
dhonia	coriander
bakhor	coriander seeds
dhoniPaTa	coriander leaf
zira	cumin
moric	chilli
gorom moshla	garam massalla
dailcini	cinnamon
elaci	cardamom
TezPaTa	bay leaf
lobong	long

(gorom moshala refers to all these items together: dailcini, elaci, lobong and TezPaTa)

gelash/glash/gollash	glass
kaP	cup
mog	mugg
zog	jugg
borTon/thala/thali/pleit	plate
bati	bowl
kula	a bamboo made item used to prepare rice
cain	sieve
Tel	oil

| dhowa | to wash |
| baca | to prepare items off undesired objects |

my home II amar barhi

barhi	home
ghor	house/flat
ghor barhi	house/household
Poribar	family/household
PoyPoribar	family/relations/household
Kamra/kutaa	room
ghumanir kutaa	bed room
Paykhana/toilet	toilet
gUsolor ghor/gUslor ghor	bathroom
Dorza	door
Qirhki/zanala/zanla	window
karPet/galica	carpet
rag	rug
PaYpush	mat
Palong	bedframe
bicna	bed
balish	pillow
razai	duvet
Kaatha	thin blanket
bicnar caDDor	bed cover
balishor usher	pillow cover
tebul	table
cheYar	chair
khat	tool
sufa	sofa
boibar ghor	living room
saf Kora	tidy up

my children II amar baichchain

baichchain/huruTa/	
huruTain/	
huruTamuruTa/	
baichchaKaichacha/	
baichchaKaichchain/	
huruTamuruTain	children
baichcha/masum/firishTa/	
bEbuz	child
geDa/bEbi/DUDor baichcha	baby
DUD	milk
mar DUD/bukor DUD	breast mil
buTolor DUD	bottle milk
gorur DUD	cow milk
Paudaror DUD	Powder milk
khelna	toys
Pala	to care/look after
rakha	to keep a baby
kul/	hold a baby in one's arm/lap
kulo rakha/	
kulo lowa/kulo Tula	
agaa	to pooh
muTa	to urinate
agaa muTa	both pooh and urination
mocoi/bocoi	a baby boy's willy
ghum Parhani	to put a baby to sleep
KanDani	to make a bay cry, not deliberately but for lack of experience
shorom	a baby girl's female organ
aamkhoirh Deowa	a baby crawling
Ubani	when a baby stands up
boa	when a baby sit up

muko BaT Deowa	to start feeding baby rice and or solid food
Pua	boy
Purhi	girl
PuTul	doll
nePi	nappy
oshUD	medicine
TaP	fever
shorDi	flu
tanda laga/baTash laga	getting a cold
ghoBoboTi	pregnant
baichcha Awa	having a baby
baichcha Pala	to raise a baby
atani	to walk a baby
khelani	to help a baby play

my emotions II amar mongoTi

Bala laga	to feel good
BaD laga	to feel bad/sick
Mon Banga	broken mind
mono aghaT laga	mind taking a hit/sever hurt
Dukko	sadness
DukkiTo	sorry
Dukki	one that is unhappy
KoPalpurha	unlucky
shuk	happiness
Qushi	happiness/joys/pleasure
annonDo	happiness/joy
aashi Qushi	happy
Qushibashi	happy
AnuBob	feelings
AnuBuTi	feelings
shel khaowa	getting severely hurt in one's being
shel laga	getting severely hurt in one's being
shul Aowa	getting severely hurt in one's being
shul khaowa	getting severely hurt in one's being
shunDor laga	something appearing beautiful/looking beautiful
bezar	unhappy
bezar Aowa	to become sad
biroKTo Aowa	to become bored/distraught
biroKTi laga	to feel bored/distraught
heran laga	to become tired
heran Aowa	to become tired
maya	love
maya Kora	to love
maya zonma	love being created
maya momoTa	lovin and affection
Balabasha	love
Balobasha	love
ghInna	hate/hatred
ghinPiT	sense of disgust
TIk	right
TIk laga	feeling alright/okay
ghInna laga	feeling a sense of disgust/hatred

my life II amar zinDegi/zibon

zibon/zinDegani/zinDegi	life
hayaaT	life span/total length of one's life
hayaaT Purhai zaowa	reaching the end of one's life
hayaaT barhi zaowa	one life's getting longer
hayaaT barha	one's life's getting longer
hayaaT Koma	one's life getting shorter
zonom	birth
zonom lowa	being born
zonom mati	one's place of birth/ one's country
zibon cinTa/	
gianshadhona	philosophy (thinking about life/quest for wisdom and knowledge)
mora/mriTTu/moiOT	death
morar duaro kharhani	standing at the door of death
baca	to live
dhormo	religion
allaakhoDa Kora/	spending time in deeds of Allah (God)
dhormoKormo Kora	
bonDegi	living a life on the path of God
bonDa/banDa	one devoted to Allah/belonging to Allah (man)
bonDi/banDi	one devoted to Allah/belonging to Allah (woman)
Bala Kam Kora	to do good deeds
BaD Kam Kora	bad deeds
PaP/gUna	sin/bad deeds
soaab	rewards for good deeds/good deeds
soaabor Kam	good deeds
Bala Kora	doing good
cinTa	thinking
DushcinTa	worry
Proshno/soaal	question
uTTor/zuab	answer
proshno Kora	to ask questions
mani	meaning
zuKTi	logic
zuKTi Torko	debating
alocona	discussion
man shomman	honour

izzoT	honour
ashman	sky/heaven
zomin	land

charity II Bala Kam

Bala Kam	good deeds/ acts of kindness/acts for common good
Dan	giving to charity
Dan Kora	to give to charity
lilla	giving to charity
lilla Deowa	to give to charity
zoKaT	giving to charity
zoKaT Deowa	to give to charity
lilla zoKaT	giving to charity
sanDa Deowa	to give to organisations for charity
sanDa Tula	to raise funds for charity
Dan Dokkina	giving to charitable purposes
Danshil/Danbir	benevolent/givig person
DaTa	one who gives to charity
Doyaban	kind one
Doyashil	kind one
dhormobir	kind one/righteous one
shaijjo	help
shaijjo Kora	help
biPoDgrosTo/ biPoDaPonno	destitute
gorib	poor
eTim	orphan
eTim esir	orphans
bidhoba	widow
Acol	disabled
andha	blind
buba	dumb
kala	deaf
aTur	limbless
niruPaay	helpless
Ashohaay	helpless
BiKari/Bikkuk	beggar
AshikkiTo	uneducated (lacking education)
Kormo	deeds/good deeds/bad deeds/Karma

Education II shikka

shikka	education
gian laB Kora	to gain an education/to tain knowledge
shikkiTo	educated
shikkok/mastor	male teacher
shikkika/mastorni	female teacher
ishkul/skul	school
kolej/mohabiDDaloy	college
inibarsiti/bishshobiDDaloy	university
maDrasha/moDorsa	religious school
moKTob	village religious school
mosjiD/mosiD	mosque
monDir	temple
girza	church
Pegoda	Pagoda
beTon	salary
beTon	school fees for students to pay
shikka bosor	academic year
Porikka	examination/test
porshoPoTro	question paper
uTTor PoTro	answer paper
Porikkok	examiner/invigilator
klaas	class (as in a class is taking place)
shreni/Bag	class (as in class of 2007 or class A)
shreni shikkok	class teacher
prodhan shikkok/hEd mastor	headteacher
uPoprodhan shikkok	deputy head
bishoy	subject
shikkagoTo unnoTi	educational progress/educational advancement
shikka bIBag	education department
shikka monTronaloy	education secretariat
shikka monTri	education secretary/minister
shikka shongkranTo/bishoyok	educational
shikka shochib	education secretary (the most senior head of the department of education who is a civil servant and not a politician, like a permanent under secretary in the UK)
shikkar man	quality of education
Porikkar fol	results of exams
faash	Pass
feil	fail

faash Kora	to pass
feil Kora	to fail
faashor aar/haar	pass rate
feilor aar/haar	fail rate
nari shikka	educating the female population
saaTro	student
saaTri	female students
saaTrosaaTri	students
Kotin	hard
shuza	easy
Paat/lesson	lesson
Paat Porikolpona	lesson plan
DorKari/proyojon	important
DorKar/proyojoniO	need
bishesh DorKar/proyojon	sepecial need
bishesh shikkagoTo proyojon	special educational need
bishesh shaijjo	special help (as in provided by a special need teacher)
maPa	to measure/assess
maPia Dekha	to assess
mark	marks
aggrogoTi/unnoTi	progress
AbonoTi	falling behind
shomoboyoshi	peers
shikkamuloK	educational
shikka bishoyok/	
shikka shongkranTo	of education or about education

Medicine II daKTori biggan

Medicine (Medical Science)   daKTori sasro, daKTori sasTro, daKTori

	biggan, cikiTshabiggan
Medicine (Drugs)	oushoD, oshuD, Duai
Pharmacy	oushoDbiggan
Anatomy	Angogoton biggan, enatomi
Pysiology	shorilkriTibiggan, fizioloji
Ilness	bemar, Ashuk, AshusToTa, bemar azar, shoril kharaP
Symptom	lokkon
Pain	beDna, bIsh, bEthaa, Kosto
Infection	Poca dhora, Pocon, infekshon
Anitbiotic	aTTorokkamulok proTirudhok, entibaiotik
Antibody	aTTorokkamulok proTirudhok zinish, entibodi
Allergy	shoriror maze roshaonik proTikria, elarji, baath
Breathing difficulty	shash Kosto, shash niTe Kosto
Asthma	shash Kosto, hafani
Fever	zor, TaP
Flu	shorDi, shorDi zor, flu
Eczema	cormorug, camrharug
Accident and Emergency	Durghotona o zorui BIbag
Caesarean	Pet Katia baichcha bar Kora, sizarian, sizarian opareshon

Nose, ear and throat	nak, Kan o gola
Chest pain	bukur beDna, bukuT beDna, bukuT bIsh, bukur bIsh
Constipation	Paykhana Koshan, Koshan Paykhana
Hard Stool	shoKTo Paykhana
Bleeding	roKTo Porha, roKTo bar Aowa, roKTo zhora
Vomiting blood	roKTo bomi Kora
Vomiting	bomi Kora
Nausea	bomi bomi Kora, bomir Bab
Morning sickness	shoKalibalakur bomi Kora, Bianibala bomi Kora/bomi bomi Kora
Dizzy/dizzying	mathaa ghurani, mathaaT ghurani, mathaaT cokkor Deowa, mathaay cokkor Deowa, mathaa ghura, mathaa ghurghur Kora, mathaa ghurani
Blood pressure	roKTo caP, roKTor cap, roKTor peshar, roKTor preshar, blad peshar, blad preshar
Weight	uzon
Weigh	uzon Kora
Body Mass Index (BMI)	shorilor uzon o uchchoTar anuPaTik shoingka, bodimas indeks
Xray	eksre
To exray	eksre Kora
Pulse	narhi, pals

Cystolic	uPormuki riDcap
Diastolic	nicmuki redcap
Heart	zanor kuta, riTPindo, riDoy (the metaphorical heart not the one surgeons hold in their hands!)
Attria	zanor Doyokuta, zanor DoyoAlinDo
Left Attrium	baUor zanor kuta
Righ Attrium	dainor zanor kuta
Left Ventricle	baUor nicor zanor kuta
Right Ventricle	dainor nicor zanor kuta
Cardiac	zanor kuta bishoyok, zanorkutar beaPar
Cardiology	zanorkutar biggan
Heart disease	riTPindor bemar, zanor kutar bemar
Heart beat	zanor kutar KaP, zanor kutar KaPa/dhorhKani, riDkompon
Blood circulation	roKTo colacol, loU colacol
Blood Circulatotry System	roKTo colacolor bebosTa/PoDDoTi
Blood clot	roKTo ghaari, ghono Ai zaowa, roKTo Acol Ai zaowa, roKTo Kala Ai zaowa
Blood thickening	roKTo ghono Aowa, loU ghono Aowa
Kidney	Kolja, Kolija, kidni
Lung	fushfush, laang
Examination	Porikka

To examine	Porikka Kora, rugi Dekha
To see a patient	rugi Dekha
Test	Porikka, test
Tablet	gulli, borhi,tablet
Capsule	kepshul, kepsul
Caplet	lomba/lamba tablet, kepshulor lakhan tablet
Liquid medicine	Torol/PaTla oshuD/oushoD
Solid medicine	shoKTo oushoD (Migh mean hard medicine meaning powerful)
To take medicine	oushoD khaowa
To take tabets	tablet/gulli khaowa
Psychitry	monorug cikiTsha shasro
Psychitrist	monorug bisheshoggo, monorug cikiTshok
Psychology	monor biggan, monobiggan
Psychologist	monosTaTTik, monosToTTobiD, monor bisheshoggo
Psychoanalysis	monobishleshonmulok manushik rugor cikiTshar eK PonTa ba Poth, psychoanalysis.
Psychosis	monorBangon, mornor poripurno Bangon, monorBumidhosh, psychosis
Nurse	shebaDanKari
Female nurse	shebika, nars, sistar
Male nurse	shebok, shebaDanKari, nars

Psychitric nurse	monorug bishoyok bisheshoggo nars
Gynocology	mohila shaisTo/rug bishoyok daKTori biggan, gaini, gainokoloji
Period pain	riTur bIsh, riTur logor beDna
Stomach pain	Peto bIsh, Petor bIsh, Petor beDna
Eye pain	cokur/cokuT bIsh
Headache	matha bIsh/ mathaaT/mathaar bIsh, mathaaT dhora, mathaa dhora
Muscle pain	manghoPeshiT beDna, mangshoT beDna
Hurting	beDna Korer, Kosto Ar
Back ache	PitiT Bish, Pito bIsh
Pain in the bone	haddiT beDna, haddiT bIsh
Depression	manushik AboshaD/klanTi, manushik AboshaDgrosToTa, monBanga, Bangamon, dipreshon
Mental illness	manushik AshusToTa
Insanity	Paglami
Insane	Pagol, mathaaT Duish, mathaaT Duish dhora Mathaa nosto Ai zoawa, unmaDona
Mad	Pagol, unmaD
Abolutely insane	boDDo unmaD, boDDo Pagol
To treat	oushuD Kora

Operation	AsroPocar, AsroPacar, opareshon
Operate	AsroPacar/ AsroPacar Kora, opareshon Kora
Course of medication	oushuDor eKta kours, nirDisto Kalor lagia oushoD

Social Services II shomaz sheba bIBag

soshal sarvis	social service
shomaz sheba biBag	Social Serivce Department
shomaz sheba	to serve the society
zhUki	risk
biPoD	danger
zhUkiPurnno	fraught with risk/danger
biPoDzonok	fraught with danger
zhUkir muko	at risk/facing risk
biPoDor muko	in face of danger
baichcha	child
Pua	boy
Purhi	girl
gEDa/bEibi	baby
Abohela	neglect
Durbeboar Kora	mistreatment
sEY seY Dur Dur Kora	active contempt and mal treatment of someone (a child)
dhOrshon/bOD Kam/ baD Kam/haram Kam PaPor Kam/gunar Kam	to rape
dhOrshon Kora/bOD Kam Kora/ baD Kam Kora/haram Kam Kora/ gUnar Kam Kora	rape
rape victim	bOD Kamor/dhOrshonor shikar
ATTacar	abuse
manushik ATTacar	emotional abuse
haram Kam/bOD Kamor ATTacar	sexual abuse
kUKam Kora	acts of sexual nature/rape/ulawful intercourse
PaloK ma	foster/adoptive mother
PaloK baP	foster/adoptive mother
PaloK ma baP	foster/adoptive parents
PalKa Deowa	to let a child be adopted or fostered
PalKa Purhi	adoptive/fostered daughter
PalKa Pua	adoptive/fostered son

(Sylheti does not differentiate between fostering and adopting. However, in case one to be made, legal, may be added before the adoption word in Sylheti to signify the legal status.)

PaloK rakha	fostering
aingoToBabe PaloK rakha	adoption

PaloK Deowa	to give a child to foster parents
aingoTo Babe PaloK Deowa	to give a child to adoptive parents
zoruri	emergency
kout odar/aDesh	court order
ukil	solicitor
nars/shebika	nurse
shomaz sheba kormi	social worker
keis	case (as in a case is being dealt with by a social worker)
mamla/keis	But if a case is at court it is a court case (there case would mean mamla)
mamla moKoDDoma	fighting at court
shohozugiTa	co-operation
shoBa/miting	conference/meeting
keisor shoBa/miting	case conference
mullayon	assessment
bemar	illness
sharorilor AKKomoTa	physical disability
manushik AKKomoTa	emotional/mental disability
mathaar AKKomoTa	nurological disability
DaKTor	doctor

Housing Services II ghorbarhir bIBag

haUzing	Housing

haUzing sarbis/	Housing Service
ghorbarhirh bIBag	
ghor	house
barhi	house
ghorbarhi	house
barhighor	house
barhi	household
Poribar	family
folat/felat/flat	flat/apartment
bashabarhi	a townhouse
basha	townhouse
Barha/rent	rent
APekka Kor/baarh caowa	wait on the waiting list
OaIting list/baarh caowar Talika	waiting list
Ubani	waiting
hoUzing ofish	housing office
haUzing ofisar	housing officer
Barha baarha	rent increase
Barha Koma	rent decrease
huUzing benifit	housing benefit
kaunsil teks benifit	countax benefit
mEramoT	repair
mEramoT Kora	to do repair work
Pani Porha	leaking
dEmp/BIza BIza Aowa/	damp
fEKna Porha/fEKna uta	
Banga	broken
Dorza Banga	broken door
Khirhki/zanala Banga	broken window
sink	sink
gusholor ghor/gushokhana	bathroom
Paykhana/toilet	toilet
ghumor kuta	bedroom
Boibar kuta	sitting room
randhar kuta/randhar ghor	kitchen
APekka Kora	to wait
Barha Deowa	to let out a house/flat/accommodation
Barha neowa/lowa	to rent a house/flat/accommodation
ghor/barhi/flat kina/lowa	to buy a house/flat/property
zomizoma	property (land)

barhighor	property (houses/flats etc)
Dam	price
morgeiz	mortgage
shuD	interest
shuDor aar/haar	interest rate
esteit egent	estate agent
ghoror malik	landlord
Par owa	to move in
Kam Korani	to get work done to a property
citi lekha	to write a letter
citi Deowa	to send/write a letter
ghor DekhaT aowa	to come to visit the house (by a housing officer)
BIrh Koria thaKa	over crowded

General II shadharon

shadharon	general

shadharonoTo	generally
ikta	this one
aik	joint
PUli	room
FUla	to swell up/ fuming with annoyance
FUli zaowa	to swell up with anger/annoyance
POI	ridde
TUTa	parrot
thUTa	chin
thUTa Kora	to argue (by a woman with her family members
Kaya	body
KaY KaY	crowing
KaY KaY Kora	Crowing
Kano/keano/Kiano/	
Kunkhano/Kunano	where
Ika	hiccup
Ika uta	to hiccup
oli	saintly/godly person/people
allaar oli	godly person
Ke	who
Ker/Kar	whose
Iaallaa	oh my God!
tUt	lip
nim	no/not
nimraza	expressing consent by silence
nimaTra	one that does not speak
nimu	(I) will take
nimi/nibi zaowa	the light to go off
nimoK	salk
nimoK haram	someone who betrays a close relation
hIla/Ilaa	to move
Kala	black/deaf
ein/en	he/she
nun	salk
Paal	sail
PaTla	light
Bala	good
Koi	where
KOi	Kai fish
khOi	fuffy rice

nein	(aPne) nein: you take
shisha	steel
shish	rice stem
shIsh	whistle (with one's mouth)
shIsh Deowa	to whistle (with one's mouth)
hUisol bazani	to whistle
alTa	footstick (if there is such a thing to colour the female feet!!!)
mEl	gathering
melaa	fete
mElaa	too much/a lot
mEua	the centre
mUs	moutache
musa	to wipe
mosa	lunch/packed lunch for a farmer
musai laowa	to delete/to wipe out
ta	the
muTra	a bamboo like plant which is used to make mats
mUTa	to urinate
mUTani	to help a child/elderly/disabled person urinate
kun	which one
kunta	which one
kUna	corner/angle
kuinguin	which ones
kunInouka	the nail that digs into the flesh
kunTa	something
kunTa naay	nothing
kun bala	what time
kun shomoy	what time
kun Din	what day
kun Tarik	what date
kunakuni	diagonal
shiTa/hITa Parha	to part one's hair
shiTan/hITan	the place where one places one's pillow on the bed
seY SeY Kora/ SeY SeY Dur Dur Kora	to show disrespect/contempt
sIta	a blob/spot
sIta Porha	to get a blob on pain on your shirt
sItani/ sItai laowa/Deowa	to spread the seeds in the field

sItkari	the inside door locker
sItkari	a weapon to hunt birds/squirrels
lama	low land/to take something down
lamani	to get something down
lamba	long
lamba maatha/	
lamba lamba maatha	to tell tales (unbelievable showing off)/telling porkies
lomba	long
mIta	sweet
mItaai	sweets
misti	sweet
mati	ground/earth/soil
mati Deowa	to burry
moiOT mati	funeral
miTa	friend
miTali	friendship
miTali PaaTa	to make friend
Tula	to pick
Tuli laowa	to finish picking up
Tula khaowa	to get easily fed/easy life
Tula khaowani	to feed a baby commercially made food/drink
Tulani	to get someone pick something
Tulshi gash	the famous Tushi Plant that the Hindus used for their dusk prayer
Tulshi Tola	the place in front of a Tulshi Plant/ sacred place to Hindus
ToUli	towel
Tol	bottom
Tole	in the the bottom
he	he (Tui)
hEY	yes (answering yes informally
Kubai/Kuai	where
Kumir/Kumbir	crocodile
ana	to bring/a banglaDeshi penny (Poysha)
ani	(I) bring
kUm	egg yolk
kUmkUm	shining
kumrha	a vegetable
kumar	a pottery maker
kumari	a young woman (unmarried)

makha	to make dough
makhani	to make a paste/to mix (the salad)
mEki	something that is a show/lie
mEKa	rice that has gone too soft in cooking/soft
maKal	fool/naïve
maKali Kora	to act foolishly/like a naïve
maKal fol	anything that is worthless/unusable
meksi	a maxi
amona/bemona	unmindful
amon	a type of paddy
mona	dear child
moyna	myna bird
muta	big/fat
muta mathaa	big head/ a show off/ one suffering from low or vulgar taste
maana	to obey or show respect
maainnogoinno	respectable
maainnogoinno Kora	to show respect
mukam	a shrine of a godly person
moKoDoma	to lodge a case at a court
uciT	righteous/ought to be done
UcaY	high
Uzan	higher end of a river/highland
nice	below
sana	to make a mess
sani laowa	to make a mess (a child may do it on his plate)
gusT	meat
gUsa	anger/annoyance
gUsa Kora	to get angry
shangoPango	partners in crime
gusaa	a set of keys/ a set of churees (that women wear on their hand)
gusi	a set of key
hEi	oi (calling a close friend)
rOwa	to stay
rUa	to plant rice plants/to sow
roiD	sun light/sunny day
Una Deowa	to boil something/the process in which paddy is boiled to make dry boiled rice
Una caUl	boiled rice (uncooked)

Una BaT	boiled rice
alaa	the paddy that has not been boiled
alaa caUl	the rice that had not been boiled
aalna	a furniture item to hang clothes
aali	rice plants
alI	a small housebound chameleon
aail	the raised border between two pieces of a field
silan/sinal	a woman with bad social reputation/ slut
silani/sinali Kora	to get engaged in being a slut
shinan Kora	to take a bath (a Hindu would sue this word)
Tana Tana	worn out state
Tana Aowa	to get worn out/ extremely exausted
Tain	he/she (aPne)
tana	to pull
tanani	to get someone pull something
tania	having pulled
tanaa Deowa	to walk fast
tanaa Dia maatha	to speak in a funny way
Tin	three
haKa	to shout
haUkani	to shout
hOK	right/truth
hokkani beaPar	godly matter
hOKor Kotha	the truth
ki	what/which
aaK	scribble
aaKa	to draw/paint (by a child)
aaKaaki Kora	to scribble
aKal	famine/bad time
aKal Porha	famine to come
aKama/beKama	worthless/useless/pointless
aKam Kora	to do something bad
beKama Kam Kora	to do something worthless/ of no merit
bekar	unemployed/for no reason/in vain
bekaroTTo	unemployment
PuTa	to press something in the ground/ the place where a house is built
PuT	child

PuTra	a father/mother of someone married to Mr Paignton's daughter would call brothers of the daughter in law PuTra and her all sisters are to be called zhIari.
Puthi	a story/an epic/a book
Poth	path/road/street
Pothua	one that is born of no origin/lacking identity/it is a swear words (might allude to being a bastard)/low quality human being
PorU/Porshu	day after tomorrow
Por	one that is not your own relation
aarIPori	neighbour
Pia khaowa	to drink
PinDa	to wear
khanaPina	food/the act of eating and drinking
nen/nein	(aPne) nen/nein
neowa	to take
unDal	kitchen
UnDa owa	to lower one's head to look down
uthan Kora	a child to be naughty/being difficult
UDan maadhan	no sense of time/no respect to time/routine
uDdhar	rescue
uDdhar Kora	to rescue
unnish	19
nisha	night/dark
nIn	deep
nica	low
shara	all/everything
shara	to finish/complete doing something
sarha	to let go/to divorce
shaDa	white
shaDaa	dry tobacco leaf
shaadha/haadha	to make repeated request (particularly when one is guilty to the person: a guilty husband might do that to a wife)
shadhona	quest/resoluteness/resolve
shadhona Kora	to keep at something with deep resolve
shaUD/shadhu	a good person
saaT	roof
saTaani	to harass
saTaowra	one that harasses

sataani khaowa	to be at the receiving end of harassment
saTu	powder
saTu Kora	to make something into powder
saaowa	to fix one's roof
caowa	to look
caUl	rice
ruP	beauty
ruPoboTi	beautiful young woman
ruPali	silver
Pisha	to make a paste of something
Pisla	slippery
Pic	back/behind
lePa	to paint with earth one's floor in a village hut
lePaPuca Kora	to tidy up/house work
lePaPa DurusTo	one who appears like a neat and tidy as in their life was about appearance/too fashion conscious
Poylowan	a wrestler/body builder/ muscleman
Poyla	at first
KanDa	to cry
KanDani	to cause someone cry
KanDa	near
KanDaT	at the nearside
Den Dorbar	quarrel/issues
Den Dorba Kora	to quarrel
Dena	money owed
nur	light
allaar nur	God's light
ner	(hE) ner
nera	hay in the field after the paddy has been cut out
narha/larha	to stir/shake
narhani/larhani	to shake
lara Deowa/zhara Deowa	to shake
lorha	to move
lorhani	to cause movement
Koisoin	(aPne) Koisoin
kUka	a device to catch fish in fresh water
BelKa	a device to catch fish
Belcha	shovel
sEn	disrespect

sEn Dekhani	to show disrespect/ contempt/ being bold and standing up to someone
hani Kora	to do harm
hana Deowa	to attach
hanaDar	killers (refer to the Pakistani army in the liberation war of 1971)
hanja	dusk
hanjabela/bala	dusk time
hanDa/hanDani	to get in/enter
hamani	to enter
duka	to enter
Duka	cheat
Duka Deowa	to cheat
Duk Deowa	to hurt/to cause pain/heartache
KeTli	kettle
Tai	she (Tui)
Ota	this one (thing)
OTa	this
Ola	like this
Olakhan	like this
ou	this
outa	this one (thing)
AToTa	this much
OKta	this one (thing)
kucia	eel
Qucani	picking on someone/poking
kUcani	to tighten the saare
Kocani	let the curry simmer
KocKoci Kora	missing someone badly
Kaca	unripe/inexperienced/naïve
Kola	banana
Kolla	head
Koyla	charcoal
KoPol	papaya
Kona	small/young one/little one
kuti	small/little one
kutimuti	tiny
kuti shuna	dear little one
kuta	pole
Qutaa	room

Kata/gosa	fish bones
Qula	to open
Qun	murder
Qun Kora	to murder/kill
Qun/roKTo/lOu	blood
lUa	iron
mara	to beat/to discipline/ to pretend being hard on discipline matter
mair khaowa	to get beaten up
maramari Kora	to get involved in fights
ruci	taste/desire to eat
nisTar	escape
nizor	own
niz	own
nize	own
rirala	solitude
nirai	soundless
teKa	taka
tEKa	in need/in shortage/in difficulty
tEkaT Porha	to fall in hardship/difficulty
tEla	to push
tElani	to push
tiki	a black item that is used to smoke hookah
tika	immunisation
tika Deowa	to get immunisation done
cilim	a pottery item that is used to smoke hookah
maath	speech
maatha	to speak
mathaa	head
maTal	drunk
maTali Kora	to act as drunk
maTlami Kora	to act as drunk
cUna	the soft limestone past that is used to eat beetle nuts
cunkhaP	white wash
cunkhaP Deowa	to white wash
cunari	one that sells churees
cUr	thief
cUri Kora	to steal
cUri Aowa	to get burgled
cuP	silent

cuPcaP	silently
cuP thaKa	to stay silent
sUbasub/sUbasubi	hurry
sUbe	in a hurry
sobur/sobor	patience
sobur/sobor Kora	to be patient
shuTa	thread
shuD	interest
sOla	to get mad
saalla	bad advice
saalla Deowa	to give bad advice/to encourage someone to do something bad
sola Poramish Kora	to take counsel from one's own group
sholoI	match box
solaa	bag
sOlani	to cause someone go mad (mad as in get into an out burst)
sOwa	to touch
sOwani	to let someone touch
soiTe mora	sensitive (too much)
sorha	small spring/canal
sOrha	rhyme/children's poems
shoKal	morning
soal	question
shorminDa	shy
shormila	shy
shoman	likewise/equal
shomBob	possible
shomBabona	possibility
shomadhan	solution
shomproDaay	community
shima	perimeter/limit/boundary
shimana	perimeter/limit/boundary
shamanTo	border
shamna	front
shamainno	a little
shoT	honest
shoKTo	hard
shoKTi	strength
shoki	female friend

shOi	Female friend of a female
shoI	straight
shOwa	to suffer/to bear
shOijjo Kora	to tolerate
shOijjo	tolerance
shoindha	dusk
naPiT	the hairdresser (male)
naPTami Kora	doing the job of being a hairdresser (male)
kina	to buy
kI na	whether
kinTu	but
Kau	wild berry
Kau Kau Kora	children making lot of noise
Kaua	crow
KaK	hip
KaKo lowa	to hold a baby on one's person
nic zaT	lower cast/low quality people
KaKoir/ciroin	comb
KEla	who
khaas	real/true
khaash	government property
khaasha	good/the best
khaash Kori	with great anticipation/admiration
Kashi	cough
khoshi	castrated he goat
khoshir mangsho	goat meat
KOsha	simmering a curry
Koshaa	bitter
Koboz	the metal little container for putting talisman written on paper
Kobza	hinge
Kobza Kora	to get ahead (with one's enemy)/having established an upper hand
Korzo	debt
Korzo Kora	to borrow
Korzo Deowa	to lend money
Boi	book
Boi Dekha/sinema Dekha	to watch a film in a cinema
Boi	a film
suI	need

haba	dumb/mick
BIn	other
BInno	other
Bai	brother
BaT	cooked rice
haaBaT/aBaT	hungry/poor
baaT	arthritic pain
Pur	village
Pura	all
Purani	to add
furhani	to finish
Purhani	to burn
Purha	to burn
Porha	to fall
PoYrha	to read
ukoin/ukuin	headlice
Palaa/bari	turn
PaYlani	to throw away
Palla	weighing device/ weighing machine
kIra	promise/ swear
KIra Deowa/KIra Kora/	
KIra Deowa	to promise/ swear
Qirani	milking
Qir	rice pudding
Kaasa/	near
Kaas	
Kaasani	to progress
KOcani	rinsing
Kaca	unripe
Karha	to refine the rice from the paddy
kul	bank
kUl	family/family honour/dynasty
kulli	gurgle
kulli Kora	to gurgle
kuluta/	woman who lost her honour/face/brough shame
Kolongkini	
Paas	near
Pass Deowa	to side with/ to stick by
sheT	rich/merchant
OsOsi Kora	to be impatient/to hurry

Puhani/Puaani	night ending/dawn
roiD Puaani	to sit in the sun in cold/sun bathing
aaguin thaabani	to sit by the fire
Pani	water
roKTo Pani Kora	to harass
Poca	rotten
Pocani	to let something rot
Pocami	having horrible unhealthy habbits
Pocami Kora	to not be neat and tidy
BaaDami Kora	to be scruffy
lena Dena	accounts/conducting business with
man	honour
manosh Kora	to decide upon
manushik	mental/emotional
sIr	head
cira	to saw
aPa	addressing to elder sisters
amma	mummy
hUsh/	conscieousness/ sense of dignity/honour
hUshbuDdhi	
lEaaz Tomiz	sense of proper conduct/behaviour
Elaa	neglect
Elaa Kora	to commit negligence
Elomelo	disarrayed/dysfunctional
Kaaci	sickle
aukali Kora	to create a nuisense
hUPa	husband of maternal aunt
Uh	ah!/ouch!
dEldEli	abundant
Dil	heart
DilDar	great heart
PoyDole	on foot
nioT	mental aim
Kat/lakhrhi	wood
ceYli	splinters of wood for fire
Teli	telegram
noi	river
nowa	to lower one's head to look down
maaIl	epidemic/big killer
maal	goods

shiki	a quarter of a taka
sIka	a hanging item used to hang up bottles
dail	lentil
latiaal	a hired fighter
Uli	a female cat
Ulaa	a male cat
UrI	a public cry/call for help in danger (if a village is attacked by robbers the villagers might call for help by making a huge cry for help so that other villager in the night can hear them)
urI	beans
urha	to fly
Urha	to beat up
urhaa	a basket
Porota	Paratha
taK	bold head
taKa/teKa	money
PiT	liver (animals)
Kaki	Paternal uncle's wife (a Hindu would use it)
kaka	paternal uncle (a Hindu would use it)
DiDi	addressing for sister (a Hindu would use it)
DaDa	addressing for brother (a Hindu would use it)
shian	mature young man/woman
shiana	shrewd
sIna	chest
sIna uca Koria ata	to walk with head held high/with honour
nilla	a curry with a thin sauce
lilla	for free
Paiba	(aPne) Paiba (you will get)
Paowa	to get
Pai	a penny
Kar	whose

my garden II amar bagan

bagan/bagica	garden
bagan Kora	gardening
ful	flower
gas	tree
dal	branch
PaTa	leaf
khal	skin
mul/zorh	root
ziTa	alive
mora	dead
ceYra	plant
Qurha	to dig
Pani Deowa	water
Kudal	digging item
Da	big cutting knife
ghash	grass
Kobi	cabbage/cauliflower
ful Kobi	cauliflower
bandha Kobi	cabbage
alu	potato
shag/haag	spinach
folani/holani	to grow/to plant
maali	(an employed) gardener
dhora	fruit comes out

my society II amar shomaz

shomaz	society
manush	people/society
shomaz/shomproDaay	community
goinno mainno	hornourable
goinno mainno manush	leaders/respectable people of the community
mana	to show respect to the elders
moy murobbi	leaders/elders of the community
murobbian	leaders/elders of the community
murobbi	elders/leaders of the community/family
PanchaiT/Panzegana	It is a body that leads a mosque in a village in Sylhet. This body is comprised with surrounding the management committee of a mosque where the whole congregation of the area would be natural members. It does not have formal functions or meetings as such unless extraordinary circumstances occur. This generally refers almost like a living form of society. It is one of those old direct democracy where all the members of an area are part of the running of the affairs. In the UK this word should simply mean society or community
Dosh/Doshe	this literally means ten but actually it means society. Doshe kiTa Koibo? What would the society say? (people say?)
zOmaT	the congregation of a mosque
zonom mirTu	birth and death
zonoza	the prayer before burial/ the whole service of burial
moron mati/moiOiT mati	burial
Kobor	grave
Kolima Porha	pray before one is dying
mora	to die
Koral	the coffin
mati Deowa	to bury/to place a little earth to the grave of the deceased
PoyPoricoy	known
PoyPoricoyor manush	known people
shomazor Bai	one of the community
shomazor Boin	one of the community

shoshan	grave yard for the followers of Hinduism
shoishsha	problem
agrogoTi	progress
unnoTi	progress/advancement
bekaroTTo	unemployment
bekar	unemployed
Kam	work
bebsha	business
bebshaI	business man/person
Dukan	shop
DukanDar	shopkeeper
DaKghor/Pustafish	post office
thana/Pulish steshon	police station
resturent	restaurant
Kamla	worker
ofisar	officer
neTa	leader
neTri	female leader
Dol	Party

my festivals II amar uTshob

uTshob	festival
anonDo/Qushi	happiness
ID	eid
ruzar ID	eid following Ramadan
boKra ID/Kurbanir ID	the second eid
ruza	fasting
romzan	fasting
romzan mash/ruza mash	the month of Ramadan
ruza rakha/ ruza thaKa	to fast
ifTar/isTar	the meal at the breaking of the fast
ifTar/isTar Kora	to eat after breaking the fast
isTar/ifTar parti	social gathering to break fast as a party
kurbani	the sacrifice of animal at the second eid
kurbani Deowa	to sacrifice animal
kurbani bata	to give out meat from the sacrificed animal to neighbours and relatives
noya bosor	new year
noboborshor uTsho	new year's festival
zonom Din/zonmor Din	birthday
shinni	is a feast given in memory of the dead or for other religious purposes
bia	wedding
biashaDi	wedding
bia Kora	to get married (a man getting married)
bia bOYowa	to get married (a woman getting married)
Pancini/ciniPan	an occasion before the wedding
gaE OloiD	an even when bride and bridgegroom gets a turmeric treatment by their in laws (before the wedding)
akhT	some time the religious part of the wedding is organised on a separate occasion before the social wedding gathering where actually the marriage is solemnised
bia/shaDi mubarok	the wedding
borzaTra	wedding party starting out
borzaTri	the wedding party
zamai	bridegroom
Koina/Koinna/Bou	bride

zamair Pokko	bridegroom's side
Koina Pokko	bride's side
ukil	ukil means lawyer but at a wedding someone needs to be an ukil taking the proposal of the bridegroom to the bride
shakki	witness
firazaTra	when the bride goes back to her parents after she has been to her in laws
bouBaT	the feast is offered cooked by the new bride
misti	sweet
shube boraT	the night when one's future year is given out by God
shobe KoDor	The holly night
siratunnobi	the Prophet's birthday
Puza Parbon	the pooja festivals celebrated by Hindus and others
Puza	worship
Durga Puza	the worship of goddess Durga
shoroshshoTi Puza	the worship of goddess Shorashwati
Kali Puza	the worship of goddess Kali
BouDDo Purnima	celebrated by the Buddhists
BorhoDin	Christmass
muhammed (Sallahialaisallam)	the prophet Mohammed (Rasul is the prophet with a holly book given to him)
Isa (Alaihiassallam)	Prophet Christ (Rasul is the prophet with a holly book given to him)
musa (Alaihiassallam)	Prophet Moses (Rasul is the prophet with a holly book given to him)
nuYh (Alaihiassallam)	Prophet Noah
BuDDoDev	Buddha
guru nanok	Guru Nanak
moshjiD/mosiD	mosque
sinagog	cinagauge
monDir	Temple
guruduar	gurdwara
ashmani KiTab	holly book
allaa	Allah (God)
nobi	prophet without a holly book given to him
rosul	prophets with a holly book given to him
nomaz	prayer (muslims pray five times a day)
zoKaT/zaKaT	giving to charity as a duty
hoz	going to pilgrimage to Makkah as a duty

kiTab kuran	the guidance of Allah
kuran shorif	The Holly Quran
haDis/haDisT/hoDis	Hadith comprised of sayings, doings and guidance of the prophet Muhammed

my politics II amar razniTi

razniTi	politics
nazniTi Kora	to be involved in politics
Politiks Kora	to be nasty to one/ doing dirty tricks
gonoTonTro	democracy
shonghshoD	parliament
shorKar	government
sTanio shorKar	local government
shongshoD shoDoishsho	MP
monTri	Secretary of State
uPomonTri/PoTimonTri	junior ministers
shochib	civil servant secretary
But/ilekshon	election/Polls
But Deowa	to cast one's vote
But Paowa	to get votes
zonomoT	public opinion
khobror Kagoz	newspapers
redio	radio
telivishon	television
Dol/razniTik Dol	party/political party
neTa	male leader
neTri	female leader
Desh	country
zila	district
zaTi	nation
uPozaTi	smaller/tribal nation
uPozila/thana	local county administrative district
Iunion porishoD	local administrative parish council
dainPonTi	rightwing
bamPonTi	leftwing
moiDDoPonTi	centrist
uDarPonTi	liberal
kottorPonTi	emtremist
PeshaDari razniTi	professional politics
alaP alocona	discussion
Tork biTork	debate
anDolon	movement
ArTal	strike

dhormoghot	strike
dhoni	rich/upper class
moiDDobiTTo	middle class
shromozibi	working class
raza	king
rani	queen
razkumar	prince
razkumari	princess
razTonTro	monarchy
shomazTonTro	socialism
shaimmobaD	communism
shomazniTi	policy/public policy
shaDa PoTro	white paper
shobuz PoTro	green paper
bil	bill
ain	law
ain Pash Kora	to pass a law
bicar	justice
niaay bicar	justice
niaay	fair
shomoTa/shaimmo	equality
mukTi	liberty
shadhinoTa	freedom
ainor shashon	rule of law
ainbiDDa	Jurrisprudence
ain shringkhola	public order
Pulish	Police
shena bahini	army
nou bahini	navy
biman bahini	air force
ashPaTal	hospital

my economics II amar ArToniTi

ArToniTi	economy/economics/fiscal policy
ArToniTik	financial/fiscal
ArTo	currency/money/finance
teKa	taka is the Bangladeshi currency from which Sylheti teKa. But it means taka, money, currency, finance
benk	bank
zoma	deposit
Korzo/dhar	loan/lending
Korzodhar/dharKorzo	in debt
zoma Deowa/zoma thOYowa	
zoma rakha	deposit
amanoT	deposit of faith. This is a sacred process of depositing something (not necessarily money or wealth) to someone who one has absolute trust based on simple trust and faith without any paper or documentary support to keep it safe and secure. The person taking the amanoT becomes the custodian of it with such a great religious duty of the highest nature that he ought to look aftet it and keep it exactly at the state he was given it and must ensure that it was returned safely back to the owner or their heir. This happens a great deal in Sylhet. From there banks tried to use this term as safe depositing accounts. amanoT is not a Sylheti world but it is in the soul of Sylhetis to have that much faith in people.
QianoT	If on the other hand one then fails the person depositing the amanoT he is deemed to have done the act of QianoT or betrayal of faith or trust. No one shall seek any social, legal or earthly compensation for the act of QianoT other than leaving it to God for God is deemed to take the act of QianoT terribly severely and thus no other punishment is good enough for it, althouth the society/community despises someone who does the act of QianoT which is the worst kind of social reprimand one can get!
laB	profit
khoTi	loss

laBkhoTi	profit and loss
mal	goods/commodities
caYowa	demand
kina/lowa	buying
kinabeca	buying and selling
becakina	buying and selling
Poysha	primarily means change but it means money/capital
Poysha khatani	investing capital
Poysha Deowa	to give out money
Poysha neowa	to take in money
Poysha Korhi	money/capital
Dabi	demand as in asking for money from the bank
Dabinama	demand note
inshurens	insurance
shuD	interest
shuDkur	someone who lends money to people and charges interest on it. Culturally speaking shuDkur is not viewed kindly. In fact, shuDkur is quite a derogatory swear word used in everyday day.
shuD lowa	to charge interest
shuD Deowa	to pay interest
cokrobriDDi har	the process in which the interst continues generating more interest as they are added to the loan as they accrue
DeUlia	bankruptcy
bebsha Kora	to do business
bebsha	business
bebshaI/beboshaI/bePari	businessman
bazar	market
bazar Bala	market is good
bazar baD	market is down
monDa/manDa	slow down/down turn/sluggish
DorKar	need
niraPoTTa	security
zibon bima	life insurance

my london II amar bilaT

london/bilaT	London
londoni	a Sylheti who either lives in London or anywhere in the UK
bara	boroughs
taowar hemlet	tower hamlets
hekni	hackney
niUham	newham
Pon	pound sterling
lebar/laibor	benefits/ Labour Party
Kachrha	racist/skinhead/bad people/dirty
bornobaDi/reisist	racist
tiub	tube
rel garhi	train
bas	bus

My england II amar inglend

inglend	England
bilaT	England/UK
zukToraijjo	United Kingdom
skotlend	Scotland
Ueils	Wales
inglish	the English
inglish/ingrezi/ingrez Buli	English language
manchestar	Manchester
barminggam/baringgam	Birmingham
sentalbon/ sent alban	St Alban
luton	Luton
bristol/biristol	Bristol
sandarlend	Sunderland
niU kasol	New Castle
oldam	Oldham
Kardif	Cardif
sUansi	Swansea
edinbora	Edinburgh
tems/temos noDi	The Thames

my uk II amar Iuke

zukTo raijj	United Kingdom
gonoTonTro	Democracy
amlaTonTro	Bureaucracy
prozaTonTro	Republic
razTonTro	Monarchy
shongshoDiO gonoTonTro	Parliamentary democracy
razar shashon	King's rule
ranir shashon	Queen's rule
ranir Desh	Queen's Country/United Kingdom
raza uzir	Ruling class
empi	MP
monTri	minister
proDan monTri	Prime Minister
uPo/proTi monTri	Junior Minister
shorKar	government
sTaniO shorKar	Local Government
kenDriO shorKar	central government
Pulish	Police
telifon	telephone
mobail	mobile
intarnet	internet
redio	radio
Kagoz/khobror Kagoz	newspaper

my sylhet II amar silet

Sylhet has many names!

silet
sillot
silot
silhot
shilhot
shilhat
shilahat
shrihotto
shrihat

And shoDolara offers an affectionate name for Sylhet: silara: Beautiful Sylheti.

Sylheti Language has like Sylhet has many names, too!

Sylheti: sileti
Sylhoti: siloti
Sylhotia: silotia
Sylhetia: siletia
Sylheti Zoban: Sylheti Tongue/Language
Sylheti buli: Sylheti Tongue/Language

sileti, however, is the most commonly used name of the language of Sylheti. sileti amar silara zoban.

Sylhet is an Administrative Region or Division of Bangladesh which is now referred as Greater Sylhet comprised with four districts:

Sylhet/Sylhet Central District
Moulovibazar District
Shunamgonjo District
Hobigonjo District

kenDrio silet (Central Sylhet) is comprised of these administrative units, called Upazilas (literally means sub districts) which used to be referred as thana (which means Police Station since each of these administrative unit had a Police Station in them) that we are spelling using Sylheti alphabet so that you can pronounce these names as native Sylheti speakers would:

silet shoDor, balaagonj, Bianibazar, bishshonaT (bishnaT), Kumpanigonj, fenchugonj (fEcugonj) gulaPgonj, guainghat, zoinTaPur, Kanaighat, zokigonj.

moulovibazar is comprised of borholekha (borhlekha), Komolgonj, kulaUrha, moulovibazar shoDor, raznogor, srimongol

shunamgonj is comprised of shunamgonj shoDor, saaToK, BishshomBorPur, dhIrai, dhormoPasha (dhoromPasha), Duarabazar, zogonnaTPur, jamalgonj, TahirPur, shallaa

hOBigonj is comprised of hOBigonj shoDor, azmirigonj, baniacong, bahubol, cunarughat, laakhai, nObigonj, maadhobPur

my europe II amar iUruP

iUruP/iUrUPor manush	Europe/European
mohaDesh	continent
biDesh	foreign land
diDeshi	foregner
Deshor manush	own country folks
frans/fransor manush	France/French
jarmani/jarmanir manush	Germany/German
Portugal/Portugalor manush	Portugal/Portugese
spEin/spEinor manush	Spain/Spanish
itali/italir manush	Italy
grIs/grIsor manush	Greece
Polaand/Polaandor manush	Poland
rumania/rumaniar manush	Romania
Astria/Astriar manush	Austria
norUYey/norUYeyr manush	Norway
suiden/suidenor manush	Sweden
finlend/finlendor manush	Finland
aislend/aislendor manush	Iceland/Icelandic
luksembarg	Luxemburg
beljiam/beljiamor manush	Belgium/Belgian
denmark/denmarkor manush	Danmark/Danish
malta/maltar manush	Malta/Maltese

My World II amar Dunia

Dunia	earth/world
dhora	earth
Bubon	earth
dhorama	mother earth
ashman	sky/heaven
zomin	land
PaTal	underworld
Tin Dunia	three worlds (heaven, earth and underworld)
mati	soil/earth
zonom mati	birth place

My Universe II amar mohaDunia

moha Dunia	Universe
moha Pritheebi	Universe
canD/can	Moon
Tera/Tara	stars
shuruz/shurzo	Sun
mohaKal	eternity/eternal
Kal	cosmic epoch
can Tera	Moon and stars
ashaman zomin	Heaven Earth

God's World II allaar Dunia

Allaar Dunia	natural world
prokriTi	nature
noDi/gang	river
sorha	spring
zolproBaT	waterfall
zalai/zola	marsh
bil	lake
aaOr	shell sea
shagor/shomuDro	sea
mohashagor	ocean
canDor grohon/Amaboishsha	lunar eclipse
shurzor grohon	solar eclipse
canD/can	moon
shuruz/shurzo	sun
ashman	sky/heaven
zomin/mati	land
Dunia	earth/world
mohaDunia	universe
canni raiT/jusna raiT	moon lit night
jusna/canni	moon lights
andhair	darkness
megh	rain/cloud
Qua	fog
shishir	dew
boroP	ice
Tushar	snow
zuarBata	tide
zuar uzan	high tide
zuar Bati	low tide
Parh	hill
PorboT	mountain
nala	canal
kua	well
Pukoir/Pushkunni/Pushkundi	pond
Tera	star
groho	planet
Tera Porha	shooting star

| DIP | island |
| khaal | canal |

Sylheti Naming

Sylheti Place Names

Sylheti naming has certain simplicity in which places are named. Lot of paces have a single name like silet, saaToK, longla, zurhi, zaflong, Patharia etc. These names are singular and nouns. However, it appears that long itself is used a naming suffix as well as in zaflong,

Then places use naming suffixes like gram (village), gau (village), ga, Pur (village), gonj (meaning market place/town/city), ghat (dock), nogor (town/city), bazar (market), Parha (small section of a village), Toli (beneath/under), Tola (beneath/under), Baag (fraction/part), aalI (a bunch of four), gul (field/marsh)that are added to a word (often some sort of name), la (a suffix and prefix), mara (to beat/kill) places derive their names relating to infamous murders), aaor (lake), bil (lake), KanDi (a bunch), KanDa (banch), sOrha (brook), khana (home/house/accommodation), zangal (the higher border raised from earth to separate two pieces of lands owned by different people), bag (garden), gorh (design), ghor (home/house), cor (island), Ura (a place), Pasha (king), long (long is a suffix though it means a tiny fruit used as a massalla but might have derived from lobong), basha (house in a city or town), kundo (waterfall/fall/whirlpool)

Komorgram
Komorgau
Komorga
KomorPur
Komor gonj
Komorghat
Komornogor
Komorbazar (which might take the form of Komrorbazar as is Komor's market)
KomorParha
KomorTola
KomorToli
KomorBaag
KomoraalI
Komorgul
Komorla
Komormara
Komoraaor (which might take the form of Komroraaor or even KomorKataraaor)
Komorbil(which might take the form of Komrorbil)
KomorKanDi
KomorKanDa
KomorsOrha

Komorkhana
Komorzangal
Komorbaag
Komorgorh
Komorghor
Komorcor/Komrorcor
KomorUra
KomorPasha
zaflong
Komorbasha
Komorkundo

Some places are named in relation to a widely known place and the name would signify the position of the place in relation to the original famous place. So daKaDokkin literally means south of Dhaka but the place is no where near Dhaka but actually in gulaPgonj, Sylhet!

silet/silot/sillot/silhot/silhat   Sylhet
silet shoDor   Central Sylhet (administrative centre in central uPozila of current Sylhet District)

uPozila's in Sylhet Central

silet shoDor

balaagonj

Bianibazar

bishshonaT (bishnaT)

Kumpanigonj

fenchugonj (fEcugonj)

gulaPgonj

guainghat

zoinTaPur

Kanaighat

zokigonj

uPozila's in mouloBizazar

mouloBibazar shoDor

borholekha (borhlekha)

Komolgonj

kulaUrha

raznogor

srimongol

uPozila's in shunamgonj

shunamgonj shoDor

saaToK

BishshomBorPur

dhIrai

dhormoPasha (dhoromPasha)

Duarabazar

zogonnaTPur

jamalgonj

TahirPur

Shallaa

uPozila's hOBigonj

hOBigonj shoDor

azmirigonj

baniacong

bahubol

cunarughat

laakhai

nObigonj

maadhobPur

People's Names

People's Names

The naming system used in Sylhet has not at all been like the European system. People's names were given as multiple names added in one without relation to any to the other and it seems that the name belongs to the person alone and he does not appear to bear his family or father's names though that started to change after the British went into the subcontinent.

Generally, people, Muslims would have names like Abdul Malik: even if these are Arabic names and Abdul Malik does not make sense if seen in Arabic meaning.
Abu Taher: which in Arabic means father of Taher where is the person than who is perhaps a baby called Abu Taher!

And a lot of Arabic names have been Sylheticised hence pronounced differently than Arabic. Most people of Islamic origin did not have a family name so they would be:

Using two names like

abDur razzak
abDullah Ismail
abDul husein
abul husein
Ikram Ahmed etc

Female names would be
aysha akTar/akhTar
aysha begom
amina khaTun
shaisTa khanum
faTima iasmin etc

Where as people with family name would have names, however, some people add the family names at the beginning of their name (in Europe people might treat it as the first name, though it is like the European system when one is referred as Lord Karl Champion or Sir Maximus Mandelson or Lady Elizabeth Curtis etc) and some add it at the end of their names:

Male names

soioD ashraful husein (though ashraful and husein both part of the name belong to the person)
coudhuri rofikul islam
TalukDar ashraf boKTiar
TorofDar salikur rohman
TofaDar enaeT husein
zuarDar abdullaa islam
bishshash alimul Ibrahim
DofaDar absar usman
Pir BokTiar ahmoD
PataDar anwarul habib
ṭikaDar boshirul umor
khan korimulla ahsan
khanbahaDur rohmulla ali
khondoKar zobbarul islam

However, the modern use is that it is becoming more and more common to use the family name or title at the end of the name. However, people still are not using father's name with their names other than people who have settled in the UK.

Female names with family titles were different than the above system.

They used to be

soioDa aysha akhTar (as opposed to soioD)
amina khanom (as opposed to khan)

but asia coudhurani (as opposed to coudhri)

But modern system is that the family tiles are no longer made feminine so today

It is ahsanur rohman coudhuri for the man and aysha coudhuri for the woman. Same applies to all other family names. A lot of people do not use their family titles but get referred to by it by other people. So a TalukDar may not use the family title but the villagers may still refer their household as TalukDarbarhi etc.

However, family names were added to the names of people who were born in families that had titles as family titles.

Hindu naming systems were a bit more systematic in that the families that have a title would use the titles with their names:

So
boshuDeb cokroborTi
boshonTokumar bonDoPaaDDaay
horihorkumar chottoPaaDDaay
binoykumar Dash
Abinash acairjo
noboshib Pal

And female name would be

Anila rani cokroborTi and so on though these days it would be Anila cokroborTi etc. However, those that have no family titles would be Anilkumar biDDaPoTi bilash and so on and so forth.

In old documents people's names were written as, for man, sri AshiTkumar coudhuri (sri meaning Mr) and srimoTi asharani cottoPaaDDaay (as miss/ms/Mrs) etc which came almost to create an equivalent addressing to Mr etc. That's how Muslim names begun to be written. That went on for a long while and then somehow some muslim document copywriters encouraged by debates about it started writing mohammed before any muslim name instead of sri and musammaT before any female name.

That was then taken on by the public and then it became a common practise for people to use mohammoD at the beginning of their names and for female musammoT. And therefore, when no one should be named mohammoD ahmoD there became hundreds of them as they were forced to write mohammed before their names! Then came the shortening of mohammod and it became MD or md and that caused impossible confusions when people began to leave the country and landed in foreign lands and could not explain the sociology of things back home to the immigration officials. That has begun to get filtered through back home and it began to change.

There are certain cultural niceties that go with names that everyone learns as they grow in society.

If one's name is abDul Korim no one would call them abDul but Korim as that's what effectively is his name.

If one's name is mohammed osman no one would in Sylhet call him mohammoD but osman.

sileti Kobirun KobiTa

o shurmar Kobi kushiaarar baul monor caYnni shikari
siletor zoban zeno futia ute TumaTanor Kolomor maze
Kolomor langolor mayar mukTo tane tane ar zonmo loy
zeno TumaTanor monor matir Dunia thaki agamir Duniar

madhobkundo-bahar ar longlar caYbagan zeno longlara
Aia mishe gia aaKaluki aOror nilua deUOr sOnDe sOnDe
bokulTolar gan zeno shaalla soia sriPuror shobuzo gia bOy
shurmar caYPaTar moioThin Qushi zeno Ay eK nayagra

kundor badhahin shaDa shaDa modhu ar bOia zaay zibonor
eK ABinashi bohoTa ganor sruTor lakhan uTlia PaTlia zeno
TumaTanor zoban shunDoror cera ar ceragbaTTir bebsha Kore

TumaTanor KolPonar Kolomor cakku zeno Kate baTTir martiT
thaki anonDor shunDor shuBon shob Bashkorz foshol benozir
ar gorhia ute sileti Kobirun KobiTar eK mohamaya mayalara

November 12, 2011

silara shurma sOnet

Other Books By This Author

Novel
Laranska The Anatomy of Fear: Novel

Philosophy
Dehumanisation of Humanity: Philosophy

Children's Poetry
That Fish is a Cat! That Cat is a Fish: Children's Poetry

Poetry
Eteläranta My Emmarsmith Blues
My Elämä Valentine
Ljubljana's Laurels
The Emm Lines
High Representative
Ideaphor
Ellvassalo Pleasanstrand
O Rain La Rain
Imsidina Songs: I-Lines Collection
Mississippi Magnolia: Ionnets Collection
Laranskan Elleesium
El Libro Del Arroyo De Sus Sonrisas
Illumine My Ithaca
A Traveller's Guide to Pollypsychophinadalium
Ink-Spring Ithaca Iguana
Neverbridge Stone Roses
Poetry of Ruins and Rains
Poetica Rainbow Ryder
The Geography of Time
The Son of Eternity
Command the Moon

Screenplay
United Colours of Blood: Screenplay

Ellarans
Ellaran Emmaphires: Ellarans Collection

Songs

La Ciela Songs of Spheres: Songs Collection

Sonnets
Prometheus and Orpheus: Sonnets

Poetic Romantic Fiction
Immonsima: Romantic Poetic Fiction

Prozzitries
Indira's Heart

Anthologies
London Poetry Pearl: London Poetry Festival 2009 Poetry Anthology: Editor
Commit the Savannah-Sunset and the Restless Sea: English Translations of Contemporary Spanish Poetry, Editor

Languages
shobDolara My Sylheti Dictionary
Baanglara My Bangla Tutor
Sylara My Sylheti Tutor

shobDolara My Sylheti Dictionary

shobDolara My Sylheti Dictionary

By Munayem Mayenin, London, United Kingdom

ISBN: 978-1-4709-4924-2

First Published: November 12, 2011

Price: £27

la ciela: singing the sacred words: la ciela

Book: Between your pages I carry hidden oceans, impossible islands, awesome landscapes, soul changing symphonies, miraculous openings and made up imsoniums. La ciela you are: voice of the sacred words, sublime words forever singing

Imsonium Books

Printed in Great Britain
by Amazon.co.uk, Ltd.,
Marston Gate.